INTERNATIONAL
Vital Records
Handbook

INTERNATIONAL
Vital Records Handbook

Thomas Jay Kemp

Librarian of the
Historical Society of Pennsylvania

GENEALOGICAL PUBLISHING CO., INC.

Dedicated to my wife Vi
and son Andrew

CONTENTS

2. British Isles
and Related Countries

3. Europe

INTRODUCTION

At one time or another all of us need copies of birth, marriage, or death certificates for driver's licenses, passports, jobs, social security, family history research, or for simple proof of identity. But the fact is that the application forms needed to obtain copies of vital records vary from state to state and from country to country, often necessitating a tedious and time-wasting exchange of correspondence before the appropriate forms can be obtained and the correct procedures followed. The *International Vital Records Handbook* is designed to put an end to all that, as it offers a complete, up-to-date collection of vital records application forms from nations throughout the world, thus simplifying and speeding up the process by which vital records are obtained, regardless of the number or type of application forms required.

Divided into three parts, the book covers some sixty-seven countries and territories: (1) North America, including the United States, United States Trust Territories, Canada, and the English-speaking Caribbean; (2) the British Isles and related countries, including England and Wales, Scotland, Northern Ireland, Ireland, Australia, New Zealand, and South Africa; and (3) Europe, featuring the thirty-one countries from Albania to Yugoslavia with references to their key archives and libraries.

Application forms issued by the various civil registration offices and the current procedures for obtaining a birth, marriage, or death certificate are given for each state, province, territory, or country. Simply photocopy the form you need, follow the instructions, and send the fee and the completed form to the appropriate record office. In the case of European countries— the majority of which have neither a centralized vital records registration system nor application forms of any kind—a list of national and provincial record repositories is provided.

In obtaining copies of vital records it should be borne in mind that copies of the original certificate might be on file in any one of several different jurisdictions, depending on the country. For example, if a vital record is not available from a state office of vital records, you should check with the appropriate county or city office to see if they have a copy. Similar records are also kept by the various religious denominations, and some copies and originals are held by archives and libraries the world over.

As a matter of policy, the Family History Library of The Church of Jesus Christ of Latter-day Saints in Salt Lake City (commonly called the Morman Church) has microfilmed millions of vital records from church and civil registers all over the world. This ongoing and extraordinary program has made the Family History Library the world's largest repository of vital records. A catalog of its microfilm holdings can be viewed at any of the 1,800 Family History Centers here and abroad. For further information on the library system write to: The Family History Library, 35 North West Temple Street, Salt Lake City, Utah 84150.

1. North America

UNITED STATES—
Citizens Abroad

Send your requests to:

Passport Services
Correspondence Branch
U.S. Department of State
Washington, DC 20524

(202) 647-0518

Cost for a certified Birth Certificate	$4.00
Cost for a certified Death Certificate	$4.00

If the person was a member of the Armed Forces write to the Secretary of Defense, Washington, DC 20301 (Army, Navy or Air Force) or to Commandant, P.S., U.S. Coast Guard, Washington, DC 20226 (Coast Guard). If the event occurred on the high seas write to the U.S. Department of State, Washington, DC 20520, if the vessel or aircraft was outbound or at a foreign port. If the vessel was inbound, and first docked in the U.S., then write to the Bureau of Vital Records in the State where it arrived.

Send your requests to:

Alabama Department of Public Health
Bureau of Vital Statistics
State Office Building
434 Monroe Street, Room 215
Montgomery, Alabama 36130-1701

(205) 261-5033

For earlier records write to:

County Clerk
County Court House
(County where the event occurred)

Cost for a certified Birth Certificate	$5.00
Cost for a certified Marriage Certificate	$5.00
Cost for a certified Death Certificate	$5.00
Cost for a duplicate copy, when ordered at the same time	$2.00

Birth and death records are on file from January 1908. Births are filed under the father's name by the date and place the event occurred. Marriage records are on file from August 1, 1936. NO PERSONAL CHECKS ARE ACCEPTED. Send a money order payable to "Alabama State Board of Health."

If your request is urgent you may call and charge your certificates to your Visa or MasterCard. There is an $18.50 charge for this service.

ALABAMA DEPARTMENT OF PUBLIC HEALTH—VITAL STATISTICS
APPLICATION FOR BIRTH RECORD

TYPE OR PRINT

DATE: _____

Full name: _____
First   Middle   Last

Date of birth: _____ Sex: _____

Place of birth: _____
Hospital   City   County

This was the _____ child born to this mother. Is this an adopted child? _____
1st, 2nd, 3rd, 4th, etc.

What changes are you requesting? _____

Next older sister or brother _____ Younger _____

Full name of father _____ / _____
First   Middle   Last   Race

Full maiden name of mother _____ / _____
First   Middle   Last (Maiden)   Race

AMOUNT ENCLOSED $ _____ (NO PERSONAL CHECKS ACCEPTED)

MAIL RECORD TO:

Name: _____

Street: _____

City or Town: _____
Zip

Signature of person making request: _____

DO NOT WRITE IN THESE SPACES
(File Number)
Additional information requested
Evidence Requested
Amendment Form Mailed
Informational letter mailed
Advised record not on file
CERTIFIED COPY ISSUED

- -

DO NOT TEAR

The fee for a record search is $5.00 each. This fee covers the issuance of one certified copy, if found. Additional copies of the same record ordered at the same time are $2.00 each. The fee is $8.00 to amend a record, prepare a new certificate of birth after adoption or legitimation or to file a delayed certificate. NO PERSONAL CHECKS ACCEPTED. FEES ARE NOT REFUNDABLE. DO NOT REMOVE ANY PART OF THIS FORM. Please send money order payable to the STATE BOARD OF HEALTH.

Certificate of _____

(This is a mailing insert. PRINT name and address of person to whom the certified copy is to be mailed)

MAIL TO:

Name: _____

Street: _____

City or Town: _____
Zip

DO NOT WRITE IN THIS SPACE

THIS WILL BE YOUR RECEIPT AFTER WE PROCESS IT AND RETURN IT TO YOU.

DO NOT TEAR   **(TYPE OR PRINT)**

MAIL TO:

Name: _____

Street: _____

City or Town: _____
Zip

MAIL APPLICATION TO.

ALABAMA DEPARTMENT OF PUBLIC HEALTH
BUREAU OF VITAL STATISTICS
434 MONROE STREET, ROOM ■ 215
MONTGOMERY, ALABAMA 36130-1701

ADPH-F-VS-14/Rev. 1-88

ALABAMA DEPARTMENT OF PUBLIC HEALTH—VITAL STATISTICS
APPLICATION FOR MARRIAGE RECORD

TYPE OR PRINT

Full name of groom _____
First   Middle   Last

Birthday of groom _____ Color or Race _____

Groom's Mother _____
First   Middle   Last (Maiden name)

Groom's Father _____
First   Middle   Last

Full name of bride _____
First   Middle   Last

Birthday of bride _____ Color or Race _____

Bride's Mother _____
First   Middle   Last (Maiden name)

Bride's Father _____
First   Middle   Last

License obtained in _____
County   State

Date of marriage _____
Month   Day   Year

Place of marriage _____
City   County   State

AMOUNT ENCLOSED $ _____ (NO PERSONAL CHECKS ACCEPTED)

Signature of person making request: _____

Street: _____

City or Town: _____
Zip

(DO NOT WRITE IN THESE SPACES)

(File Number)

Additional information requested

Evidence Requested

Amendment Form Mailed

Informational letter mailed

Advised record not on file

CERTIFIED COPY ISSUED

- -
DO NOT TEAR

The service fee is $5.00 for a record search and one (1) certified copy; $2.00 each for additional copies of the same record ordered at the same time.

Fees must be paid in advance and are not refundable. Payment should be made by MONEY ORDER payable to the State Board of Health.

DO NOT SEND CASH. NO PERSONAL CHECKS ACCEPTED.

(DO NOT WRITE IN THIS SPACE)
(Validating machine only)

MAIL TO: Name: _____

Street: _____

City or Town: _____
Zip

- -
DO NOT TEAR   (TYPE OR PRINT)

MAIL TO: SEND TO:

Name: _____

Street: _____

City or Town: _____
Zip

DEPARTMENT OF PUBLIC HEALTH
BUREAU OF VITAL STATISTICS
434 MONROE STREET, RM. 215
MONTGOMERY, ALABAMA 36130-170

ADPH-F-VS-12/Rev. 10-88

ALABAMA DEPARTMENT OF PUBLIC HEALTH—VITAL STATISTICS
APPLICATION FOR DEATH RECORD

TYPE OR PRINT

Full name of deceased _____

      First   Middle   Last (Jr., Sr., Etc.)

Social Security No. of Deceased _____

Date of death _____ Age: _____ Sex: _____ Race: _____

Place of death _____

      City   County

Name of
Husband or Wife _____

      First   Middle   Last

Name of Funeral Home _____

Full Name of Father _____

      First   Middle   Last

Full maiden name of mother _____

      First   Middle   Last (Maiden)

AMOUNT ENCLOSED $ _____ NUMBER OF COPIES _____
(NO PERSONAL CHECKS ACCEPTED)

MAIL RECORD TO:

    Name: _____

    Street: _____

    City or Town: _____ Zip

_____
Signature of person making request   Relationship to Deceased

DO NOT TEAR

DO NOT WRITE IN THIS SPACE
File No.
Additional Information Requested
Evidence Requested
Amendment Form Mailed
Informational Letter Mailed
Advised Record Not On File
Certified Copy Issued

The service fee is $5.00 for a record search and one (1) certified copy; $2.00 each for additional copies of the same record ordered at the same time.

Fees must be paid in advance and are not refundable. Payment should be made by MONEY ORDER payable to the State Board of Health.

DO NOT SEND CASH. NO PERSONAL CHECKS ACCEPTED.

MAIL TO:

    Name: _____

    Street: _____

    City or Town: _____ Zip

DO NOT WRITE IN THIS SPACE

THIS WILL BE YOUR RECEIPT AFTER WE PROCESS IT AND RETURN IT TO YOU.

DO NOT REMOVE THIS STUB ▲

TYPE OR PRINT MAILING ADDRESS ON BOTH INSERTS

▼

MAIL TO:

    Name: _____

    Street: _____

    City or Town: _____ Zip

SEND TO:

ALABAMA DEPARTMENT OF PUBLIC HEALTH
BUREAU OF VITAL STATISTICS
434 MONROE, ROOM ▇ 215
MONTGOMERY, ALABAMA 36130-1701

ADPH-F-VS-18 Rev 1-88

ALASKA

Send your requests to:

Alaska Department of Health and Social Services
Bureau of Vital Statistics
P.O. Box H
Juneau, Alaska 99811-0675

(907) 465-3392

Cost for a certified Birth Certificate	$5.00
Cost for a plastic Birth Certificate	$5.00
Cost for a certified Marriage Certificate	$5.00
Cost for a certified Death Certificate	$5.00
Cost for a duplicate copy, when ordered at the same time	$2.00

The State Bureau of Vital Statistics has records from January 1, 1913.

If your request is urgent you may call and charge your certificates to your Visa or MasterCard. There is a $5.00 fee for this service.

VITAL RECORDS ORDER FORM
PLEASE SPECIFY TYPE OF RECORD YOU WANT AND HOW MANY

	HOW MANY
BIRTH CARD	
BIRTH-FULL COPY	

	HOW MANY
MARRIAGE	
DIVORCE	

	HOW MANY
DEATH	

1. NAME ON RECORD: (First)	(Middle)	(Last)	
2. NAME OF SPOUSE: (Death, Marriage, Divorce only)			
3. DATE OF EVENT: (Mo.) (Day) (Yr.)	HOSPITAL:		SEX:
4. PLACE OF EVENT: (City)		ALASKA	
5. FATHER'S NAME:			
6. MOTHER'S FIRST & MAIDEN NAME:			
7. NAME OF AGENCY OR PERSON ORDERING RECORD:			
8. YOUR RELATIONSHIP TO LINE 1:		DAYTIME PHONE NUMBER	

Birth card $5.00 each. First certified copy is $5.00, each additional copy is $2.00, if requested at the same time.

PLEASE NOTE: The fee for each item requested is $5.00. If the requested record cannot be found a $5.00 search fee must be retained.

PLEASE ENCLOSE THE CORRECT FEE WITH THIS APPLICATION FORM

Make checks or money orders payable to: **BUREAU OF VITAL STATISTICS**

The Alaska Vital Records Office has the following records:

Birth in Alaska since 1913
Marriage in Alaska since 1913

Death in Alaska since 1913
Divorce in Alaska since 1950

In accordance with Alaska Statute 18.50, in addition to having one's own record, a birth record can be furnished to the parents, guardian or respective representative. If you do not fall into one of the above categories, we will need written permission from one of the above eligible persons. The written consent must accompany return of this form. We can send the copy directly to the registrant if the address is available.

*YOUR MAILING ADDRESS MUST BE ENTERED BELOW:

NAME		
STREET		
CITY	STATE	ZIP CODE

*MAIL TO: VITAL STATISTICS, P.O. BOX H   JUNEAU, ALASKA 99811-0675

Form 06-8000
VS-7 (Rev. 4/86)

Send your requests to:

Arizona Department of Health Services
Office of Vital Records
1740 West Avenue
P.O. Box 3887
Phoenix, Arizona 85030-3887

(602) 255-1072

Send your requests for Marriage Certificates to:

Clerk
Superior Court
(County where the Marriage License was issued)

Cost for a certified Birth Certificate	$8.00
Cost for a short form Birth Certificate	$5.00
Cost for a plastic Birth Certificate	$5.00
Cost for a certified Death Certificate	$5.00

The Arizona Office of Vital Records began keeping records in July of 1909. They do have abstracts of some records filed in the County Clerk's Office before that date. Your request must be accompanied by a copy of a photo ID card witnessed by a notary public. Payment must be by certified check or money order. If the Office does not have the records you want contact the County Clerk in the county where the event occurred.

If your request is urgent you may call and charge your certificates to your Visa or MasterCard. There is a $4.50 fee for this service.

ARIZONA DEPARTMENT OF HEALTH SERVICES
VITAL RECORDS SECTION

REQUEST FOR COPY OF BIRTH CERTIFICATE

DATE _____

ENCLOSED $ _____ IN _____ FOR _____

CERTIFIED COPY $8   COMPUTERIZED COPY $5

AMOUNT

I. BIRTH CERTIFICATE OF:

FULL NAME AT BIRTH

DATE OF BIRTH   SEX

PLACE OF BIRTH (City, County, State, Hospital)

MOTHER'S MAIDEN NAME (First, Middle, Last)   MOTHER'S BIRTHPLACE

HOSPITAL OR FACILITY

FATHER'S FULL NAME   FATHER'S BIRTHPLACE

II. PERSON MAKING REQUEST

WARNING: Ta obtain application for a birth certificate is a punishable offense.

For the protection of the individual certificates of vital events are NOT open to public inspection. Therefore, applicant MUST BE NOTARIZED OR this form must be accompanied by a copy of a valid picture I.D. which contains the applicant's signature.

Your Signature

YOUR NAME

YOUR ADDRESS (Number and Street)

(Town, State)   (Zip Code)

RELATIONSHIP TO PERSON NAMED IN CERTIFICATE (e.g., parent, attorney, etc.)

FOR WHAT PURPOSE DO YOU NEED THIS COPY?   TELEPHONE NO. (Optional)

Send completed application and correct fee to
OFFICE OF VITAL RECORDS
Arizona Department of Health Services
P.O. Box 3887
Phoenix, Arizona 85030

FOR OFFICE USE ONLY

DATE ISSUED

STATE FILE NUMBER

SUBSCRIBED AND SWORN TO OR AFFIRMED BEFORE ME THIS _____ DAY OF _____

NOTARY'S SIGNATURE

MY COMMISSION EXPIRES

ARIZONA DEPARTMENT OF HEALTH SERVICES
OFFICE OF VITAL RECORDS

APPLICATION FOR COPY OF DEATH CERTIFICATE

FOR OFFICE USE ONLY
STATE FILE NUMBER
DATE ISSUED

THE FEE IS $5 FOR EACH CERTIFIED COPY

DATE _____

ENCLOSED $ _____   IN _____   FOR _____   COPIES OF THE FOLLOWING DEATH CERTIFICATE

AMOUNT

1 NAME OF DECEASED - First, Middle, Last

IF ANOTHER LAST NAME (except by marriage) WAS EVER USED ENTER HERE

2 DATE OF DEATH - Month, Day, Year

SEX

SOCIAL SECURITY NUMBER (necessary for positive identification)

3 PLACE OF DEATH - Hospital or Residence

Town or City   County   ARIZONA

4 IF MARRIED, IS WIFE/HUSBAND OF DECEASED NOW LIVING? ☐ YES ☐ NO

IF YES, LIST NAME - First, Middle, Last

5 HOW WILL COPIES BE USED?

ARE COPIES TO BE USED FOR U.S. GOV'T CLAIMS? ☐ YES ☐ NO

IF YES, LIST EACH TYPE OF CLAIM

WARNING: False application for a death certificate is a punishable offense.

For the protection of the individual certificates of vital events are NOT open to public inspection. Signature of applicant MUST BE NOTARIZED OR this form must be accompanied by a copy of a valid picture I.D. which contains the applicant's signature.

6. SIGNATURE OF APPLICANT (The regulations require a signed application)

RELATIONSHIP TO THE DECEASED?

7 TYPE OR PRINT NAME AND CORRECT MAIL ADDRESS BELOW

NAME

STREET ADDRESS OR P.O. BOX NUMBER

CITY AND STATE   ZIP CODE

SEND COMPLETED APPLICATION AND CORRECT FEE TO:

OFFICE OF VITAL RECORDS
Arizona Dept. of Health Services
P.O. Box 3887
Phoenix, AZ 85030-3887

SUBSCRIBED AND SWORN TO OR AFFIRMED BEFORE ME THIS _____ DAY OF _____

_____
NOTARY'S SIGNATURE

MY COMMISSION EXPIRES _____

ADHS/ADM/Vital Records
VS-15B (Rev. 9-88)

ARKANSAS

Send your requests to:

Arkansas Department of Health
Division of Vital Records
4815 West Markham Street
Little Rock, Arkansas 72205-3867

(501) 661-2371

For earlier records contact:

County Clerk
County Court House
(County where the event occurred)

Cost for a certified Birth Certificate	$5.00
Cost for a plastic Birth Card	$5.00
Cost for a certified Marriage Certificate	$5.00
Cost for a certified Death Certificate	$4.00
Cost for a duplicate copy, when ordered at the same time	$1.00

The Arkansas Department of Health began filing birth and death records February 1, 1914 and marriage records January 1, 1917. They do have some birth records for individuals that were filed as delayed certificates. The Arkansas History Commission (Multi-Agency Complex, Capitol Mall, 2nd Floor, Little Rock 72201) has some marriage records from selected counties from 1814.

ARKANSAS DEPARTMENT OF HEALTH
DIVISION OF VITAL RECORDS
4815 WEST MARKHAM STREET
LITTLE ROCK, ARKANSAS 72205-3867

APPLICATION FOR CERTIFIED COPY OF CERTIFICATE OF BIRTH

Only Arkansas births are recorded in this office. There are no original birth records for events which occurred before February 1, 1914. The fee is per certificate copy or birth registration card. This fee must accompany the application. Send check or money order payable to the Arkansas Department of Health. DO NOT SEND CASH. Of the total fee you send, $5.00 will be kept in this office to cover search charges if no record of the birth is found.

INFORMATION ABOUT PERSON WHOSE BIRTH CERTIFICATE IS REQUESTED (Type or Print)				
1. FULL NAME AT BIRTH	FIRST NAME	MIDDLE NAME	LAST NAME	
2. DATE OF BIRTH	MONTH DAY YEAR		SEX & RACE	AGE LAST BIRTHDAY
3. PLACE OF BIRTH	CITY OR TOWN COUNTY	STATE	ORDER OF THIS BIRTH (1st, 2nd, 3rd, etc.)	
	NAME OF HOSPITAL OR STREET ADDRESS		ATTENDANT AT BIRTH	
4. FULL NAME OF FATHER	FIRST NAME	MIDDLE NAME	LAST NAME	
5. FULL MAIDEN NAME OF MOTHER (NAME BEFORE MARRIAGE)	FIRST NAME	MIDDLE NAME	MAIDEN NAME	

If this child has been adopted, please give original name if known.

_____

Has a copy of this certificate been received before? _____

If this is a delayed certificate, when was it filed? _____

What is your relationship to the person whose certificate is being requested?

_____

What is your reason for requesting this certificate? _____

_____

Is the person whose record is being requested still living? _____

If the birth was not recorded, do you wish to file a delayed birth record? _____

Signature and telephone number of person requesting this certificate:

_____

DO NOT WRITE IN THIS SPACE	
Searcher _____	
Index _____	
Delayed	Prior
Volume No.	
Page No.	Yr.

DO NOT DETACH

Please **PRINT** below the name and address of the person who is to receive the copy(s) or card(s).

THERE ARE TWO TYPES OF CERTIFICATE COPIES AVAILABLE: (1) A PAPER COPY. AND, (2) A PLASTIC, BILLFOLD-SIZE BIRTH CARD WITHOUT NAMES OF PARENTS. BOTH TYPES OF COPIES ARE LEGAL PROOF OF THE EVENT OF BIRTH.

COPIES REQUESTED	
PAPER COPY	HOW MANY ☐
BIRTH CARD	HOW MANY ☐
AMOUNT OF MONEY ENCLOSED	$

_____

_____

ZIP _____

VR-7 🅰 —3702

Any person who willfully and knowingly makes any false statement in an application certified copy of a vital record filed in this state is subject to a fine of not more than thousand dollars ($10,000) or imprisoned not more than five (5) years, or both. (Ark. Stat 82-527)

ARKANSAS DEPARTMENT OF HEALTH
DIVISION OF VITAL RECORDS
4815 WEST MARKHAM STREET
LITTLE ROCK, ARKANSAS 72205-3867

APPLICATION FOR CERTIFIED COPY OF MARRIAGE OR DIVORCE RECORD

nly Arkansas events of marriage or divorce are filed in this office. Marriage records start with 1917 and divorce records with 1923. The fee is
er certified copy of a marriage or divorce coupon. This fee must accompany the application. Send check or money order payable to the Arkansas
epartment of Health. DO NOT SEND CASH. Of the total fee you send, $5.00 will be kept in this office to cover search charges for each record not
und in our files.

FILL IN FOR A MARRIAGE RECORD

IAME OF GROOM _____

IAIDEN NAME OF BRIDE _____

ATE OF MARRIAGE _____
         Month   Day   Year

OUNTY IN WHICH LICENSE WAS ISSUED _____

FILL IN FOR A DIVORCE RECORD

IAME OF HUSBAND_____

IAME OF WIFE _____

)ATE OF DIVORCE OR DISMISSAL _____
                          Month   Day   Year

:OUNTY IN WHICH DIVORCE WAS GRANTED/DISMISSED _____

_____

PLEASE ANSWER ALL QUESTIONS

DO NOT WRITE IN THIS SPACE	
Searcher _____	
Index _____	

Vhat is your relationship to the parties named on the requested record?

_____

Vhat is your reason for requesting a copy of this record?_____

_____

iignature and telephone number of person requesting this record:

Volume No. _____	
Page No. _____	Yr. _____

- -

DO NOT DETACH

NO. OF COPIES REQUESTED

THIS IS A MAILING INSERT. **PRINT** NAME AND ADDRESS OF
PERSON TO WHOM THE CERTIFIED COPY IS TO BE MAILED.

THIS IS NOT AN INVOICE.

Marriage _____

Divorce _____

Amount of
Money Enclosed _____

AME _____

)DRESS _____

TY _____ STATE _____ ZIP _____

Any person who willfully and knowingly makes any false statement in an application fo
certified copy of a vital record filed in this state is subject to a fine of not more than t
thousand dollars ($10,000) or imprisoned not more than five (5) years, or both. (Ark. Statut
82:527)

R-9

A—3689

ARKANSAS DEPARTMENT OF HEALTH
DIVISION OF VITAL RECORDS
4815 WEST MARKHAM STREET
LITTLE ROCK, ARKANSAS 72205-3867

APPLICATION FOR CERTIFIED COPY OF CERTIFICATE OF DEATH

Only Arkansas deaths are recorded in this office. There are no original death records for events which occurred before February 1, 1914. The fee is for the first copy and   for each additional copy of the same record ordered at the same time. The fee must accompany the application. Send check or money order payable to the Arkansas Department of Health. DO NOT SEND CASH. Of the total fee you send, $4.00 will be kept in this office to cover search charges if no record of the death is found.

FULL NAME OF DECEASED _____
First   Middle   Last

DATE OF DEATH _____ AGE OF DECEASED _____ SEX _____ RACE _____

PLACE WHERE DEATH OCCURRED _____
City   County   State

If Unknown,
Give Last Place of Residence _____
City   County   State

NAME OF FUNERAL HOME _____

ADDRESS _____

NAME OF ATTENDING PHYSICIAN _____

ADDRESS _____

What is your relationship to the person whose certificate is being requested?

_____   _____

What is your reason for requesting a copy of this record? _____

_____

If the death was not recorded, do you wish to file a delayed death record? _____

Signature and telephone number of person requesting this certificate:

_____

DO NOT WRITE IN THIS SPACE	
Searcher	
Index	
Delayed	Prior
Volume No.	
Page No.	Yr.

DO NOT DETACH

THIS IS A MAILING INSERT. PRINT NAME AND ADDRESS OF
PERSON WHO IS TO RECEIVE THE COPY OR COPIES.

THIS IS NOT AN INVOICE

COPIES REQUESTED	
	HOW MANY
ONE COPY ADDITIONAL COPIES	☐
AMOUNT OF MONEY ENCLOSED	$

NAME _____

ADDRESS _____

CITY _____ **STATE** _____ **ZIP** _____

VR-8

Ⓐ—3688

Any person who willfully and knowingly makes any false statement in an application certified copy of a vital record filed in this state is subject to a fine of not more than thousand dollars ($10,000) or imprisoned not more than five (5) years, or both. (Ark. St. 82 527).

CALIFORNIA

Send your requests to:

Office of the State Registrar of Vital Statistics
Department of Health Services
410 N Street
Sacramento, California 95814-4381

(916) 445-2684

Vital Statistics Section
Dept of Health Service
P.O. Box 730241
Sacramento, CA
94244-0241
(916) 445-2684

Send your requests for Marriage Certificates from April 1, 1986 to date to:

County Clerk
County Court House
(County where the Marriage License was issued)

Cost for a certified Birth Certificate	$11.00
Cost for a certified Marriage Certificate	$11.00
Cost for a certified Death Certificate	$ 7.00

The Registrar has birth and death records from July 1, 1905 to the present and marriage records from July 1, 1905 to March 31, 1986. For earlier records contact the County Clerk in the county where the event occurred.

If your request is urgent you may call and charge your certificates to your Visa or MasterCard. There is an additional $4.50 charge for this service.

The Family History Library of the Church of Jesus Christ of Latter-day Saints (Mormon Church) in Salt Lake City, Utah has microfilmed many of the original and published vital records and church registers of California's cities and counties. They have made microfiche copies of the statewide marriage indexes from 1960 to 1981 and the statewide death indexes from 1940 to 1983. For details on their holdings please consult your nearest Family History Center.

APPLICATION FOR CERTIFIED COPY OF BIRTH RECORD

INFORMATION

Birth records have been maintained in the Office of the State Registrar of Vital Statistics since July 1, 1905. The only records of earlier events are delayed birth certificates and court order delayed birth certificates registered as provided by law.

INSTRUCTIONS

1. Use a separate application blank for each different record of birth for which you are requesting a certified copy. Send $11.00 for each certified copy requested. If no record of the birth is found, the $11.00 fee will be retained for searching as required by statute and a Certification of No Record will be sent.

2. Give all the information you have available for the identification of the record of the registrant in the spaces under registrant information. If the information you furnish is incomplete or inaccurate, it may be impossible to locate the record. If this person has been adopted, please make the request in the adopted name.

3. Complete the applicant information section.

4. Indicate the number of certified copies you wish and include with this application sufficient money in the form of a personal check, postal or bank money order (international money order only for out-of-country requests), made payable to the State Registrar of Vital Statistics; the fee is $11.00 for each certified copy. Mail this application with the fee to Office of State Registrar, 410 N St., Sacramento, CA 95814.

5. All copies are certified and have a raised state seal.

CERTIFICATE INFORMATION – PLEASE PRINT OR TYPE

Name on Certificate—First Name	Middle Name	Last Name or Birth Name If Married
City or Town of Birth		Place of Birth—County
Date of Birth—Month, Day, Year (If Unknown, Enter Approximate Date of Birth)		Sex
Name of Father—First Name	Middle Name	Last Name
Birth Name of Mother—First Name	Middle Name	Last Name

APPLICANT INFORMATION – PLEASE PRINT OR TYPE

Purpose for Which Certified Copy Is to Be Used	Today's Date	Phone Number—Area Code First
Please Print—Name of Person Completing Application	Signature of Person Requesting Record/s—Your Signature ➤	
Address—Street	City	State—Zip Code
Name of Person Receiving Copies If Different From Above:	Number of Certified Copies Requested	Amount of Money Enclosed
Mailing Address for Copies If Different From Above—Street	City	State—Zip Code

DO NOT WRITE IN SPACES BELOW – FOR REGISTRAR

BIRTH

APPLICATION FOR CERTIFIED COPY OF MARRIAGE RECORD

INFORMATION

Marriage records have been maintained in the Office of the State Registrar of Vital Statistics since July 1, 1905 through __*1985*__.

INSTRUCTIONS

1. Use a separate application blank for each different record of marriage for which you are requesting a certified copy. Send $11.00 for each certified copy requested. If no record of the marriage is found, the $11.00 fee will be retained for searching as required by statute and a certificate of search will be sent.

2. Give all the information you have available for the identification of the record of marriage in the spaces under bride and groom information. If the information you furnish is incomplete or inaccurate, it may be impossible to locate the record.

3. Complete the applicant information section.

4. Indicate the number of certified copies you wish and include with this application sufficient money in the form of a postal or bank money order (International Money Order only for out-of-country requests), made payable to the State Registrar of Vital Statistics; the fee is $11.00 for each certified copy. Enclose a self-addressed, stamped envelope to expedite filling your request.

5. All copies are certified and have a raised state seal.

BRIDE AND GROOM INFORMATION—PLEASE PRINT

Name of Groom — First Name	Middle Name	Last Name	
Date of Birth	Place of Birth	Name of Father of Groom	
Maiden Name of Bride—First Name	Middle Name	Last Name	
Date of Birth	Place of Birth	Name of Father of Bride	
Date of Marriage—Month, Day, Year	If Date Unknown, Enter Year(s) to be Searched	County of Issue of License	County of Marriage

---

APPLICANT INFORMATION—PLEASE TYPE OR PRINT

Enter Purpose for Which Certified Copy is to be Used	Today's Date	Your Phone Number—Area Code First
Please Print—Name of Person Completing Application	Signature of Person Requesting Record/s—Your Signature	
Address—Street	City	State—Zip Code
Mailing Address For Copies If Different Than Above	Number of Certified Copies Requested	Amount of Money Enclosed
Mailing Address—Street	City	State—Zip Code

DO NOT WRITE IN SPACES BELOW—FOR REGISTRAR

VS 113 (10/87)

APPLICATION FOR CERTIFIED COPY OF DEATH RECORD

INFORMATION

Death records have been maintained in the Office of the State Registrar of Vital Statistics since July 1, 1905.

INSTRUCTIONS

1. Use a separate application blank for each different record of death for which you are requesting a certified copy. Send $7.00 for each certified copy requested. If no record of the death is found, the $7.00 fee will be retained for searching as required by statute and a certificate of search will be sent.

2. Give all the information you have available for the identification of the record of the decedent in the spaces under Decedent Information. If the information you furnish is incomplete or inaccurate, it may be impossible to locate the record.

3. Complete the Applicant Information section.

4. Indicate the number of certified copies you wish and include with this application sufficient money in the form of a personal check or postal or bank money order (International Money Order only for out-of-country requests), made payable to the State Registrar of Vital Statistics; the fee is $7.00 for each certified copy. Mail this application with fee to Office of State Registrar, 410 N Street, Sacramento, CA 95814.

5. All copies are certified and have a raised state seal.

DECEDENT INFORMATION   *(PLEASE TYPE OR PRINT.)*

Name of Decedent--First Name	Middle Name	Last Name	Sex
Place of Death—City or Town	Place of Death—County	Place of Birth	Date of Birth—Month, Day, Year
Date of Death—Month, Day, Year—or Period of Years to be Searched			Social Security Number
Mother's Maiden Name		Name of Spouse (Husband or Wife of Decedent)	

APPLICANT INFORMATION   *(PLEASE TYPE OR PRINT.)*

Enter Purpose for Which Certified Copy is to be Used	Today's Date	Your Phone Number ( )
Name of Person Completing Application	Signature of Person Requesting Record(s)—Your Signature	
Address—Street	City	State	ZIP Code
Name of Person Receiving Copies If Different From Above	Number of Certified Copies Requested	Amount of Money Enclosed
Mailing Address for Copies If Different From Above—Street	City	State	ZIP Code

DO NOT WRITE IN SPACE BELOW—FOR REGISTRAR USE ONLY

COLORADO

Send your requests to:

    Colorado Department of Health
    Vital Records Section
    4210 East 11th Avenue, Room 100
    Denver, Colorado 80220-3786

(303) 320-8474

Send your requests for Marriage Certificates and early vital records to:

    County Clerk
    County Court House
    (County where the Marriage License was issued)

Cost for a certified Birth Certificate	$ 6.00
Cost for a wallet-size Birth Card	$10.00
Cost for a certified Death Certificate	$ 6.00

If you apply for a birth or death certificate in person and wait for the certificate to be prepared, the fee is $10.00. The Vital Records Section requests that you include a self-addressed stamped envelope with your orders by mail. The Vital Records Section has an index to marriage records from 1900 through 1939 and from 1975 through 1987. The index gives the names of the persons married, date and county of the marriage. The fee is $6.00 to search the index. Contact the County Clerk for a copy of the marriage certificate.

If your request is urgent you may call and charge your certificates to your Visa or MasterCard. There is a $10.00 fee for this service. Call the Vital Records Section at (303) 331-4890 to arrange for this service.

Vital Records Section, Colorado Department of Health
4210 East 11th Avenue, Room 100, Denver, Colorado 80220

APPLICATION FOR CERTIFIED COPY OF BIRTH CERTIFICATE
(This form must be completed IN FULL. PLEASE PRINT OR TYPE.)

Colorado has birth records for the entire state since 1910. Legislation passed in 1943 provides for the filing of delayed birth certificates for persons who were born prior to that date or whose births were not recorded at the time of birth.

$ 6.00 REGULAR SERVICE Record mailed within 4 weeks or less. $6.00 per copy or per search of files if no record is found.

$10.00 PRIORITY SERVICE Record mailed within 5 days. $10.00 per copy or per search of files if no record is found.

$ 1.00 PER YEAR SEARCHED beyond one year when date of birth is unknown.

FULL name at birth
(If adopted, give new name) _____

Place of Birth _____ Date of Birth _____

Full name of father_____ Maiden name of mother_____

Is this person deceased? If yes, date and state of death_____

Is this the record of an adopted person?_____

Purpose for this copy:_____

These records are confidential. Please state your relationship to the person named on the record. See other side for a list of persons who may obtain birth certificates. _____

Pursuant to Colorado Revised Statutes, 1982, 25-2-118 and as defined by Colorado Board of Health Rules and Regulations, I hereby certify that I have a direct and tangible interest in the birth record requested. I understand that there are penalties by law (CRS 25-2-118) for obtaining a record under false pretenses.

YOUR SIGNATURE_____ _____
                                               Street

(   )_____ _____
Your day time telephone number   City   State   Zip

PENALTY BY LAW if any person alters, uses, attempts to use or furnishes to another for deceptive use or supplies false information for any vital statistics certificate.

If possible, please include a self-addressed, long envelope with your order. Make your check or money order payable to Vital Records. We cannot be responsible for cash sent through the mail.

Number of copies ordered _____   Amount enclosed $_____

AD RS 2 (Rev. 10/87)

APPLICATION FOR A VERIFICATION OF A MARRIAGE RECORD

(Please complete the form as far as your information will allow.)
(Please Print or Type.)

Vital Records Section
Colorado Department of Health
4210 East 11th Avenue, Room 100
Denver, Colorado 80220

Fees	
Regular Service:	Record mailed or search completed within 4 weeks or less. $6.00 per copy or per search of files if no record is found.
Priority Service:	Record mailed or search completed within 5 days. $10.00 per copy or per search of files if no record is found.

When date of the event is unknown, an additional $1 per year searched beyond one year is charged.
THE SEARCHING FEE OF $6.00 or $10.00 WILL BE CHARGED IF NO RECORD IS FOUND

Name of Bride _____

Name of Groom _____

Date of Marriage _____

Place of Marriage _____

This office will not have a record of the marriage if the county did not forward the information for the State Index.

Your signature _____

_____ , _____
                          Street

( )
Your day time telephone number   City   State   ZIP

If possible, please include a self-addressed, long envelope with your order.
Make your check or money order payable to Vital Records.

APPLICATION FOR CERTIFIED COPY OF DEATH CERTIFICATE
(This form must be completed IN FULL. PLEASE PRINT)

Vital Records Section
Colorado Department of Health
4210 East 11th Avenue, Room 100
Denver, Colorado 80220

FEES
Regular Service: Record mailed within 4 weeks or less. $6.00 per copy or per search of files if no record is found.
Priority Service: Record mailed within 5 days after order is received. $10.00 per copy or per search of files if no record is found.
When date of death is unknown, there is an an additional charge of $1 per year searched beyond one year.

FULL Name of Deceased Person:
(At Time of Death) _____

Place of Death _____   Date of Death _____

Place of Birth _____   Date of Birth _____

Maiden Name of Decedent if applicable _____   Mother's Maiden Name _____

Father's Name _____

Purpose for this copy _____   Social Security No. _____
These records are confidential.
Please state your relationship to the deceased: _____

If possible, please include a long, self-addressed envelope with your order. Make your check or money order payable to Vital Records.

PENALTY BY LAW if any person alters, uses, or attempts to use or furnishes to another for deceptive use or supplies false information for any vital statistics certificate.

Your signature _____

( )
Your daytime telephone number

Address _____
Street _____   City _____   State _____   Zip _____

AD RS 1 (Rev. 10/87)   Number of Copies _____   Amount Enclosed $ _____

CONNECTICUT

Send your requests to:

Connecticut State Department of Health Services
Vital Records Section
150 Washington Street
Hartford, Connecticut 06106-4476

(203) 566-1124

Earlier records are available from:

Town Clerk
Town Hall
(Town where the event occurred)

Cost for a certified Birth Certificate	$5.00
Cost for a short form Birth Certificate	$5.00
Cost for a certified Marriage Certificate	$5.00
Cost for a certified Death Certificate	$5.00

The Connecticut State Department of Health Services has copies of vital records from July 1, 1897. For earlier records contact the town where the event occurred. The Connecticut State Library has the Barbour Index to Connecticut Vital Records which covers the 1600s to the mid 1800s. They also have the Hale Index to Cemetery Inscriptions and the Hale Index to Marriage and Death Notices (which appeared in early newspapers).

REQUEST FOR COPY OF BIRTH CERTIFICATE

VS-39B 3-88

Mail request with fee or bring to:

STATE OF CONNECTICUT, DEPT. OF HEALTH SERVICES

Vital Records Section

150 Washington Street, Hartford, Conn. 06106

PLEASE PRINT　　　　*DO NOT MAIL CASH*

I. BIRTH CERTIFICATE OF:

FULL NAME AT BIRTH

DATE OF BIRTH　　　SEX

PLACE OF BIRTH *(Town, Hospital)*

II. PARENTS OF PERSON NAMED IN BIRTH CERTIFICATE:

FATHER'S FULL NAME　　　FATHER'S BIRTHPLACE *(State)*

MOTHER'S MAIDEN NAME　　　MOTHER'S BIRTHPLACE *(State)*

RESIDENCE OF PARENTS AT TIME OF THIS BIRTH

TYPE OF COPY (See explanation below)	LEGAL FEE	NO. OF COPIES	AMOUNT ATTACHED
Full Certified Copy	$		$
Certification of birth	$		$

III. PERSON MAKING THIS REQUEST

Your Name

Your Address

(No. and Street)

(Town, State)　　　*(Zip Code)*

▲ Your Signature

Full certified copy: Sufficient for all legal purposes. If requestor is a minor (under 18 years of age), parent or guardian must sign this request.

Certification of birth: Wallet-size certificate; sufficient for Social Security, school driver's license, and working papers.

*For the protection of the individual, certificates of vital events are **not** open to public inspection.*
A full certified copy can be obtained by registrant 18 or over, parent, or legal representative.
A birth certification can be obtained by registrant 16 or over, parent, spouse or legal representative.

RELATIONSHIP TO PERSON NAMED IN CERTIFICATE
(e.g. parents, attorney)

REASON FOR MAKING REQUEST

REQUEST FOR COPY OF MARRIAGE CERTIFICATE

VS-39M 3-88

Mail request with fee or bring to:

STATE OF CONNECTICUT, DEPT. OF HEALTH SERVICES

Vital Records Section

150 Washington Street, Hartford, Conn. 06106

PLEASE PRINT

	FULL NAME (First)	(Middle)	(Last)
GROOM			
BRIDE	FULL NAME BEFORE MARRIAGE (First)	(Middle)	(Last)

DATE OF MARRIAGE (Mo./Day/Year/)   PLACE OF MARRIAGE (Town)

	YOUR NAME
PERSON	
MAKING	YOUR ADDRESS (No. and Street)
THIS	
REQUEST	(Town, State) (Zip Code)

NO. OF COPIES WANTED | AMOUNT ATTACHED
$

YOUR SIGNATURE ▲

For the protection of the individual, certificates of vital events are **not** *open to public inspection.*

If the person making this request is not the person named in the certificate,

the following must be completed in order to permit this office to comply with the request.

RELATIONSHIP TO PERSON NAMED IN CERTIFICATE   REASON FOR MAKING REQUEST
(e.g. attorney)

REQUEST FOR COPY OF DEATH CERTIFICATE

VS-39D 3-88

Mail request with fee or bring to:

STATE OF CONNECTICUT, DEPT. OF HEALTH SERVICES

Vital Records Section

150 Washington Street, Hartford, Conn. 06106

PLEASE PRINT

	FULL NAME (First)	(Last)	Sex	DATE OF DEATH (OR DATE LAST KNOWN TO BE ALIVE) *(Month, Day, Year)*
DEATH CERTIF- ICATE OF:	PLACE OF DEATH (Town)	DATE OF BIRTH (Month, Day, Year)		PLACE OF BIRTH *(Town, State or Foreign Country)*
	FATHER'S NAME	MOTHER'S NAME		IF MARRIED, SPOUSE'S NAME

	YOUR NAME		NO. OF COPIES WANTED	AMOUNT ATTACHED $
PERSON MAKING THIS REQUEST	YOUR ADDRESS (No. and Street)		YOUR SIGNATURE ▲	
	(Town, State)	(Zip Code)		

For the protection of the individual, certificates of vital events are **not** *open to public inspection.*

RELATIONSHIP TO PERSON NAMED IN CERTIFICATE *(e.g. funeral director, attorney, next-of-kin)*	REASON FOR MAKING REQUEST

DELAWARE

Send your requests to:

Office of Vital Statistics
Division of Public Health
P.O. Box 637
Dover, Delaware 19903-0637

(302) 736-4721

Cost for a certified Birth Certificate	$5.00
Cost for a certified Marriage Certificate	$5.00
Cost for a certified Death Certificate	$5.00
Cost for a duplicate copy, when ordered at the same time	$3.00

The Delaware Office of Vital Statistics has birth and death records from January 1, 1861 to December 31, 1863 and January 1, 1881 to the present. They hold marriage records from January 1, 1847.

If your request is urgent you may call and charge your certificates to your Visa or MasterCard. There is a $5.00 fee for this service, plus the express mail charges.

The Family History Library of the Church of Jesus Christ of Latter-day Saints (Mormon Church) in Salt Lake City, Utah has microfilmed many of the original and published vital records and church registers of Delaware's cities and counties. They have made microfilm copies of the statewide birth records and indexes from 1861-1913, marriage records and indexes from 1680-1850, and death records and indexes from 1855-1910. For details on their holdings please consult your nearest Family History Center.

Today's Date

_____

Number of Copies

APPLICATION FOR BIRTH CERTIFICATE
COMPLETE ALL ITEMS REQUESTED BELOW AS ACCURATELY AS POSSIBLE

_____

Full Name at Birth of Person Whose Record is Requested - If Name Has Ever Been Changed Please Give Details on Back

_____

Date of Birth (Month, Day, Year)   *Place of Birth (Hospital)*

_____

Full Maiden Name of Mother

_____

Full Name of Father

_____

If Known, Name of Doctor or Midwife

_____

For What Purpose is Certificate Needed

PLEASE COMPLETE
YOUR NAME AND
MAILING ADDRESS

NAME ....

STREET ADDRESS ....

TOWN .... STATE ....

ZIP CODE ....

FEE: $5.00 for first copy. $3.00 for each additional copy of same record requested at same time.

A certified copy of the original birth record has entered thereon the name, birthdate, birthplace, names of parents and personal particulars. This copy is used for all purposes.

If the record is not found $5.00 will be retained as the search fee.

Insufficient fee being returned $ ....

If a check with the incorrect fee is being returned do not alter. make another check.

_____
Today's Date

_____
Number of Copies

APPLICATION FOR MARRIAGE CERTIFICATE
COMPLETE ALL ITEMS REQUESTED BELOW AS ACCURATELY AS POSSIBLE

FULL NAME OF GROOM _____

FULL MAIDEN NAME OF BRIDE _____

PLACE OF MARRIAGE _____

DATE OF MARRIAGE _____

NAME OF OFFICIATING MINISTER _____

* * * * *

MAIL COPY TO . . . .   NAME _____

STREET ADDRESS _____

TOWN _____

STATE _____ ZIP CODE _____

Fee for a certified copy is $5.00 for the first copy.

$3.00 for each additional copy of same record requested at same time.

Include fee with appplication - Make payable to the Office of Vital Statistics.

If the record is not found $5.00 will be retained as the search fee.

Insufficient fee being returned.

Document Control No.: 35-05-002-86-02-19-PH-

Today's Date

Number of Copies

APPLICATION FOR A CERTIFIED COPY OF A DEATH CERTIFICATE
(Complete items requested below accurately as possible)

Name of decedent

Race

Date of decease

Place of decease

Full name of decedent's father

Full maiden name of mother

For what purpose is certificate needed

SEND COPY TO . . . .

Name

Street/Development/Rural Delivery/Box Number

City/Town

State

Zip Code

Fee - $5.00 for first copy. $3.00 for each additional copies of same record requested at same time.

Payable to. . . . OFFICE OF VITAL STATISTICS

If the record is not found the fee will be retained for the search.

Insufficient fee being returned _____

If a check with the incorrect fee is being returned do not alter. Make another check.

DISTRICT OF COLUMBIA

Send your requests to:

> Government of the District of Columbia
> Department of Human Services
> Vital Records Branch
> 425 I Street, N.W., Room 3007
> Washington, DC 20001-2585

(202) 727-5314

Send your requests for Marriage Certificates to:

> Marriage Bureau
> Superior Court of the District of Columbia
> 515 5th Street, N.W., Room 111
> Washington, DC 20001

(202) 879-2839

Cost for a certified Birth Certificate	$16.00
Cost for a computerized short form Birth Certificate	$ 8.00
Cost for a certified Marriage Certificate	$5.00
Cost for a certified Death Certificate	$8.00

The Vital Records Branch has birth and death records from January 1, 1874. Marriage records are available from January 1, 1982 and must be ordered from the Superior Court.

If your request is urgent you may call and charge your certificates to your Visa or MasterCard. There is a $5.00 charge for this service.

GOVERNMENT OF THE DISTRICT OF COLUMBIA
Department of Human Services
Vital Records Branch

★ ★ ★
▆▆▆

APPLICATION FOR CERTIFIED COPY OF BIRTH
CERTIFICATE (*Use Only for D.C. Births*)

FEE:
Computer(short) $8.00; Archival(Long) $16.00

Full Name of Child

Sex	Date of Birth (Mo-Day-Yr)	Age at Last Birthday:	Certificate Number, If known:

Full Name of Mother BEFORE ANY MARRIAGE

Full Name of Father

Name of Hospital		Married Name of Mother at time of this birth:

DID BIRTH OCCUR   Yes   or   No
IN WASH., D.C.?   ☐   ☐

Purpose   Relationship of Applicant to Child:

Number and Type of
Copies: ▆▆▆
SHORT— Computer Form $8.00 _____
LONG— Full Form $16.00 _____

Signature of Applicant

Adress of Applicant

DHS-230 Rev. 7/85

SELF-MAILER REQUEST FOR DEATH TRANSCRIPTS

			Date
Full Name of Deceased (First, Middle, Last)	Sex	Date of Death	Place of Death

		VITAL RECORDS USE ONLY
No. Copies Requested:	Death Certificate No.	
Signature of Requestor		Amount
Purpose	Relationship to Deceased	( ) Check ( ) M. Order ( ) Cash
		Mail Control Number
		Date Mailed to Requestor:

⋆⋆⋆ ▬▬

GOVERNMENT OF THE DISTRICT OF COLUMBIA   DEPARTMENT OF HUMAN SERVICES

DHS-499 9/83

FLORIDA

Send your requests to:

> State of Florida
> Department of Health and Rehabilitation Services
> Vital Statistics
> P.O. Box 210
> Jacksonville, Florida 32231-0042

(904) 359-6900

Earlier records are available from:

> County Clerk
> County Court House
> (County where the event occurred)

Cost for a certified Birth Certificate	$ 8.00
Cost for a commemorative Birth Certificate	$25.00
Cost for a certified Marriage Certificate	$ 4.00
Cost for a certified Death Certificate	$ 4.00
Cost for a duplicate copy, when ordered at the same time	$ 3.00

The first State law requiring registration was passed in 1899. However, the Office of Vital Statistics has birth records from April 1865 and death records from August 1877 to the present. The Office has marriage records from June 6, 1927 to date.

If your request is urgent you may charge your certificates to your Visa or MasterCard for an additional $10.00 ($6.00 "rush" fee plus $4.00 credit card fee). Telephone the Department at (904) 359-6911 to arrange for this service.

HRS

State of Florida, Department of Health and Rehabilitative Services
APPLICATION FOR BIRTH RECORD FOR PERSON BORN IN FLORIDA

PLEASE TYPE OR PRINT CLEARLY

	First	Middle	Last	
FULL NAME AT BIRTH (Registrant)				
BIRTH NUMBER (if known)			Social Security Number (if known)	Age
DATE OF BIRTH (required for search)	Month	Day	Year	Sex
PLACE OF BIRTH	Hospital	City	County	FLORIDA
FATHER'S NAME	First	Middle	Last	
MOTHER'S MAIDEN NAME (name before marriage)	First	Middle	Last (Maiden)	

BEFORE ORDERING, please read the back of this form.
FEES ARE NONREFUNDABLE and subject to change without notice.

ONE CERTIFIED RECORD or WALLET SIZE CARD .... Record [ ]   Wallet Card [ ]   **$8.00***

ADDITIONAL CERTIFIED RECORDS or CARDS: $3.00 .... Number of Records [ ]   Number of Wallet Cards [ ]

RUSH ORDERS (optional): $6 per order. Envelope must be marked "RUSH" .... [ ]

COMMEMORATIVE CERTIFICATE NOW AVAILABLE: signed by the Governor of Florida; large size suitable for framing; $25 if ordered at the same time as certified record, $33 if ordered separately, allow 4-6 weeks for delivery [ ]

TOTAL ENCLOSED: Check or money order payable in U.S. dollars to Vital Statistics. ....   PLEASE DO NOT MAIL CASH   [ ]

Florida Law imposes an additional service charge of $10 for dishonored checks.

Applicant's Signature	Applicant's relationship to registrant
Applicant's Name (must be typed or printed)	Name and Address for mailing, if different from residence
Residence Address	Apt. No.	
City, State, Zip	Telephone No.	

*$2 of this fee is for Crimes Against Children; $1.50 is for Child Welfare Training

HRS Form 726, Oct 88 (Obsoletes previous editions which may not be used)
(Stock Number: 5740-000-0726-8)

HRS

State of Florida, Department of Health and Rehabilitative Services
APPLICATION FOR MARRIAGE RECORD FOR LICENSES ISSUED IN FLORIDA

	First	Middle	Last	Race
NAME OF GROOM				
NAME OF BRIDE	First	Middle	Last	Race
DATE OF MARRIAGE (approximate month & day)	Month	Day	Specify exact year or series of years to be searched	
PLACE LICENSE ISSUED	City or Town		County	FLORIDA

AVAILABILITY: Marriage records from June 6, 1927 are available at this office. Beginning with 1972, the marriage application is an integral part of the record issued here. Other marriage documents are obtainable only from the county court which issued them.

FIRST YEAR SEARCH FEE: (includes one certified record or a "no record found" statement).............

ADDITIONAL YEARS: $1 per year. The maximum search fee is $53 regardless of the total number of years to be searched

DUPLICATE RECORDS: when ordered at the same time. $2 each............

EXPEDITED PROCESSING: $5 per order (optional). Envelope must be marked "EXPEDITE"............

FOR JACKSONVILLE PICKUP SERVICE OR FOR MASTERCARD OR VISA CHARGES, TELEPHONE (904) 359-6911

COMMEMORATIVE CERTIFICATE NOW AVAILABLE: signed by the Governor of Florida; large size suitable for framing; $25 if ordered at the same time as certified record, $28 if ordered separately, allow 4-6 weeks for delivery.

PLEASE DO NOT MAIL CASH

TOTAL ENCLOSED: Check or money order payable in U.S. dollars to Vital Statistics.............
Florida Law imposes an additional service charge of $10 for dishonored checks.

	Name and Address for mailing, if different from residence
Applicant's Signature	
Applicant's Name (must be typed or printed)	
Residence Address	Apt. No.
City, State, Zip	Telephone No.

MAIL THIS APPLICATION TO VITAL STATISTICS, P.O. BOX 210, JACKSONVILLE, FL 32231-0042

PLEASE TYPE OR PRINT CLEARLY

State of Florida, Department of Health and Rehabilitative Services

APPLICATION FOR DEATH RECORD FOR DEATH WHICH OCCURRED IN FLORIDA

NAME OF DECEASED (Registrant)	First	Middle	Last	Race
SOCIAL SECURITY NO. (if known)				Sex
DATE OF DEATH (approximate month & day)	Month	Day	Specify exact year or series of years to be searched	
PLACE OF DEATH	City or Town		County	FLORIDA
NAME OF FUNERAL DIRECTOR				

BEFORE ORDERING, please read the back of this form. FEES ARE NONREFUNDABLE and subject to change without notice.

FIRST YEAR SEARCH FEE: (includes one certified record or a "no record found" statement) $4.00

ADDITIONAL YEARS: $2 per year. The maximum search fee is $54 regardless of the total number of years to be searched ...

ADDITIONAL RECORDS: when ordered at the same time. $3 each ...

RUSH ORDERS: $6 per order (optional). Envelope must be marked "RUSH" ...

FOR JACKSONVILLE PICKUP SERVICE OR FOR MASTERCARD OR VISA CHARGES, TELEPHONE (904) 359-6911

TOTAL ENCLOSED: Check or money order payable in U.S. dollars to Vital Statistics ...
Florida Law imposes an additional service charge of $10 for dishonored checks.

PLEASE DO NOT MAIL CASH

Applicant's Signature	Applicant's relationship to registrant
Applicant's Name (must be typed or printed)	Name and Address for mailing, if different from residence
Residence Address	Apt. No.
City, State, Zip	Telephone No.

MAIL THIS APPLICATION TO VITAL STATISTICS, P.O. BOX 210, JACKSONVILLE, FL 32231-0042

HRS FORM 727 Oct 88 (Obsoletes previous editions which may not be used)

PLEASE TYPE OR PRINT CLEARLY

GEORGIA

Send your requests to:

Georgia Department of Human Resources
Vital Records Unit
Room 217-H, Health Building
47 Trinity Avenue, S.W.
Atlanta, Georgia 30334-1201

(404) 656-4750

Earlier records are available from:

County Clerk
County Court House
(County where the event occurred)

Cost for a certified Birth Certificate	$3.00
Cost for a certified Birth Card	$4.00
Cost for an additional copy of Birth Card	$1.00
Cost for a certified Marriage Certificate	$3.00
Cost for a certified Death Certificate	$3.00
Cost for a duplicate birth, marriage or death certificate, when ordered at the same time	$1.00

The Georgia Department of Human Resources has birth and death records from January 1, 1919 to the present. They also hold marriage records from June 9, 1952 to the present. The Department requires payment in the form of a U.S. postal money order, cashier's check, or certified check.

If your request is urgent you may call and charge your certificates to your Visa or MasterCard. There is a $22.00 fee for this service, which includes the postal costs.

REQUEST FOR SEARCH OF
VITAL RECORDS — GEORGIA
CERTIFICATES ONLY

**THIS SPACE
FOR OFFICE USE ONLY**

FILL IN INFORMATION BELOW CONCERNING PERSON WHOSE CERTIFICATE IS REQUESTED —
PLEASE FOLLOW THE NUMBERS AND PRINT ALL INFORMATION.

Certificate Number

Years Searched

Clerk's Initials

1 CHECK THE TYPE OF CERTIFICATE REQUESTED. *(ONE Request Form Per Certificate)*

☐ BIRTH   ☐ DEATH   ☐ MARRIAGE   ☐ DIVORCE   ☐ OTHER

(1919 To Present)   *(1952 To Present)*

2 ENTER THE NUMBER OF CERTIFIED COPIES REQUESTED:

☐ FULL Certified Copy
of Certificate

☐ Birth Registration
Card (Wallet Size)

☐ Total Number
of Copies Requested

Amount Received

$_____

Search Fee

NOTE:
IF DELAYED CERTIFICATE OF
BIRTH WAS PREVIOUSLY
FILED, GIVE DATE _____

$_____

Amendment Fee

3 Name on Certificate

4 Date of Event

$_____

Filing Fee, Delayed

5 Age **6** Race **7** Sex **8** Place of Event (County) (State)

$_____

Replacement Fee

9 Full Name of Father (if this is a Marriage or Divorce Request, enter spouse's name here)

$_____

Total Fees

10 Full Name of Mother (include maiden name)

$_____

Refund (if any)

11

(Signature of Requester)

$_____

MACHINE VALIDATION

MACHINE VALIDATION

NOTE:
Fill in only the MAIL TO: information below.
This label will be used to mail your certificate
to you.
PLEASE PRINT NAME AND ADDRESS
CORRECTLY AND LEGIBLY.

Address Correspondence to:
Georgia Department of Human Resources
VITAL RECORDS SERVICE
Room 217-H, 47 Trinity Ave., S.W.
Atlanta, Georgia 30334

OFFICE USE ONLY

NAME ON CERTIFICATE _____

DATE OF EVENT _____

Certificate Number

MAIL TO:

_____

_____

_____

☐ Copy(ies) Issued

☐ Search Fee

☐ Voucher

☐ Refund

Amount
Refunded $_____

Form 3918 (Rev. 12-82)

Georgia Department of Human Resources
Vital Records Unit
Room 217—H, Health Building, 47 Trinity Avenue, S.W.
Atlanta, Georgia 30334
REQUEST FOR SEARCH OF DEATH RECORDS

PLEASE INDICATE BELOW THE NUMBER OF COPIES NEEDED AND FORWARD THIS FORM WITH EITHER A MONEY ORDER OR CHECK FOR THE CORRECT AMOUNT MADE PAYABLE TO THE GEORGIA DEPARTMENT OF HUMAN RESOURCES.

Total Number of Copies

Amount Received $ _____

FILL IN INFORMATION BELOW CONCERNING PERSON WHOSE CERTIFICATE IS REQUESTED

Name_____Date of Death _____
         (First)   (Middle)   (Last)

Age_____Race_____Sex_____Place of Death _____
                                                        (Hospital)   (City)   (County)   (State)

If Married, Name of Husband or Wife _____

Occupation of Deceased _____ Funeral Director's Name _____

Name of Doctor_____ Place of Burial _____
                                                        (City)   (County)   (State)

List below name and address of person to whom certificate is to be mailed.

Name _____

Address _____
            (No. & Street or RFD and Box No.)   (Apt. No.)

_____
         (City)   (State)   (Zip Code)

OAS(5)—17 (Rev. 9-74)

DO NOT WRITE IN SPACE BELOW

Georgia Department of Human Resources
Vital Records Unit
Room 217—H, Health Building, 47 Trinity Avenue, S.W.
Atlanta, Georgia 30334

Name

DOD

OAS(5)—17 (Rev. 9-74)

HAWAII

Send your requests to:

State Department of Health
Research and Statistics Office
Vital Records Section
1250 Punchbowl Street, Room 103
P.O. Box 3378
Honolulu, Hawaii 96801

(808) 961-7327

Cost for a certified Birth Certificate	$2.00
Cost for a certified Marriage Certificate	$2.00
Cost for a certified Death Certificate	$2.00

The Hawaii Vital Records Section has birth, marriage, and death records from 1853.

The Family History Library of the Church of Jesus Christ of Latter-day Saints (Mormon Church) in Salt Lake City, Utah has microfilmed many of the original and published vital records and church registers of Hawaii's cities and counties. They have made microfilm copies of the statewide birth registers from 1896 to 1903 and death registers from 1896 to 1909. For details on their holdings please consult your nearest Family History Center.

STATE OF HAWAII, DEPARTMENT OF HEALTH
RESEARCH AND STATISTICS OFFICE

REQUEST FOR CERTIFIED COPY OF **BIRTH** RECORD
(ATTACH $2.00 FOR EACH COPY. DO NOT SEND CASH BY MAIL)

	FIRST	MIDDLE	LAST
NAME ON CERTIFICATE			

	MONTH	DAY	YEAR		CITY OR TOWN	ISLAND
DATE OF BIRTH:				PLACE OF BIRTH:		

	FIRST	MIDDLE	LAST
FATHER'S NAME:			

	FIRST	MIDDLE	MAIDEN NAME
MOTHER'S NAME:			

NUMBER OF COPIES	AMOUNT ATTACHED $ ....

ALL ITEMS MUST BE COMPLETED IN FULL TO PERMIT THIS OFFICE TO COMPLY WITH THIS REQUEST. FOR THE PROTECTION OF THE INDIVIDUAL, CERTIFICATES OF VITAL EVENTS ARE NOT OPEN TO PUBLIC INSPECTION.

RELATIONSHIP OF REQUESTOR TO PERSON NAMED ON CERTIFICATE

REASON FOR REQUESTING A CERTIFIED COPY

	TELEPHONE NUMBERS
SIGNATURE OF REQUESTOR:	RES.:
PRINT OR TYPE NAME OF REQUESTOR:	BUS.:

MAIL TO:
NAME

NO. AND STREET OR P. O. BOX

CITY   STATE   ZIP

FOR OFFICE USE ONLY			
Index Searched		Volumes Searched	Date Copy Prepared
From To		From To	
Year	Volume	Certificate	Receipt Number

RS 135 (Rev. 1/84)

STATE OF HAWAII, DEPARTMENT OF HEALTH
RESEARCH AND STATISTICS OFFICE

REQUEST FOR COPY OF **MARRIAGE** OR **DIVORCE** RECORD
(ATTACH $2.00 FOR CERTIFIED COPY)

	MARRIAGE	DIVORCE
AMOUNT ATTACHED $ _____	NO. OF COPIES _____	NO. OF COPIES _____

		FIRST	MIDDLE	LAST
GROOM'S NAME:				

		FIRST	MIDDLE	LAST
BRIDE'S NAME:				

		MONTH	DAY	YEAR
DATE OF	MARRIAGE: OR DIVORCE:			

		CITY OR TOWN	ISLAND
PLACE OF	MARRIAGE: OR DIVORCE		

ALL ITEMS MUST BE COMPLETED IN FULL TO PERMIT THIS OFFICE TO COMPLY WITH THIS REQUEST. FOR THE PROTECTION OF THE INDIVIDUAL, CERTIFICATES OF VITAL EVENTS ARE NOT OPEN TO PUBLIC INSPECTION.

RELATIONSHIP OF REQUESTOR TO PERSONS NAMED ON CERTIFICATE

REASON FOR REQUESTING A CERTIFIED COPY

	TELEPHONE NUMBERS
SIGNATURE OF REQUESTOR:	RES.:
PRINT OR TYPE NAME OF REQUESTOR:	BUS.:

MAIL TO:

NAME

NO. AND STREET OR P. O. BOX

CITY	STATE	ZIP

FOR OFFICE USE ONLY		
Index Searched	Volumes Searched	Date Copy Prepared
From To	From To	
Year	Volume	Certificate	Receipt Number

RS 137 (Rev. 1/84)

STATE OF HAWAII, DEPARTMENT OF HEALTH
RESEARCH AND STATISTICS OFFICE

REQUEST FOR CERTIFIED COPY OF **DEATH** RECORD

ATTACH $2.00 FOR EACH CERTIFIED COPY	AMOUNT ATTACHED $ _____	NUMBER OF COPIES REQUESTED: _____

	FIRST	MIDDLE	LAST
NAME OF DECEASED:			

	MONTH	DAY	YEAR
DATE OF DEATH:			

	CITY OR TOWN	ISLAND
PLACE OF DEATH:		

ALL ITEMS MUST BE COMPLETED IN FULL TO PERMIT THIS OFFICE TO COMPLY WITH THIS REQUEST. FOR THE PROTECTION OF THE INDIVIDUAL, CERTIFICATES OF VITAL EVENTS ARE NOT OPEN TO PUBLIC INSPECTION.

RELATIONSHIP OF REQUESTOR TO DECEASED

REASON FOR REQUESTING A CERTIFIED COPY

	TELEPHONE NUMBERS
SIGNATURE OF REQUESTOR:	RES.:
PRINT OR TYPE NAME OF REQUESTOR:	BUS.:

MAIL TO:

NAME

NO. AND STREET OR P. O. BOX

CITY	STATE	ZIP

FOR OFFICE USE ONLY		
Index Searched	Volumes Searched	Date Copy Prepared
From To	From To	
Year	Volume	Certificate	Receipt Number

RS 136 (Rev. 1/84)

IDAHO

Send your requests to:

State of Idaho
Department of Health and Welfare
Bureau of Vital Statistics
(450 West State Street)
State House
Boise, Idaho 83720-6056

(208) 334-5980

Earlier records are available from:

County Clerk
County Court House
(County where the event occurred)

Cost for a certified Birth Certificate	$6.00
Cost for a plastic Birth Certificate	$6.00
Cost for a certified Marriage Certificate	$6.00
Cost for a certified Death Certificate	$6.00

The Idaho State Office of Vital Statistics has birth and death records from July 1911 and marriage records from May 1947.

BIRTH CERTIFICATE APPLICATION
(For Persons Born in Idaho)

MAIL TO: **VITAL STATISTICS**
450 W. State Street
Boise, ID 83720

Name on Certificate _____
(First)   (Middle)   (Last)

Place of Birth _____ File Number _____
(City)   (County)   (If Known)

If Home Birth Give Exact Address _____

Date of Birth _____ Sex _____
(Month)   (Day)   (Year)

Father's Name _____

Mother's Maiden Name _____

Purpose _____ Circle if Applicable: a. RUSH
                                                                 b. Twin Birth

Signature of Applicant _____

Address _____
(Street)   (City)   (State)   (Zip)

Relationship _____

Number of Copies Requested: Certified Copy _____ Plastic Wallet Card _____

PLEASE COMPLETE THE FOLLOWING IF THE CERTIFICATE IS TO BE MAILED
(Please Print Clearly)

_____
Name

_____
Street

_____
City   State   Zip   HWH 0160

APPLICATION FOR A MARRIAGE CERTIFICATE

Address correspondence and make money order payable to:

BUREAU OF VITAL STATISTICS, STANDARDS AND LOCAL HEALTH SERVICES
Department of Health and Welfare

Boise, Idaho   83720

FULL NAME OF GROOM _____

FULL NAME OF BRIDE _____

DATE OF MARRIAGE _____

CITY OF LICENSE APPLICATION _____

SIGNATURE OF APPLICANT _____

ADDRESS _____

RELATIONSHIP TO ABOVE PERSONS _____

Number of certified copies requested: _____
The fee for each certified copy and/or search is

NOTE: *Marriages have been filed with the State office since May, 1947. Prior to that time, they are filed with the County Recorder of each County in the State.*

HW-0161

APPLICATION FOR AN IDAHO DEATH CERTIFICATE

Note: Death records have been filed in Idaho since July 1911.

ADDRESS CORRESPONDENCE AND MAKE MONEY ORDER PAYABLE TO:

VITAL STATISTICS
450 W. State Street
Boise, ID   83720

1. Full name of deceased at death _____

2. Place of death _____ _____
   (City/Town)   (County)

3. Date of death _____
   (Month/Day/Year)   (If unknown, need approximate year or range to search)

4. Signature of applicant _____

   Address _____

   Relationship to person named in item #1 _____

   Number of certified copies requested: _____ The fee for each certified copy and/or search is _____

FOR DEATHS PRIOR TO 1969 PLEASE COMPLETE THE FOLLOWING: Purpose _____

Birth Date _____ Birth Place _____ Spouse _____
           (Month./Day/Year)   (City/State)

Mother's Maiden Name _____ Father's Name _____

ILLINOIS

Send your requests to:

Illinois Department of Public Health
Division of Vital Records
605 West Jefferson Street
Springfield, Illinois 62702-5035

(217) 782-6553

Send your requests for Marriage Certificates to:

County Clerk
Superior Court
(County where the Marriage License was issued)

Cost for a certified Birth Certificate	$15.00
Cost for a short form Birth Certificate	$10.00
Cost for a certified Birth Card	$10.00
Cost for an uncertified record	$10.00
Cost for a verified Marriage Certificate	$ 5.00
Cost for a certified Death Certificate	$15.00
Cost for a duplicate copy, when ordered at the same time	$ 2.00

The Illinois Department of Public Health has birth and death records from January 1, 1916. They hold marriage records from January 1, 1962. The Department will verify a marriage record but will not issue a certificate. For a Marriage Certificate write to the Superior Court. For copies of vital records before 1916 write to the County Clerk of the county where the event occurred.

If your request is urgent you may call and charge your certificates to your Visa or MasterCard. There is an additional $14.75 fee for this, which includes the postal charges.

APPLICATION FOR SEARCH OF BIRTH RECORD FILES

The fee for a search of the files is $10.00. If the record is found one CERTIFICATION or BIRTH CARD is issued at no additional charge. Additional certifications or birth cards of the same record ordered at the same time are $2.00 each. The fee for a FULL CERTIFIED COPY is $15.00 Additional certified copies of the same record ordered at the same time are $2.00 each. Please indicate below the type and number of copies requested and return this form with the proper fee. DO NOT SEND CASH. Make check or money order payable to: Illinois Department of Public Health.

CERTIFIED COPY $15.00 Each	CERTIFICATION $10.00 Each	BIRTH CARD (wallet size) $10.00 Each
Amount Enclosed:$_____ for _____copies	Amount Enclosed:$_____ for _____copies	Amount Enclosed:$_____ for _____copies

FULL NAME: First   Middle   Last

PLACE OF BIRTH: Street, RFD., Hosp.   City or Town   County

DATE OF BIRTH: Month   Day   Year   SEX: BIRTH NUMBER IF KNOWN:

FATHER:

MOTHER: Maiden Name   Married Name

Application Made By:

NAME:
(written signature)

STREET ADDRESS:

CITY: STATE: ZIP

YOUR RELATIONSHIP TO PERSON:

Mail Copy to (if other than applicant):

NAME:

STREET ADDRESS:

CITY   STATE: ZIP

INTENDED USE OF DOCUMENT:

NOTE: Birth certificates are confidential records, and copies can be issued only to persons entitled to receive them. The application must indicate the requestor's relationship to the person and the intended use of the document.

VR. 180 (5/87R)–DIVISION OF VITAL RECORDS–605 WEST JEFFERSON STREET–ILLINOIS DEPARTMENT OF PUBLIC HEALTH, SPRINGFIELD, ILLINOIS 62702

APPLICATION FOR SEARCH OF DEATH RECORD FILES

The fee for a search of the files is $10.00. If the record is found, one *CERTIFICATION is issued at no additional charge. Additional certifications of the same record ordered at the same time are $2.00 each. The fee for a **FULL CERTIFIED COPY is $15.00. Additional certified copies of the same record ordered at the same time are $2.00 each.

The fee for a 5 years search for genealogical research is $10.00. If found, one UNCERTIFIED copy of the record will be issued at no additional charge. Each additional year searched is $1.00. NOTE: STATE DEATH RECORDS BEGAN JANUARY 1, 1916.

A CERTIFICATION shows only the name of deceased, sex, place of death, date of death, date filed, and certificate number.

A FULL CERTIFIED COPY is an exact photographic copy of the original death certificate.

CERTIFIED COPY $15.00 Each	CERTIFICATION $10.00 Each	GENEALOGICAL RESEARCH
Amount Enclosed:$_____	Amount Enclosed:$_____	Amount Enclosed:$_____
for_____ copies	for_____ copies	for_____ year search

(DO NOT SEND CASH) Make check or money order payable to: Illinois Department of Public Health.

FULL NAME OF DECEASED:	First	Middle	Last

PLACE OF DEATH:	Hospital	City or Town	County

DATE OF DEATH:	Month Day Year	SEX:	RACE:	OCCUPATION:
DATE LAST KNOWN TO BE ALIVE:	Month Day Year	LAST KNOWN ADDRESS:		MARITAL STATUS:
DATE OF BIRTH:	Month Day Year	BIRTHPLACE: (City and State)		NAME OF HUSBAND OR WIFE:

FULL NAME OF FATHER OF DECEASED:	FULL MAIDEN NAME OF MOTHER OF DECEASED:

APPLICATION MADE BY:	MAIL COPY TO: (if other than applicant)
NAME:	NAME:
FIRM NAME: (if any)	FIRM NAME: (if any)
STREET ADDRESS:	STREET ADDRESS:
CITY: STATE: ZIP:	CITY: STATE: ZIP:

280 (5/87R) DIV. OF VITAL RECORDS, ILLINOIS DEPT. OF PUBLIC HEALTH, SPRINGFIELD, IL. 62702

Send your requests to:

Indiana State Board of Health
1330 West Michigan Street
P.O. Box 1964
Indianapolis, Indiana 46206-1964

(317) 633-0276

Send your requests for earlier vital records and Marriage Certificates to:

Clerk of the Court
County Court House
(County where the Marriage License was issued)

Cost for a certified Birth Certificate	$6.00
Cost for a certified Death Certificate	$4.00
Cost for a duplicate copy, when ordered at the same time	$1.00

The Indiana State Board of Health has birth certificates from October 1907 and death records from January 1900. While marriage records are located only in the courts in each county, the State does have an index to marriages from January 1958 to the present. The Board of Health, at this time, only issues an application form for birth certificates.

STATE of INDIANA

INDIANAPOLIS

STATE BOARD OF HEALTH

AN EQUAL OPPORTUNITY EMPLOYER

Address Reply to:
Indiana State Board of Health
1330 West Michigan Street
P. O. Box 1964
Indianapolis, IN 46206

MR# _____ Date Rec'd _____

☐ Your fee of $_____ was received
and is being held pending return of information
requested below.

☐ Please remit additional fee of
$ _____

Application for Search and Certified Copy of Birth Record. Please Complete All Items Below.

Full Name at Birth _____

 Could this birth be recorded under any other name? If so, please give name:

_____

Has this Person Ever Been Adopted? Yes _____ No _____ If YES, please give name **AFTER** adoption

_____

Place of Birth: City _____ County _____

Date of Birth: _____ Age Last Birthday _____

Full Name of Father: _____ _____
     (If adopted, give name of adoptive father)

Full Name of Mother Before Marriage: _____
       (If adopted, give name of adoptive mother)

Purpose For Which Record Is To Be Used: _____

Your Relationship to person whose birth record is requested _____

FOR STATE OFFICE USE

Vol. _____

Cert. # _____

Filed _____

Am. Date _____

S. Clerk _____

_____

Total Certificates _____ Total Fee $ _____

Signature of Applicant _____

Mailing Address _____

City and State _____ Zip _____

Original birth records filed with this office begin October 1907. If birth occurred before this date, contact the
health officer in the county where the birth occurred.

SBH06-040 2/79
State Form 35485

VR-12

Send your requests to:

Iowa State Department of Public Health
Vital Records Section
Lucas State Office Building
Des Moines, Iowa 50319-0075

(515) 281-4944

For earlier vital records write to:

County Clerk
County Court House
(County where the event occurred)

Cost for a certified Birth Certificate	$6.00
Cost for a certified Marriage Certificate	$6.00
Cost for a certified Death Certificate	$6.00
Cost for a duplicate copy, when ordered at the same time	$6.00

The Iowa State Department of Public Health has birth records from July 1, 1880, marriages from July 1, 1916, and deaths from January 1, 1891. However, the State did not make registration mandatory until July 1921, consequently less than 50% of the vital records were recorded before that date.

If your request is urgent you may call and charge your certificates to your Visa or MasterCard. There is a $5.00 fee plus an additional express mail charge for this service.

THIS IS AN APPLICATION FOR CERTIFIED COPY OF RECORD OF:

BIRTH ☐

(Please check ONLY one)　DEATH ☐

MARRIAGE ☐

1. Name on Record _____
   (If marriage record application, please provide both bride's and groom's names and
   county in which license was applied for)

2. Date of Event _____

3. City and/or County of Event _____

4. Father's Name _____
   (Please complete ONLY if this is a birth or death record application)

5. Mother's Maiden Name _____
   (Please complete ONLY if this is a birth or death record application)

6. Purpose for this copy _____

7. Has a copy of this record ever been received from this office? _____

8. Has name on certificate applied for ever been changed by court procedure? If so,
   please provide the name change _____

9. If this is a birth record application, is this the first-born child of this mother? ____
   or the ___2nd? ___3rd? ___4th? ___5th?

10. Number of copies requested at $6.00 per copy? _____

    Iowa Law requires a searching fee of $6.00 per record search and includes one certified
    copy, if found. Additional copies are $6.00 each. If a record is not found, the $6.00
    fee shall be retained for the search. Please make check or money order payable to the
    "Iowa Department of Public Health".

    (When mailing in an applica-　　Applicant's Signature _____
    tion, please enclose a
    stamped, self-addressed　　　 Applicant's Relationship _____ Tel.No._____
    envelope)

NO ORIGINAL RECORDS ARE ON FILE IN THIS OFFICE PRIOR TO JULY 1, 1880.

NAME AND ADDRESS:

_____　　　PICKUP ☐

_____

_____　　　MAIL ☐

588-0225 (7/86)
CPE-69365

Send your requests to:

Kansas State Department of Health and Environment
Office of Vital Statistics
900 S.W. Jackson
Topeka, Kansas 66612-1290

(913) 296-1400

For earlier records write to:

County Clerk
County Court House
(County where the event occurred)

Cost for a certified Birth Certificate	$6.00
Cost for a wallet-size Birth Certificate	$6.00
Cost for a certified Marriage Certificate	$6.00
Cost for a certified Death Certificate	$6.00
Cost for a duplicate copy, when ordered at the same time	$3.00

The Kansas Office of Vital Statistics has birth and death records from July 1, 1911. They hold marriage records from May 1, 1913.

If your request is urgent you may call and charge your certificates to your Visa or MasterCard. There is a $5.00 fee for this service.

APPLICATION FOR CERTIFIED COPY OF BIRTH CERTIFICATE

INSTRUCTIONS: Provisions of K.A.R. 28-17-6 require a fee of _____ for the first certified copy of a birth certificate and _____ for each additional copy of the same certificate requested at the same time. The certified copy fee must accompany this request. Make check payable to State Registrar of Vital Statistics. Cash sent by mail will be at applicant's risk.

If no birth record is located, the form and instructions for filing a Delayed Birth Certificate will be sent. The fee will be temporarily retained and may be applied to the cost of filing a delayed certificate. Fees expire 12 months from date paid.

FACTS CONCERNING THIS BIRTH

Full name on certificate _____

Date of birth _____ Present age of this person _____
       (Month)   (Day)   (Year)

Place of birth _____ Sex _____
       (City)   (County)   (State)

Full name of father _____ Birthplace _____

Full maiden name of mother _____ Birthplace _____

Is this birth certificate for an adopted child? _____ Legal change of name, other than by marriage? _____

If so, state original name (if known) _____

NOTICE: It is a violation of State and Federal Laws for anyone to make, sell or offer for sale any birth record for false identification purposes.

I hereby declare that as the applicant for a certified copy of the above described certificate, I have direct interest in the matter recorded and that the information therein contained is necessary for determination of personal or property rights, as per K.S.A. 65-2422(c).

....

Signature of person making request _____

Date of request _____

Relationship to person whose certificate is requested _____

PLEASE ENCLOSE SELF-ADDRESSED STAMPED ENVELOPE

COPIES REQUESTED:

Number

Complete Copy .... [____]
Wallet Size Card .... [____]
  (Not including Parents)

PLEASE PRINT CORRECT MAILING ADDRESS:

_____
       (Name)

_____
   (Street Address)

_____
(City)   (State)   (Zip)

REASON FOR REQUEST:

Social Security .... (____)
Passport .... (____)
Genealogy .... (____)
Other (School, Drivers License, etc.) ... (____)

Total fee enclosed .. $_____

Form VS-235 Rev. 7-1983

KANSAS STATE DEPARTMENT OF HEALTH AND ENVIRONMENT

Vital Statistics

APPLICATION FOR CERTIFIED COPY OF MARRIAGE LICENSE

Marriage records are on file from May 1, 1913. Provisions of K.A.R. 28-17-6 require a fee of _____ for the first certified copy of a marriage record and _____ for each additional copy of the same record ordered at the same time. Check or money order should be made payable to the State Registrar of Vital Statistics. Cash sent by mail will be at applicant's risk.

FACTS CONCERNING THIS MARRIAGE

Name of groom_____ Age at time of marriage_____

Maiden name of bride_____ Age at time of marriage_____

Date of marriage_____ _____

County in which marriage license was issued_____

City or town in which marriage took place_____

Notice: It is a violation of State and Federal Laws for anyone to make, sell, or offer for sale, any marriage record for false identification purposes.

I hereby declare that as the applicant for a certified copy of the above described certificate, I have direct interest in the matter recorded and that the information therein contained is necessary for determination of personal or property rights, as per K.S.A. 65-2422(c).

....

Signature of person making request_____

Relationship_____ Reason for request_____

┌─────────────────────────────────┐
│   PLEASE ENCLOSE SELF-ADDRESSED │   Number of copies_____
│   STAMPED ENVELOPE   │
└─────────────────────────────────┘   Total fee enclosed $_____

(All fees expire 12 months from date paid.)

PLEASE PRINT CORRECT MAILING ADDRESS:

_____   Date of request_____
          (Name)

_____
       (Street Address)

_____ _____ _____
  (City)   (State)   (Zip)

Form VS-237 Rev 7-1983

KANSAS STATE DEPARTMENT OF HEALTH AND ENVIRONMENT

Vital Statistics

APPLICATION FOR CERTIFIED COPY OF DEATH CERTIFICATE

Death Certificates are on file from July 1, 1911. Provisions of K.A.R. 28-17-6 require a fee of   for the first certified copy of a death certificate and for each additional copy of the same certificate ordered at the same time. Check or money order should be made payable to the State Registrar of Vital Statistics. Cash sent by mail will be at applicant's risk.

FACTS CONCERNING THIS DEATH

Full name of deceased_____

Place of death_____Date of death_____
              (City)   (County)   (State)   (Month) (Day) (Year)

(ADDITIONAL INFORMATION, IF KNOWN)

Age at time of death_____Place of birth_____
  (or birthdate)

Name of husband or maiden name of wife_____

Usual place of residence_____

Funeral Director's name_____

NOTICE: It is a violation of State and Federal Laws for anyone to make, sell, or offer for sale any death record for false identification purposes.

. . . .
I hereby declare that as the applicant for a certified copy of the above described certificate, I have direct interest in the matter recorded and that the information therein contained is necessary for determination of personal or property rights, as per K.S.A. 65-2422(c).

Signature of person making request_____
                                   Reason
Relationship_____for request_____

┌─────────────────────────────────┐
│ PLEASE ENCLOSE SELF-ADDRESSED │
│   STAMPED ENVELOPE   │   Number of copies_____
└─────────────────────────────────┘

PLEASE PRINT CORRECT MAILING ADDRESS: Total fee enclosed $_____
                                           (All fees expire 12 months from date paid.)

_____
          (Name)
                                           Date of request_____
_____
        (Street Address)

_____
(City)   (State)   (Zip Code)

Form VS-236 Rev 7-1983

KENTUCKY

Cost for a certified Birth Certificate	$5.00
Cost for a wallet-size Birth Certificate	$5.00
Cost for a certified Marriage Certificate	$4.00
Cost for a certified Death Certificate	$4.00

The Kentucky Office of Vital Statistics has birth and death records from January 1, 1911. They hold marriage records from June 1, 1958. Prior to this marriage records are available from the County Clerk of the county where the license was issued. The Public Records Division of the Kentucky Department for Libraries and Archives has microfilm copies of the vital records from 1852 to 1910 and indexes to vital records from January 1, 1911 through 1954.

The Family History Library of the Church of Jesus Christ of Latter-day Saints (Mormon Church) in Salt Lake City, Utah has microfilmed many of the original and published vital records and church registers of Kentucky's cities and counties. They have microfilm of birth records from 1874-1878, 1907-1910, 1939-1954; marriage records from 1875-1878, 1906-1914; and death records from 1874-1878, 1905-1910, 1939-1954. There is an additional index to births and deaths from 1911-1954. For details on their holdings please consult your nearest Family History Center.

VS-37
(Rev. 9/84)

COMMONWEALTH OF KENTUCKY
DEPARTMENT FOR HEALTH SERVICES

APPLICATION FOR BIRTH CERTIFICATE

Please Print or Type All Information Required on This Form

Full Name at Birth _____ Sex _____

Date of Birth _____ Ky. County of Birth _____

Mother's Full Maiden Name _____

Father's Name _____

Name of Attending Physician or Midwife _____ Hospital _____

Has Original Certificate Been Changed? If So, To _____

Have You Ever Received a Copy Before? ☐ Yes ☐ No ☐ Unknown

If yes, When? _____
Year

Please State Purpose For Which This Certificate Is Needed: _____

_____

_____ Phone: _____
(Signature of Applicant)   (Area Code)   (Number)

Relationship to Person Named on Certificate _____

Office Use Only
Vol. _____
Cert. _____
Year _____
Date _____
Initials _____

Check Type of   ☐ Full Size Copy -   Quantity Desired _____
Copy desired
                       ☐ Billfold Size Birth Card -   - Quantity Desired _____

Print Name and Mailing Address of Person to Receive the Certificate.
This Portion is a Mailing Insert and Will be Used to Mail the Copy
you Have Requested.

_____
Name

_____
Street Number & Name

_____
City — State — Zip Code

APPLICANT'S PHONE. _____
                    (Area Code)   (Number)

VS-230
(Rev. 2-83)

COMMONWEALTH OF KENTUCKY
DEPARTMENT FOR HEALTH SERVICES

275 EAST MAIN STREET
FRANKFORT, KENTUCKY 40621

APPLICATION FOR MARRIAGE/DIVORCE CERTIFICATE

Please Print or Type All Information Given on This Form.

It must be clear which information you are requesting—whether marriage or divorce. Please circle the appropriate reference each place required below. Accurate information is necessary to enable us to locate the certificate you are requesting.

Full Name of Husband _____

Maiden Name of Wife _____

County In Which   (Marriage License)   (Divorce Decree)   Granted _____
                          (Circle One)

Date of   (Marriage) (Divorce) _____
                   (Circle One)   (Mo.)   (Day)   (Year)

Name of Applicant _____

Address _____
              (Street No.)   (City)   (State)   (Zip Code)

The Information I Am Requesting Concerns
(Marriage) (Divorce)
(Circle One)

Please Indicate Quantity Desired _____

Office Use Only
Vol. _____
Cert. _____
Year _____
Date _____
Initials _____

Print Name and Mailing Address of Person to Receive the Certificate. This Portion is a Mailing Insert and Will be Used to Mail the Copy you Have Requested.

_____
Name

_____
Street Number & Name

_____
City—State—Zip Code

VS-31
(Rev. 1-85)

COMMONWEALTH OF KENTUCKY
DEPARTMENT FOR HEALTH SERVICES

APPLICATION FOR DEATH CERTIFICATE

Please Print or Type All Information Required on This Form.

Full Name of Deceased _____

Date of Death _____ KY County in Which
          (Mo.)   (Day)   (Year)   Death Occurred _____

Did Death Occur ☐ ☐ If "Yes" Give
In a Hospital?   Yes No Name of Hospital _____

Name of Attending Physician _____

Name of Funeral Director _____

	Office Use Only
Address _____ | Vol. _____ |
(Street)   (City)   (State) | Cert. _____ |
Name of Applicant _____ | Year _____ |
Address _____ | Date _____ |
(Street)   (City)   (State) | Initials _____ |

_____ Phone _____
    Signature of Applicant   (Area Code) (Number)

Please Indicate Quantity Desired _____

Print Name and Mailing Address of Person to Receive the Certificate.
This Portion is a Mailing Insert and Will be Used to Mail the Copy
you Have Requested.

_____
                   Name

_____
        Street Number & Name

_____
       City — State — Zip Code

Send your requests to:

Louisiana State Department of Health
  and Human Resources
Office of Preventive and Public Health Services
Vital Records Registry
P.O. Box 60630
New Orleans, Louisiana 70160-0630

(504) 568-5152

For earlier vital records write to:

County Clerk
County Court House
(County where the event occurred)

Cost for a certified Birth Certificate	$8.00
Cost for a wallet-size Birth Certificate	$3.00
Cost for a certified Marriage Certificate	$5.00
Cost for a certified Death Certificate	$5.00

The Louisiana Vital Records Registry has statewide records from July 1, 1914. They also hold New Orleans birth records from 1790 and death records from 1803.

DEPARTMENT OF HEALTH AND HUMAN RESOURCES
OFFICE OF PREVENTIVE AND PUBLIC HEALTH SERVICES
VITAL RECORDS REGISTRY

APPLICATION FOR CERTIFIED COPY OF BIRTH CERTIFICATE

PHS 520A   (Rev. 4/85)

TO REQUEST SERVICE BY MAIL, SUBMIT CHECK OR MONEY ORDER PAYABLE TO VITAL RECORDS.
CASH IS SENT AT YOUR OWN RISK.
IF NO RECORD IS FOUND, YOU WILL BE NOTIFIED AND FEES WILL BE RETAINED FOR THE SEARCH.

☐ BIRTHCARD (For sample see back side of this form.)
☐ BIRTH CERTIFICATE

_____
Name at Birth

_____
Date of Birth (If Unknown Give Approximate Age)

_____
City or Parish of Birth

_____
Father's Name

_____
Mother's Name (Before Marriage)

HOW ARE YOU RELATED TO THE PERSON WHOSE RECORD YOU ARE REQUESTING? _____

WRITE YOUR ADDRESS (FOR OUR RECORDS ONLY)

Name _____

Street or
Route No. _____

City
and State _____
                              Zip Code

Number of Copies
of each Certificate
Requested: _____

Total Fees Due $_____

I AM AWARE THAT ANY PERSON WHO WILLFULLY AND KNOWINGLY MAKES ANY FALSE STATEMENT IN
AN APPLICATION FOR A CERTIFIED COPY OF A VITAL RECORD IS SUBJECT UPON CONVICTION TO
A FINE OF NOT MORE THAN $10,000 OR IMPRISONMENT OF NOT MORE THAN FIVE YEARS, OR BOTH.

(PLEASE DO NOT WRITE IN THIS SPACE)

CLIENT WAITING   _____
CLIENT WILL PICK UP   _____
NEXT DAY MAIL OUT   _____
TIME IN   _____
TIME OUT   _____

_____
Signature of Applicant

_____
Home Phone Number

_____
Office Phone Number

APPLICATION FOR CERTIFIED COPY OF MARRIAGE CERTIFICATE

PHS 520C   (Rev. 5/85)

TO REQUEST SERVICE BY MAIL, SUBMIT CHECK OR MONEY ORDER PAYABLE TO VITAL RECORDS.
CASH IS SENT AT YOUR OWN RISK.
IF NO RECORD IS FOUND, YOU WILL BE NOTIFIED AND FEES WILL BE RETAINED FOR THE SEARCH.

MARRIAGE RECORD OF:

_____

Groom

_____

Bride

_____

Parish where License was Purchased

_____

Date of Marriage

PLEASE NOTE: A MARRIAGE RECORD IS AVAILABLE FROM THE DIVISION OF VITAL RECORDS ONLY IF THE MARRIAGE LICENSE WAS PURCHASED IN ORLEANS PARISH. OTHERWISE YOU MUST CONTACT THE CLERK OF COURT IN THE PARISH WHERE THE LICENSE WAS PURCHASED.

WRITE YOUR ADDRESS (FOR OUR RECORDS ONLY)

Name _____

Street or
Route No. _____

City
and State _____

Zip Code

Number of Copies
of each Certificate
Requested: _____

Total Fees Due $_____

- -

PLEASE MAIL FORM TO:

**LOUISIANA VITAL RECORDS SECTION
P. O. BOX 60630
NEW ORLEANS, LOUISIANA 70160**

PLEASE FILL OUT THE ADDRESS BELOW ONLY IF THE CERTIFICATE IS TO BE MAILED

Certificate to be mailed to:

Name _____

Street or
Route No. _____

City
and State _____

Zip Code

APPLICATION FOR CERTIFIED COPY OF DEATH CERTIFICATE

PHS 520B   (Rev. 5/85)

TO REQUEST SERVICE BY MAIL, SUBMIT CHECK OR MONEY ORDER PAYABLE TO VITAL RECORDS.
CASH IS SENT AT YOUR OWN RISK.
IF NO RECORD IS FOUND, YOU WILL BE NOTIFIED AND FEES WILL BE RETAINED FOR THE SEARCH.

DEATH RECORD OF:

_____
Name at Death

_____
Date of Death

_____
City or Parish of Death

HOW ARE YOU RELATED TO THE PERSON WHOSE RECORD YOU ARE REQUESTING? _____

WRITE YOUR ADDRESS (FOR OUR RECORDS ONLY)

Name _____

Street or
Route No. _____

City
and State _____
                                    Zip Code

Number of Copies
of each Certificate
Requested: _____

Total Fees Due $_____

PLEASE MAIL FORM TO:

LOUISIANA VITAL RECORDS SECTION
P. O. BOX 60630
NEW ORLEANS, LOUISIANA 70160

PLEASE FILL OUT THE ADDRESS BELOW ONLY IF THE CERTIFICATE IS TO BE MAILED

Certificate to be mailed to:

Name _____

Street or
Route No. _____

City
and State _____
                                    Zip Code

MAINE

Send your requests to:

>
> Maine Department of Human Services
> Office of Vital Statistics
> (221 State Street)
> State House, Station 11
> Augusta, Maine 04333-6831

(207) 289-3184

For earlier vital records write to:

>
> County Clerk
> County Court House
> (County where the event occurred)

Cost for a certified Birth Certificate	$5.00
Cost for a certified Marriage Certificate	$5.00
Cost for a certified Death Certificate	$5.00
Cost for a duplicate copy, when ordered at the same time	$2.00

The Maine Office of Vital Statistics has records from January 1, 1892. Make your check payable to "Treasurer, State of Maine."

If your request is urgent you may call and charge your certificates to your Visa or MasterCard. There is a $6.00 fee for this service.

The Family History Library of the Church of Jesus Christ of Latter-day Saints (Mormon Church) in Salt Lake City, Utah has microfilmed many of the original and published vital records and church registers of Maine's cities and counties. They have microfilm of births, marriages, and deaths from 1670 to 1922. They also have a bride's marriage index from 1895 to 1953. For details on their holdings please consult your nearest Family History Center.

DEPARTMENT OF HUMAN SERVICES
OFFICE OF VITAL STATISTICS
STATE HOUSE STATION 11
AUGUSTA, MAINE   04333

APPLICATION FOR A SEARCH AND A CERTIFIED COPY OF A RECORD OF BIRTH

FEE $5.00

Make Checks Payable to - "TREASURER OF STATE"

Applicant: Please fill in the following items of information
for searching and record identification.

Name at Birth _____

Date of Birth _____

Place of Birth _____

Father's Full Name _____

Mother's Maiden Name _____

Signature of Applicant: _____

VS-108-B   2/87

DEPARTMENT OF HUMAN SERVICES
OFFICE OF VITAL STATISTICS
STATE HOUSE STATION 11
AUGUSTA, MAINE   04333

APPLICATION FOR A SEARCH AND A CERTIFIED COPY OF A RECORD OF MARRIAGE

FEE $5.00

Applicant: Please fill in the following items of information
for searching and record identification.

Full Name of Groom _____

Full Name of Bride _____

Date of Marriage _____

Place of Marriage _____

Reason for Requesting Record or Relationship _____

Signature of Applicant: _____

VS-108-M   2/87

DEPARTMENT OF HUMAN SERVICES
OFFICE OF VITAL STATISTICS
STATE HOUSE STATION 11
AUGUSTA, MAINE   04333

APPLICATION FOR A SEARCH AND A CERTIFIED COPY OF A RECORD OF DEATH

FEE $5.00

Make Checks Payable to "TREASURER OF STATE"

Applicant: Please fill in the following items of information
for searching and record identification.

Full Name of Decedent _____

Date of Death _____

Place of Death _____

Reason for Requesting Record or Relationship _____

Signature of Applicant: _____

VS-108-D   3/87

MARYLAND

Send your requests to:

Maryland Department of Health & Mental Hygiene
Division of Vital Records
4201 Patterson Avenue
P.O. Box 68760
Baltimore, Maryland 21215

(301) 764-3034

For abstracts of records before January 1, 1969 write to:

Maryland State Archives
Hall of Records
350 Rowe Boulevard
Annapolis, Maryland 21401

They will make an abstract of the records in their custody for $5.00.

(301) 974-3914

Cost for a certified Birth Certificate	$4.00
Cost for a wallet-size Birth Certificate	$4.00
Cost for a certified Marriage Certificate	$4.00
Cost for a certified Death Certificate	$4.00
Cost for a duplicate copy, when ordered at the same time	$4.00

The Maryland Division of Vital Records has birth and death records from August 1, 1898 and marriage records from June 1, 1951. They also hold birth and death records for Baltimore from January 1, 1875. For marriage records before June 1, 1951 write to the Clerk of the Circuit Court where the marriage license was issued. The Maryland State Archives has restrictions on birth records for 100 years and death records for 20 years. They will, however, provide an abstract of the record for a fee of $5.00.

If your request is urgent you may call and charge your certificates to your Visa or MasterCard. There is a $6.00 fee for this service, plus the postal charges.

STATE OF MARYLAND
DEPARTMENT OF HEALTH & MENTAL HYGIENE
DIVISION OF VITAL RECORDS
P.O. BOX 68760
BALTIMORE, MARYLAND 21215-0020

Send Check or Money Order Payable to:
DIVISION OF VITAL RECORDS

DO NOT WRITE IN ABOVE SPACE

APPLICATION FOR A COPY OR ABSTRACT OF BIRTH CERTIFICATE

Date: _____ 19 _____

Full name at birth: _____
                    (First)   (Middle)   (Last)

Date of birth: _____ Sex: _____
               (Month)   (Day)   (Year)

Age last birthday: _____   Certificate No. (If known): _____

Place of birth: _____   County: _____

Name of hospital (If known): _____

Number of child in order of birth: _____

Full name of father: _____

Full maiden name of mother: _____

Reason for request: _____

Your relationship to person whose birth record is requested: _____

NOTE: A non-refundable $4.00 fee is required for each certificate requested. If the
search provides no record, the $4.00 fee is not returned, and a certificate of no
record will be issued. You may apply in person or by mail. When applying by mail,
please enclose a self-addressed, stamped envelope. DO NOT SEND CASH OR STAMPS.
Birth records are on file beginning 1875 for Baltimore City and 1898 for Maryland
Counties. For County birth records prior to 1898, contact the Maryland State
Archives.

IMPORTANT: PLEASE INDICATE BELOW THE NUMBER AND TYPE OF RECORD REQUESTED.

☐	CERTIFIED PHOTOCOPY:	This can be used for all purposes.
☐	CERTIFICATION OF BIRTH CARD: (WALLET-SIZE)	This card may be used for new school enrollment, applying for social security numbers and social security benefits. (For other purposes, please contact the party involved).
	NOTE: AVAILABLE ONLY FOR YEARS 1973 AND AFTER.	

APPLICANT'S NAME (Print): _____

APPLICANT'S SIGNATURE: _____

MAILING ADDRESS: _____

CITY AND STATE: _____

VR C-31
DHMH 1526
REV. 7/89

ZIP CODE: _____

STATE OF MARYLAND
DEPARTMENT OF HEALTH & MENTAL HYGIENE
DIVISION OF VITAL RECORDS
P.O. BOX 68760
BALTIMORE, MARYLAND 21215-0020

Send Check or Money Order Payable to:
DIVISION OF VITAL RECORDS

DO NOT WRITE IN ABOVE SPACE

APPLICATION FOR A COPY OF MARRIAGE CERTIFICATE

Date: _____ 19 _____

Groom's name: _____
(First)   (Middle)   (Last)

Bride's maiden name: _____
(First)   (Middle)   (Last)

Date of marriage: _____
(Month)   (Day)   (Year)

Place of marriage: _____
(Town)   (County)

Reason for request: _____

Whom do you represent: _____

NOTE: A non-refundable $4.00 fee is required for each certificate requested. If the
search provides no record, the $4.00 fee is not returned, and a certificate of no
record will be issued. You may apply in person or by mail. When applying by mail
please enclose a self-addressed, stamped envelope. DO NOT SEND CASH OR STAMPS.
For marriages performed PRIOR TO JUNE, 1951, certified copies of certificates are
available only from the Circuit Court of the County in which the marriage took
place.

IMPORTANT: PLEASE INDICATE BELOW THE NUMBER OF COPIES REQUESTED.

☐   CERTIFIED PHOTOCOPY

APPLICANT'S NAME (Print): _____

APPLICANT'S SIGNATURE: _____

MAILING ADDRESS: _____

CITY AND STATE: _____

ZIP CODE: _____

VR C-80
DHMH 1937
REV. 7/89

STATE OF MARYLAND
DEPARTMENT OF HEALTH & MENTAL HYGIENE
DIVISION OF VITAL RECORDS
P. O. BOX 68760
BALTIMORE, MARYLAND 21215-0020

Send check or money order payable to:
DIVISION OF VITAL RECORDS   DO NOT WRITE IN ABOVE SPACE

APPLICATION FOR A COPY OF A DEATH CERTIFICATE

DATE:_____

NOTE: A non-refundable $4.00 fee is required for each certificate requested
If the search provides no record, the $4.00 fee is not returned, and a
Certificate of No Record will be issued. You may apply in person or by
mail. When applying by mail, please enclose a self-addressed, stamped
envelope. DO NOT SEND CASH OR STAMPS. We do not issue records prior to
1969 for genealogical purposes. If you desire a death certificate for
genealogical purposes, please contact the Maryland Hall of Records,
350 Rowe Boulevard, Annapolis, Maryland 21401.

Name of deceased: _____
                    (First)   (Middle)   (Last)

Date of death:_____
                    (Month)   (Day)   (Year)

Place of death regardless of residence:_____
                                         (Town)   (County)

Reason for request:_____

Your relation to deceased:_____

IMPORTANT: PLEASE INDICATE BELOW THE NUMBER OF COPIES REQUESTED.

CERTIFIED PHOTOCOPY

        APPLICANT'S NAME (Print):_____

        APPLICANT'S SIGNATURE:_____

        MAILING ADDRESS:_____

        CITY, STATE AND ZIP CODE:_____

CR C-34
DHMH 4326
REV 7/89

MASSACHUSETTS

Send your requests to:

Massachusetts Executive Office of Human Services
Division of Health Statistics and Research
Registry of Vital Records and Statistics
150 Tremont Street, Room B-3
Boston, Massachusetts 02111-1197

(617) 727-0036

For records from 1841 to 1895 write to:

Massachusetts State Archives
220 Morrissey Blvd.
Boston, Massachusetts 02125

The fee for certified copies from the Archives is $3.00.

(617) 727-2816

Cost for a certified Birth Certificate	$6.00
Cost for a certified Marriage Certificate	$6.00
Cost for a certified Death Certificate	$6.00
Cost for a duplicate copy, when ordered at the same time	$6.00

While Massachusetts has vital records available from the 1600s, the Massachusetts Registry of Vital Records and Statistics has records only from January 1, 1896. The State Archives has records from January 1, 1841 to the end of 1895. For earlier records write to the town where the event occurred or consult the hundreds of published town vital records for the State. The Registry of Vital Records and Statistics does not currently provide application forms for vital records.

The Family History Library of the Church of Jesus Christ of Latter-day Saints (Mormon Church) in Salt Lake City, Utah has microfilmed many of the original and published vital records and church registers of Massachusett's cities and counties. They have microfilm of the vital records from 1841 to 1899; corrections of the vital records made from 1893 to 1970; and indexes from 1891 to 1971. For details on their holdings please consult your nearest Family History Center.

MICHIGAN

Send your requests to:

Michigan Department of Public Health
Office of the State Registrar
   and Center for Health Statistics
3423 North Logan Street
P.O. Box 30035
Lansing, Michigan 48909

(517) 335-8656

Vital records are also kept by:

County Clerk
County Court House
(County where the event occurred)

Cost for a certified Birth Certificate	$10.00
Cost for a wallet-size Birth Certificate	$10.00
Cost for a certified Marriage Certificate	$10.00
Cost for a certified Death Certificate	$10.00
Cost for a duplicate copy, when ordered at the same time	$ 3.00

The Michigan State Registrar has birth and death records from January 1, 1867 and marriage records from April 1867. If you are doing genealogical research the fee for the first record requested is $10.00, and the additional records requested are $6.00 each if requested in the same envelope.

If your request is urgent you may call and charge your certificates to your Visa or MasterCard. There is a $5.00 fee for this service, plus the postal charges.

APPLICATION FOR A CERTIFICATE OF REGISTRATION OR A CERTIFIED COPY OF A BIRTH RECORD

PLEASE READ INSTRUCTIONS ON REVERSE SIDE

PRINT CLEARLY

1. Name at Birth_____ Date of Birth: _____
   Or adopted name: First   Middle   Last   Mo   Day   Year

2. Place of Birth: _____
                   Hospital (if known)   City   County

3. Mother's Maiden Name: _____
                         First   Middle   Last

4. Father's Name: _____
                  First   Middle   Last

5. Is the individual named in No. 1 adopted?   ☐ yes   ☐ no   ☐ maybe

   If the information is available and you are the individual named in No. 1, or if the record is being sent to the individual named in No. 1, do you wish to receive the name and location of the court where the adoption took place?   ☐ yes   ☐ no

6.
   PLEASE PROVIDE IN THIS SPACE ANY ADDITIONAL INFORMATION THAT WOULD HELP US LOCATE THE RECORD, FOR EXAMPLE, A LEGAL CHANGE OF NAME.

RECORDS CAN BE PROVIDED ONLY TO ELIGIBLE PERSONS (SEE INSTRUCTIONS ON REVERSE.)

7. Please place an "X" in the appropriate area and follow additional instructions.
   My Relationship To The Person In Line 1 Is:

   ☐ INDIVIDUAL NAMED IN LINE 1   ☐ PARENT NAMED ON RECORD   ☐ LEGAL GUARDIAN

   ☐ LEGAL REPRESENTATIVE — Whom Are You Representing? _____

   ☐ HEIR — Specify Your Relationship To The Person In Line 1? _____

   IF YOU STATE YOUR RELATIONSHIP AS AN HEIR PLEASE PROVIDE THE DATE AND PLACE OF DEATH OF THE PERSON NAMED IN LINE 1.

   DATE _____

   PLACE _____

8. Applicant's Signature: _____
                          Signature of Applicant   Date

   Applicant's Address: _____
                        Street   City   State   Zip   Area Code   Phone

   (APPLICATION MUST BE SIGNED TO PROCESS YOUR REQUEST)

   THIS BOX FOR INTERNAL USE ONLY

   DP INFORMATION

   YEAR _____

   REGISTRATION NUMBER _____

(PLEASE DO NOT REMOVE THIS STUB)

PRINT THE NAME AND MAILING ADDRESS OF THE PERSON TO WHOM THE RECORD(S) ARE TO BE SENT.

THIS IS A MAILING INSERT AND WILL BE USED TO MAIL THE RECORDS

PLEASE SEND THE FOLLOWING

Fee

☐ Certificate of Registration (wallet size)   @ $10.00 _____

_____ Additional Certificates of Registration   @ $ 3.00 _____

☐ Certified Photocopy   @ $10.00 _____

_____ Additional Copies   @ $ 3.00 _____

_____ Additional years Searched (See instructions)   @ $ 3.00 Per Year _____

* See Instructions for Special Fees

TOTAL _____

9. Name: _____

   Street: _____

   City: _____

   State: _____ Zip: _____

MAKE CHECK OR MONEY ORDER PAYABLE TO **STATE OF MICHIGAN**

APPLICATION FOR A CERTIFIED COPY OF A MARRIAGE CERTIFICATE

We are required by Act 368 of 1978 as amended, to collect the statutory fee before a search may be made for any record. Fee schedule is itemized below. Please make check or money order payable to the STATE OF MICHIGAN.

Minimum fee for ONE CERTIFIED COPY — $10.00 Minimum fee includes a 3 year search	
ADDITIONAL CERTIFIED COPIES of the same record ordered at the same time — $3.00 each	
ADDITIONAL YEARS searched over 3 years — $3.00 each (when exact year is not known and more than a 3 year search is required, remit — $3.00 FOR EACH additional year over the minimum 3 years searched)	
TOTAL	

FEES PAID TO SEARCH THE FILES ARE NOT REFUNDABLE.

When a record is not found, the applicant will receive notification that the record as requested is not on file in this office.

PLEASE PRINT

Please send me a certified copy of the marriage certificate of:

Name of groom _____

Name of bride at time of
application for marriage license _____

Date of marriage _____
                        (Month)   (Day)   (Year)

If exact year is unknown _____
                                        (Years to be searched)

Place where license was obtained _____
                                                    (County)

_____   _____
        Applicant's Signature   Date

- -

(PLEASE DO NOT REMOVE THIS STUB)   **ADDITIONAL INFORMATION**
PRINT THE NAME AND MAILING ADDRESS OF THE PERSON TO WHOM
THE RECORD(S) ARE TO BE SENT.
THIS IS A MAILING INSERT AND WILL BE USED TO MAIL THE RECORDS.
                                    ▼

NAME _____

STREET _____

CITY _____

STATE _____ ZIP _____

B-225-C 10/84

APPLICATION FOR A CERTIFIED COPY OF A DEATH CERTIFICATE

We are required by Act 368 of 1978 as amended, to collect the statutory fee before a search may be made for any record. Fee schedule is itemized below. Please make check or money order payable to the STATE OF MICHIGAN.

Minimum fee for ONE CERTIFIED COPY — $10.00 Minimum fee includes a 3 year search	
ADDITIONAL CERTIFIED COPIES of the same record ordered at the same time — $3.00 each	
ADDITIONAL YEARS searched over 3 years — $3.00 each (when exact year is not known and more than a 3 year search is required, remit — $3.00 FOR EACH additional year over the minimum 3 years searched	
TOTAL	

FEES PAID TO SEARCH THE FILES ARE NOT REFUNDABLE

WHEN A RECORD IS NOT FOUND, THE APPLICANT WILL RECEIVE NOTIFICATION THAT THE RECORD AS REQUESTED IS NOT ON FILE IN THIS OFFICE.

PLEASE PRINT

Please send me a certified copy of the death certificate of:

Name of deceased: _____
    (First)   (Middle)   (Last)

Date of death: _____
    (Month)   (Day)   (Year)

If exact year is unknown: _____
                              (Years to be searched)

Place of death _____
                    (Township, Village, or City)   (County)

_____   _____
    Applicant's Signature   Date

IF THE INFORMATION REQUESTED ABOVE IS NOT KNOWN, please indicate in the box below any data which may be used for identifying the record, such as marital status, name of husband or wife if married, parents' names, age or birthplace.

- -

(PLEASE DO NOT REMOVE THIS STUB)

ADDITIONAL INFORMATION

PRINT THE NAME AND MAILING ADDRESS OF THE PERSON TO WHOM THE RECORD(S) ARE TO BE SENT.
THIS IS A MAILING INSERT AND WILL BE USED TO MAIL THE RECORDS

NAME: _____

STREET: _____

CITY: _____

STATE: _____ ZIP: _____

B-225B 12/84

MICHIGAN DEPARTMENT OF PUBLIC HEALTH
Office of the State Registrar & Center for Health Statistics
P.O. Box 30035
Lansing, MI 48909

APPLICATION TO REQUEST. A VITAL RECORD FOR GENEALOGICAL RESEARCH

By Law, the statutory fee must be paid before a search may be made for any Record. The fee schedule is itemized below. Please make check or money order payable to STATE OF MICHIGAN. FEES ARE NOT REFUNDABLE.

		NUMBER	FEE
First record request — fee includes 3 year search	$10.00		
Second and subsequent record requests submitted at the same time in the same envelope	$6.00 ea.		
Additional copies of the same record ordered at the same time	$3.00 ea.		
Additional years searched per record request	$3.00/year		
GENEALOGICAL RESEARCH COPIES ARE NON-CERTIFIED		TOTAL	

2. **RECORD TYPE:** ☐ Death   ☐ Marriage   ☐ Divorce

☐ Birth
{
You must satisfy the eligibility requirements required by law and supply the following information: (See other side for instructions)

3) Your relationship to person named on the birth record _____

4) The date and place the person named on the birth record died _____
   date

   _____
   place
}

5. _____
   name of registrant; name of deceased; name of groom; name of husband
   (birth)   (death)   (marriage)   (divorce)

6. Date of Event: _____ 7. Place of Event: _____
   (city, village, township and county)

8. If exact year is unknown, years to be searched: _____

9. _____
   mother's maiden name; name of bride; name of wife
   (birth)   (marriage)   (divorce)

10. Father's name (birth only): _____

11. Applicant's Signature: _____ Date: _____

IF THE INFORMATION REQUESTED ABOVE IS NOT KNOWN, please indicate in the box below any data which may be used for identifying the record, such as marital status, name of husband or wife if married, parents' names, age or birthplace.

- -

(PLEASE DO NOT REMOVE THIS STUB)

PRINT THE NAME AND MAILING ADDRESS OF THE PERSON TO WHOM THE RECORD(S) ARE TO BE SENT.

THIS IS A MAILING INSERT AND WILL BE USED TO MAIL THE RECORDS

▼

NAME: _____

STREET: _____

CITY: _____ STATE: _____ ZIP: _____

ADDITIONAL INFORMATION

B 225 G 3/85

Authority: ACT 368, P.A. 1978
Completion: Voluntary

Send your requests to:

Minnesota Department of Health
Section of Vital Statistics Registration
717 Delaware Street, S.E.
P.O. Box 9441
Minneapolis, Minnesota 55440-9441

(612) 623-5121

Send your requests for Marriage Certificates and early vital records to:

Clerk
County District Court
(County where the Marriage License was issued).

Cost for a certified Birth Certificate	$11.00
Cost for a duplicate Birth Certificate	$ 5.00
Cost for a certified Death Certificate	$ 8.00
Cost for a duplicate Death Certificate, when ordered at the same time	$ 2.00

The Minnesota Section of Vital Statistics Registration has birth records from January 1, 1900 and death records from January 1, 1908.

If your request is urgent you may call and charge your certificates to your Visa or MasterCard. There is a $5.00 fee for this service.

1. Our files include birth records since 1900 and death records since 1908 for the entire State of Minnesota. Some records prior to these years are on file with the clerk of District Court in the county of occurrence.

2. Minnesota law requires a fee of _____ for each certified copy of a record, non-certified copy of a record, verification, or statement that the record is not on file.

3. A check or money order should be made payable to "Treasurer, State of Minnesota". PLEASE NOTE: We cannot accept two-party checks, Canadian checks or Canadian currency.

(A) BIRTH

Name: _____

Date of Birth: _____

City, Town or Township of Birth: _____

County of Birth: _____

Father's Full Name: _____

Mother's Full Maiden Name: _____

(B) DEATH

Name: _____

Date of Death: _____
 (or year last known to be alive)

City, Town or Township of Death: _____

County of Death: _____

Age at the time of Death: _____

Occupation: _____

Spouse's Full Name: _____

(C) ISSUE TO

Signature: _____

Street or Route: _____

City, State & Zip Code: _____

MISSISSIPPI

Send your requests to:

> Mississippi State Department of Health
> Vital Records Office
> 2423 North State Street
> P.O. Box 1700
> Jackson, Mississippi 39205-1700

(601) 960-7981

For early vital records contact:

> County Clerk
> County Court House
> (County where the event occurred)

Cost for a certified Birth Certificate	$10.00
Cost for a short form Birth Certificate	$ 5.00
Cost for a certified Marriage Certificate	$ 5.00
Cost for a certified Death Certificate	$ 5.00
Cost for a duplicate copy, when ordered at the same time	$ 1.00

The Mississippi Office of Vital Records has birth records from November 1, 1912. Marriage records are on file from January 1, 1926 to June 30, 1938 and from January 1, 1942 to the present. Marriage records are also on file with the County Court where the license was issued. Death records are on file from November 1, 1912. The Office will only accept payment by postal money order, bank money order, or by a bank cashier's check.

If your request is urgent you may call and charge your order for birth certificates to your Visa or MasterCard. There is a $4.50 fee for this service.

MISSISSIPPI STATE DEPARTMENT OF HEALTH

Vital Records
P. O. Box 1700
Jackson, Mississippi 39205

APPLICATION FOR CERTIFIED COPY OF BIRTH CERTIFICATE

INFORMATION

Only births recorded after November 1, 1912 are on file.

We recommend that the certified ABSTRACT (Short Form) be ordered. These may be obtained for $5.00 each, and $1.00 for each additional copy ordered at the same time.

There are some instances where, for family, historical or legal reasons, additional information is required. A certified COPY of the birth certificate (Long Form) is available for $10.00 for the first copy and $1.00 for each additional copy ordered at the same time.

INSTRUCTIONS

1. Complete ALL the information sections of the form. PLEASE PRINT.

2. The application must be signed.

3. Please remit a POSTAL MONEY ORDER, BANK MONEY ORDER or BANK CASHIER'S CHECK made payable to the Mississippi State Department of Health. Personal checks and personal money orders are not accepted. *We accept no responsibility for cash sent through the mail.*

4. Send completed application, appropriate fee and self-addressed stamped legal size envelope to the address at the top of this form.

BASIC INFORMATION: DOUBLE CHECK SPELLING AND DATE

DO NOT WRITE IN THIS SPACE

FULL NAME AT BIRTH	FIRST NAME	MIDDLE NAME	LAST NAME	STATE FILING NUMBER
DATE OF BIRTH	MONTH	DAY	YEAR	
PLACE OF BIRTH	COUNTY	CITY OR TOWN	STATE	FILING DATE
Has name ever been changed other than by marriage? ☐ Yes ☐ No	If so, what was original name?			

ADDITIONAL INFORMATION REQUIRED

12 — 36

SEX		6. RACE		37 — 66
FULL NAME OF FATHER	FIRST NAME	MIDDLE NAME	LAST NAME	S.C.
FULL MAIDEN NAME OF MOTHER	FIRST NAME	MIDDLE NAME	LAST NAME	S.C.

ABOUT THE APPLICANT

S.C.

FEE
I AM ENCLOSING FEE OF $ _____ FOR _____ SHORT FORMS.

S.C.

I AM ENCLOSING FEE OF $ _____ FOR _____ LONG FORMS.

C.D.

0. RELATIONSHIP OF APPLICANT TO PERSON NAMED IN ITEM 1.

SUP.

1. PURPOSE FOR WHICH THIS COPY IS REQUESTED

P.

Pursuant to Section 41-57-2 of the Mississippi Code of 1972, Annotated, and as defined by Mississippi State Board of Health Rules and Regulations, I hereby certify that I have a legitimate and tangible interest in the birth record requested. I understand that obtaining a record under false pretenses may subject me to the penalty as described in Section 41-57-27 of the Mississippi Code of 1972, Annotated.

CWA.

2. SIGNATURE OF APPLICANT	DATE SIGNED

PRINT YOUR MAILING ADDRESS HERE

3.		Name
4.	Apt. No.	Street or Route
5.		City or Town State, Zip Code

MISSISSIPPI STATE BOARD OF HEALTH

APPLICATION FOR CERTIFIED COPY OF STATISTICAL RECORD OF MARRIAGE

INFORMATION

Marriage records have only been kept since January 1, 1926. In addition, from July 1, 1938, to December 31, 1941, records were kept only by the circuit court clerk in the county in which the marriage license was issued.

INSTRUCTIONS

1. Complete the information sections of this form. PLEASE PRINT.
2. The application must be signed.
3. Payment for certificates is preferably by Money Order. Personal checks or cash are not recommended.
4. Send (a) completed application form and
   (b) appropriate fee
   to the address at the top of this form.

INFORMATION ABOUT BRIDE AND GROOM WHOSE STATISTICAL RECORD OF MARRIAGE IS REQUESTED (Please Print)			
1. FULL NAME OF GROOM	FIRST NAME	MIDDLE NAME	LAST NAME
2. FULL NAME OF BRIDE	FIRST NAME	MIDDLE NAME	LAST NAME
3. DATE OF MARRIAGE	MONTH	DAY	YEAR
4. PLACE OF MARRIAGE	COUNTY	CITY OR TOWN	STATE
5. WHERE LICENSE WAS BOUGHT	COUNTY	CITY OR TOWN	STATE
PERSON REQUESTING CERTIFIED COPY			
6. PURPOSE FOR WHICH COPY IS TO BE USED			
7. RELATIONSHIP OR INTEREST OF PERSON REQUESTING CERTIFICATE			
8. FEE I AM ENCLOSING A FEE OF $ _____ FOR _____ CERTIFIED COPIES.			
9. SIGNATURE OF APPLICANT		10. DATE SIGNED	

PRINT OR TYPE YOUR MAILING ADDRESS HERE

11.	
12.	NAME
13.	Street Or Route
	City Or Town
	State, ZIP Code

Form No. 523
Revised 3/1/81

MISSISSIPPI STATE BOARD OF HEALTH

APPLICATION FOR CERTIFIED COPY OF DEATH CERTIFICATE

INFORMATION

1. Only deaths recorded after November 1, 1912, are on file.
2. The death certificate is the most important legal document in the settlement of the estate and insurance. It is important that the information on the certificate is correct.
3. When you receive copies of the death certificate, check particularly spelling of names and that dates are correct.
4. If there are any incorrect items on the certificate and the death has occurred less than one year ago, please notify the funeral director who filed the certificate.
5. If there are incorrect items on the certificate and the death occurred more than one year ago, a court order is required. Please contact Vital Records at the above address for additional information.

INSTRUCTIONS

1. Complete the information sections of this form. PLEASE PRINT.
2. The application must be signed.
3. Payment for certificates is preferably by Money Order. Personal checks or cash are not recommended.
4. Send (a) completed application form and
       (b) appropriate fee
   to the address at the top of this form.

INFORMATION ABOUT PERSON WHOSE DEATH CERTIFICATE IS REQUESTED (Type or Print)		
1. FULL NAME OF DECEASED — FIRST NAME	MIDDLE NAME	LAST NAME
2. DATE OF DEATH — MONTH	DAY	YEAR
3. PLACE OF DEATH — COUNTY	CITY OR TOWN	STATE
4. SEX 5. RACE	6. AGE AT DEATH	7. STATE FILE NUMBER IF KNOWN
8. NAME OF FATHER	9. NAME OF MOTHER	
10. FUNERAL DIRECTOR — NAME	ADDRESS	

11. PURPOSE FOR WHICH CERTIFIED COPY IS TO BE USED	NO. OF COPIES .... _____
12. RELATIONSHIP OR INTEREST OF PERSON REQUESTING CERTIFICATE	VETERAN'S SERVICE OR VA CLAIM NO._____
13. SIGNATURE OF APPLICANT	TOTAL .... _____
14. DATE SIGNED	FEE SUBMITTED .... $_____

PRINT OR TYPE YOUR MAILING ADDRESS HERE

15.	NAME
16.	Street Or Route
17.	City Or Town State, ZIP Code

Send your requests to:

Missouri Department of Health
Bureau of Vital Records
P.O. Box 570
Jefferson City, Missouri 65102-0570

(314) 751-6387

Send your requests for Marriage Certificates and early vital records to:

Recorder of Deeds
County Court House
(County where the Marriage License was issued)

Cost for a certified Birth Certificate	$4.00
Cost for a wallet-size Birth Certificate	$4.00
Cost for a certified Death Certificate	$4.00

The Missouri Bureau of Vital Records has birth and death records from January 1, 1910. They also have an index to marriages from July 1, 1948; however, marriage certificates can only be obtained from the county courts. The Bureau will search this index for free. The Records Management and Archives Service (100 Industrial Drive, P.O. Box 778, Jefferson City, Missouri 65102) has microfilm copies of the records of the County Recorders of Deeds. Some of these records date from the early 1800s.

If your request is urgent you may call and charge your birth certificates to your Visa or MasterCard. There is a $5.00 fee for this service.

MISSOURI DEPARTMENT OF HEALTH
BUREAU OF VITAL RECORDS
APPLICATION FOR CERTIFIED COPY OF BIRTH CERTIFICATION

INSTRUCTIONS	COPIES REQUESTED	

INSTRUCTIONS

Recording of births began in this office January 1, 1910. The law requires a fee of $4 for a search of the files. This fee entitles you to a certified copy, if available. Additional copies are $4 each. **Fee must accompany application.**

NO CASH BY MAIL PLEASE. Make check or money order payable to *Missouri Department of Health.*

Mail this application to:

Missouri Department of Health
Bureau of Vital Records
P.O. Box 570
Jefferson City, Missouri 65102-0570

COPIES REQUESTED

Birth Certification   How Many
Certification of facts of birth contained in original record. ☐

Birth Card   How Many
A nonlaminated wallet-size card that includes only information shown in sample. ☐

**Amount of
Money Enclosed $**

MISSOURI DEPARTMENT OF HEALTH
BIRTH CERTIFICATION
DATE FILED — STATE FILE NUMBER
June 22, 1955   124-41-42355
CHILD NAME
John Henry Dow
BIRTH DATE — SEX
Feb. 31, 1984   M
COUNTY OF BIRTH
Butler
DATE ISSUED
March 9, 1999
THIS IS A TRUE CERTIFICATION OF NAME AND BIRTH FACTS RECORDED IN THIS OFFICE

**ALL FORMS OF CERTIFICATE
$4.00 EACH**

INFORMATION ABOUT PERSON WHOSE BIRTH CERTIFICATE IS REQUESTED   (TYPE OR PRINT ALL ITEMS EXCEPT SIGNATURE)

1. FULL NAME OF PERSON*	FIRST NAME	MIDDLE NAME	LAST NAME (MAIDEN NAME)		
	IF THIS BIRTH COULD BE RECORDED UNDER ANOTHER NAME, PLEASE INDICATE THE NAME				
2. DATE OF BIRTH	MONTH	DAY	YEAR	3. SEX	4. RACE
5. PLACE OF BIRTH	CITY OR TOWN	COUNTY	STATE		
	HOSPITAL OR STREET NO.	ATTENDING PHYSICIAN	☐ PHYSICIAN ☐ MIDWIFE ☐ OTHER		
6. FULL NAME OF FATHER	FIRST NAME	MIDDLE NAME	LAST NAME		
7. FULL MAIDEN NAME OF MOTHER	FIRST NAME	MIDDLE NAME	LAST NAME (MAIDEN)		

*IF NEWBORN, PLEASE WAIT 6 TO 8 WEEKS BEFORE REQUESTING.

PERSON REQUESTING CERTIFIED COPY (IF LEGAL GUARDIAN OF REGISTRANT, SEND ALONG GUARDIANSHIP PAPERS.)

8. PURPOSE FOR WHICH CERTIFIED COPY IS TO BE USED	9. RELATIONSHIP (MUST BE REGISTRANT, MEMBER OF IMMEDIATE FAMILY, LEGAL GUARDIAN, OR LEGAL REPRESENTATIVE)
10. SIGNATURE OF APPLICANT ▶	DATE SIGNED

12. ADDRESS OF APPLICANT (TYPE OR PRINT)	STREET ADDRESS		
	CITY OR TOWN	STATE	ZIP CODE

THIS COUPON MUST BE COMPLETED AND WILL BE USED TO ADDRESS OUR REPLY

NAME OF PERSON CERTIFICATION IS REQUESTED FOR

PLEASE PRINT OR TYPE THE NAME AND ADDRESS OF THE PERSON TO WHOM THE RECORD IS TO BE RETURNED.

▶ NAME

ADDRESS (NUMBER AND STREET)

CITY   STATE   ZIP CODE

MISSOURI DEPARTMENT OF HEALTH
BUREAU OF VITAL RECORDS
APPLICATION FOR SEARCH OF MARRIAGE INDEXES

THE BUREAU OF VITAL RECORDS IS AUTHORIZED NO FEE FOR THIS SERVICE

NAME OF GROOM

MAIDEN NAME OF BRIDE

COUNTY ISSUING THE LICENSE

DATE OR APPROXIMATE DATE THE LICENSE WAS ISSUED

NOTE: THESE INDEXES BEGIN ON JULY 1, 1948. MARRIAGE INFORMATION PRIOR TO THAT DATE MAY BE OBTAINED ONLY FROM THE RECORDER OF DEEDS OF THE COUNTY THAT ISSUED THE LICENSE.

MO 580-0692 (1-86)

VS-705 (8-75)

MISSOURI DEPARTMENT OF HEALTH
BUREAU OF VITAL RECORDS
Jefferson City, Missouri 65102

APPLICATION FOR CERTIFIED COPY OF DEATH CERTIFICATION

<table>
<tr>
<td colspan="2">

INSTRUCTIONS

<u>No Cash Please.</u> Make check or money order payable to:
Missouri Department of Health

Mail this application to:
Missouri Department of Health
Bureau of Vital Records
P. O. Box 570
Jefferson City, Missouri 65102-0570

</td>
<td colspan="2">

COPIES REQUESTED

Death Certification   How Many
(Certification of facts of death contained in original record)

Amount of Money Enclosed

</td>
<td>

THE RECORDING OF DEATHS BEGAN IN THIS OFFICE ON JAN. 1, 1910. RECORDS ARE FILED BY YEAR OF DEATH AND ALPHABETICALLY BY THE NAME OF THE DECEASED AT THE TIME OF DEATH. THEREFORE, AT LEAST THE APPROXIMATE YEAR OF DEATH OR LAST YEAR IN WHICH THE DECEASED WAS KNOWN TO BE ALIVE MUST BE GIVEN.

</td>
</tr>
</table>

INFORMATION ABOUT PERSON WHOSE DEATH CERTIFICATE IS REQUESTED *(TYPE or PRINT all items EXCEPT SIGNATURE)*

1. FULL NAME OF DECEASED	FIRST NAME	MIDDLE NAME	LAST NAME AT TIME OF DEATH		
2. DATE OF DEATH	MONTH	DAY	YEAR	3. SEX	RACE / AGE
4. PLACE OF DEATH	CITY OR TOWN	COUNTY	STATE		
5. FULL NAME OF SPOUSE	FIRST NAME	MIDDLE NAME	LAST NAME		
6. FULL NAME OF FATHER	FIRST NAME	MIDDLE NAME	LAST NAME		
7. FULL MAIDEN NAME OF MOTHER	FIRST NAME	MIDDLE NAME	LAST NAME (MAIDEN)		

PERSON REQUESTING CERTIFIED COPY OF DEATH RECORD

8. PURPOSE FOR WHICH CERTIFIED COPY IS TO BE USED	Please check: ☐ Insurance claim on policy issued within 2 years of death ☐ Other insurance claims ☐ Other (specify) _____
9. RELATIONSHIP TO REGISTRANT OR INTEREST OF PERSON REQUESTING CERTIFICATION	10. SIGNATURE OF APPLICANT

11. NAME AND ADDRESS WHERE COPIES ARE TO BE MAILED (TYPE or PRINT)	NAME	12. NAME AND ADDRESS OF FUNERAL HOME	
	STREET ADDRESS		13. DATE SIGNED
	CITY OR TOWN	STATE	ZIP CODE

THIS COUPON MUST BE COMPLETED AND WILL BE USED TO ADDRESS OUR REPLY.

Please print or type the name and address of the person to whom the record is to be furnished.

_____
NAME

_____
NUMBER   STREET

_____
CITY   STATE   ZIP CODE

Name of person certificate is requested for:

_____

MO 580-0640 (9-85)   VS-351 (R9-85)

MONTANA

Send your requests to:

Montana Department of Health
and Environmental Sciences
Bureau of Records and Statistics
Cogswell Building, Room C-118
Helena, Montana 59620

(406) 444-2614

Send your requests for Marriage Certificates and early vital records to:

Clerk
County District Court
(County where the Marriage License was issued).

Cost for a certified Birth Certificate	$ 5.00
Cost for a wallet-size Birth Certificate	$ 5.00
Cost for searching the Marriage Index	$10.00
Cost for a certified Death Certificate	$ 5.00

The Montana Bureau of Records has birth and death records from late 1907. They have an index to marriages from January 1, 1943 to the present which they will search for a fee of $10.00. The marriage certificate must be obtained from the County Clerk.

If your request is urgent you may call and charge your certificates to your Visa, Discover or MasterCard. There is a $5.00 charge for this service. With the express mail charges the total cost is usually $24.00

APPLICATION FOR A CERTIFIED COPY OF A BIRTH CERTIFICATE

Department of Health and Environmental Sciences
Bureau of Records and Statistics
Cogswell Building, Room C-118
Helena, Montana 59620

Date: _____

I am related to the person named on the certificate as: _____
                                                    (self, parent, other relative/specify

The purpose for which this record is needed: _____

_____   _____
        Signature of Applicant   Applicant's name typed or printed

                                          ( )
_____   _____
        Street Address   Applicant's phone number

_____
City or Town   State   Zip

The following information is necessary to verify a personal right to this certificate, t
locate the proper record, and to verify the information on the record.

NAME AS IT APPEARS
ON THE RECORD: _____
               First   Middle   Last (if married, give maiden name

DATE OF BIRTH: _____
            Month   Day   Year

PLACE OF BIRTH: _____
             City or Town   County   Hospital name, at home/specify

NAME OF FATHER: _____
             First   Middle   Last

NAME OF MOTHER: _____
             First   Middle   Maiden Surname

Please issue: (check one)

_____ Standard Certified Copy

_____ Wallet Size Card

****

FOR STATE USE ONLY:

Application approved ____Yes____No   By: _____

                                           Date: _____

Amount enclosed or attached $_____(Fee is $5.00 per copy)
(NOTE: The fee will be refunded in the event this application is not approved.)

DHES R&S 2 (August 1988)

APPLICATION FOR A CERTIFIED COPY OF A DEATH CERTIFICATE

Department of Health and Environmental Sciences
Bureau of Records and Statistics
Cogswell Building, Room C-118
Helena, Montana 59620   Date:_____

I am related to the decedent as:_____
                        (spouse, parent, other relative or interested party/specify

The purpose for which this record is needed:_____

_____   _____
    Signature of Applicant   Applicant's name typed or printed

_____   ( )_____
       Street Address   Applicant's phone number

_____
City or Town   State   Zip

The following information is necessary to verify a personal or property right to th
certificate, to locate the proper record, and to verify the information on the record.

NAME OF DECEDENT:_____ _____
                    First   Middle   Last

DATE OF DEATH:_____ PLACE OF DEATH:_____
              Month   Day   Year

SPOUSE NAME:_____
            First   Middle   Last

AGE OF DECEDENT AT DEATH: (approximate)_____

DATE AND PLACE OF BIRTH OF DECEDENT:_____

DECEDENT'S OCCUPATION:_____

PARENT'S NAMES:_____ _____
                    Father   Mother

****

FOR STATE USE ONLY:

Application approved ____Yes____No   By:_____

                                                 Date:_____

Amount enclosed or attached $_____(Fee is $5.00 per copy)
(NOTE: The fee will be refunded in the event this application is not approved.)

DHES R&S 3 (August 1988)

NEBRASKA

Send your requests to:

Nebraska State Department of Health
Bureau of Vital Statistics
P.O. Box 95007
Lincoln, Nebraska 68509-5007

(402) 471-2871

For early vital records contact:

County Clerk
County Court House
(County where the event occurred)

Cost for a certified Birth Certificate	$6.00
Cost for a wallet-size Birth Certificate	$6.00
Cost for a certified Marriage Certificate	$5.00
Cost for a certified Death Certificate	$5.00

The Nebraska Bureau of Vital Statistics has birth and death records from 1904 and marriage records from January 1, 1909.

BVS-C-1
Rev. July 1983
020-08-038

Bureau of Vital Statistics
P. O. Box 95007
Lincoln, Nebraska 68509-5007
(402) 471-2871

APPLICATION FOR BIRTH CERTIFICATE

Nebraska has been registering births with this office since <u>1904</u>. 1941 legislation provided for the filing of delayed birth registrations for births not previously filed; however, there are very few filed for births occurring prior to 1875.

Full name at birth _____
(If adopted, list adoptive name and adoptive parents)

Full date of birth _____

City or county of birth _____

Father's full name _____

Mother's full maiden name _____
Is this the record of an adopted child? _____
Has a delayed birth registration been filed? _____
Purpose record is to be used? _____
How are you related to this person? _____

Certified photocopies   Number _____
Plastic billfold-size birth registration
cards (acceptable for passport purpose)   Number _____

PLEASE ENCLOSE A STAMPED   Signature _____
ADDRESSED ENVELOPE.
                                   Type or print name _____

                                   Firm name _____

                                   Street address _____

Date _____   City, State, Zip _____

Section 71-649, Nebraska Revised Statutes: It is a felony to obtain, possess, use, sell, furnish, or attempt to obtain any vital record for purposes of deception.

BVS-C-6
REV 11/83
020-08-043

Bureau of Vital Statistics
P.O. Box 95007
Lincoln, Nebraska 68509-95007
(402) 471-2871

APPLICATION FOR MARRIAGE RECORD

Nebraska has been registering marriages in this office since 1909. For records occurring prior to that date, contact the county court of the county in which the marriage license was issued.

Full name of groom _____

Full name of bride _____

City of County of marriage _____

Month, day, year of marriage _____

City or county where marriage license issued _____

Purpose record is to be used? _____
If this is not your marriage record, how are you
related to these persons? _____

Signature _____
Typed or printed
name _____

| PLEASE ENCLOSE A STAMPED |
| ADDRESSED ENVELOPE. |

Street address _____

City, State, Zip _____

Section 71-649, Nebraska Revised Statutes: It is a felony to attempt to obtain, possess, or use any copy of a vital record for purposes of deception.

BVS-C-4
Rev. July 1983
020-08-034

BUREAU OF VITAL STATISTICS
P.O. Box 95007
Lincoln, Nebraska 68509-5007
(402)471-2871

APPLICATION FOR DEATH CERTIFICATE

Nebraska has been registering deaths in this office since 1904.

Full name of deceased_____

City or county of death_____

Month, day, year of death_____

Year of birth_____Color_____Birthplace_____

Spouse_____Home address_____

Funeral director:_____

      City_____

For what purpose is record to be used?_____

      Number of certified copies_____

PLEASE ENCLOSE A STAMPED ADDRESSED ENVELOPE	Signature_____ Typed or printed name_____
If to be mailed to another	Firm name_____
address, enter that mailing	Street address_____
address.	City, state, zip_____
	Date_____

Name_____
Street address_____
City, state, zip_____

Section 71-649, Nebraska Revised statutes: It is a felony to attempt
to obtain, possess or use any copy of a vital record for purposes of
deception.

NEVADA

Send your requests to:

Nevada State Department of Human Resources
State Health Division
Section of Vital Statistics
505 East King Street
Carson City, Nevada 89710-4761

(702) 885-4480

Send your requests for Marriage Certificates and early vital records to:

County Recorder
County Court House
(County where the Marriage License was issued).

Cost for a certified Birth Certificate	$6.00
Cost for a wallet-size Birth Certificate	$6.00
Cost to search the Marriage Index (1968–)	$2.00
Cost for a certified Death Certificate	$6.00

The Nevada Section of Vital Statistics has birth and death records from July 1, 1911. They also have an index to Marriage Certificates from 1968 to date. The Marriage Certificate must be requested from the County Recorder. There is a $2.00 charge to search this index. The cost of a Marriage Certificate from the County Recorder is $3.00.

If your request is urgent you may call and charge your certificates to your Visa or MasterCard. There is a $5.00 fee for this service, plus the postal charges.

NEVADA STATE HEALTH DIVISION
Section of Vital Statistics
Carson City, Nevada 89710
(702) 885-4480

BIRTH CERTIFICATE APPLICATION   No. of Copies____

Search fee when no record is found ...   /name

FULL NAME AT BIRTH_____

DATE of Birth_____

PLACE of Birth_____

Name of Father_____

Maiden Name of Mother_____

Attending Physician or Midwife_____

Purpose for which certificate is to be used_____

_____

_____

Mailing Address_____

_____

Signature of Applicant_____

Relationship_____

XXXXXXXXXXXXXXXXXXXXXXXXXXXXXXXXXXXXXXXXXXXXXXXXXXXXXXX

For Office Use Only:

Amount Received_____
Copies Ordered_____
Receipt Number_____   (Date)
Refunded_____

NEVADA STATE HEALTH DIVISION
Section of Vital Statistics
Carson City, Nevada 89710
(702) 885-4480

DEATH CERTIFICATE APPLICATION   No. of Copies___

Search Fee when no record is found -   /name

FULL NAME OF DECEASED_____

Place of Death_____

Date of Death_____

Name of Father of Deceased_____

Maiden Name of Mother_____

Mortuary in Charge of Arrangements_____

Address:_____

Purpose for which certificate is to be used____

_____

Certificate is to be mailed to:_____

_____

Signature of Applicant_____

RELATIONSHIP to Deceased_____

///
For Office use only:

Amount Received:_____   (Date)
Copies Ordered_____
Receipt Number_____
Refunded_____

NEW HAMPSHIRE

Send your requests to:

New Hampshire Division of Public Health Services
Department of Health and Human Services
Bureau of Vital Records and Health Statistics
6 Hazen Drive
Concord, New Hampshire 03301-6527

(603) 271-4650

Vital records are also maintained by:

Town Clerk
Town Hall
(Town where the event occurred)

Cost for a certified Birth Certificate	$3.00
Cost for a certified Marriage Certificate	$3.00
Cost for a certified Death Certificate	$3.00

New Hampshire has copies of vital records from 1640. Make your check payable to "Treasurer, State of New Hampshire."

If your request is urgent you may call and charge your certificates to your Visa or MasterCard. There is a $5.00 fee for this service.

The Family History Library of the Church of Jesus Christ of Latter-day Saints (Mormon Church) in Salt Lake City, Utah has microfilmed many of the original and published vital records and church registers of New Hampshire's cities and counties. They have microfilm of birth, marriage, and death records from 1640 to 1900 and an index to early town records from 1639 to 1910. For details on their holdings please consult your nearest Family History Center.

BIRTHS

BUREAU OF VITAL RECORDS & HEALTH STATISTICS

CONCORD, NEW HAMPSHIRE 03301

APPLICATION FOR COPY OF BIRTH RETURN

PLEASE PRINT PLAINLY

NAME AT
BIRTH . . . .
           (FIRST NAME)   (MIDDLE NAME)   (LAST NAME)

DATE OF
BIRTH . . . .
          (MONTH)   (DAY)   (YEAR)

PLACE OF
BIRTH . . . .

FATHER'S
NAME . . . .
               (FIRST NAME)   (LAST NAME)

MOTHER'S
MAIDEN NAME . . . .
               (FIRST NAME)   (LAST NAME)

PURPOSE FOR WHICH CERTIFICATE IS REQUESTED . . . .

BY WHOM . . . . RELATIONSHIP TO REGISTRANT. . . . .

      A FEE OF   **DOLLARS IS REQUIRED BY LAW FOR THE SEARCH OF THE FILE FOR ANY ONE RECORD**

NOTICE: ANY PERSON SHALL BE GUILTY OF A CLASS B FELONY IF HE/SHE WILLFULLY AND KNOWINGLY MAKE ANY FALSE STATEMENT IN AN APPLICATION FOR A CERTIFIED COPY OF A VITAL RECORD. (RSA 126:24)

VS A-1

MARRIAGES

BUREAU OF VITAL RECORDS & HEALTH STATISTICS

CONCORD, NEW HAMPSHIRE 03301

APPLICATION FOR COPY OF MARRIAGE RETURN

PLEASE PRINT PLAINLY

GROOM'S
NAME . . . .
        (FIRST NAME)   (LAST NAME)

BRIDE'S
NAME . . . .
        (FIRST NAME)   (LAST NAME)

DATE OF
MARRIAGE . . . .
      (MONTH)   (DAY)   (YEAR)

PLACE OF
MARRIAGE . . . .
             (COUNTY)

PURPOSE FOR WHICH CERTIFICATE IS REQUESTED . . . .

BY WHOM . . . . RELATIONSHIP TO REGISTRANT. . . . .

    A FEE OF   **DOLLARS IS REQUIRED BY LAW FOR THE SEARCH OF THE FILE FOR ANY ONE RECORD**

NOTICE: ANY PERSON SHALL BE GUILTY OF A CLASS B FELONY IF HE/SHE WILLFULLY AND KNOWINGLY
MAKE ANY FALSE STATEMENT IN AN APPLICATION FOR A CERTIFIED COPY OF A VITAL RECORD.
(RSA 126:24)

-VS B-1

DEATHS

NUMBER
REQUESTED
ISSUED

CONCORD, NEW HAMPSHIRE 03301

APPLICATION FOR COPY OF DEATH RETURN

PLEASE PRINT PLAINLY

NAME OF
DECEASED...
          (FIRST NAME)   (MIDDLE NAME)   (LAST NAME)

DATE OF
DEATH..
                    (MONTH)   (DAY)   (YEAR)

PLACE OF
DEATH..
                                        (COUNTY)

PURPOSE FOR WHICH CERTIFICATE IS REQUESTED ....

BY WHOM .... RELATIONSHIP TO REGISTRANT................................

A FEE OF _____ DOLLARS IS REQUIRED BY LAW FOR THE SEARCH OF THE FILE FOR ANY ONE RECORD

NOTICE: ANY PERSON SHALL BE GUILTY OF A CLASS B FELONY IF HE/SHE WILLFULLY AND KNOWINGLY MAKE ANY FALSE STATEMENT IN AN APPLICATION FOR A CERTIFIED COPY OF A VITAL RECORD. (RSA 126:24)

VS C-1

Send your requests to:

> New Jersey Department of Health
> State Registrar–Search Unit
> Bureau of Vital Records
> CN 360
> Trenton, New Jersey 08625-0360

(609) 292-4087

Send your requests for records from May 1848 to May 1878 to:

> Division of Archives and Records Management
> Archives Section
> Department of State
> CN 307
> Trenton, New Jersey 08625-0307

(609) 530-3200

Cost for a certified Birth Certificate	$4.00
Cost for a certified Marriage Certificate	$4.00
Cost for a certified Death Certificate	$4.00

The Division of Archives and Records Management has a statewide index to the May 1848–May 1878 records in their custody. They also have incomplete marriage records back to 1665. The Division has indexes to the 1665-1800 and 1848-1878 marriage records. The index and abstract of marriages from 1665 to 1800 was published in *New Jersey Archives* Volume 22.

The State Registrar has an index to the vital records in their custody from May 1878 to December 31, 1900 and thereafter annual indexes.

The Family History Library of the Church of Jesus Christ of Latter-day Saints (Mormon Church) in Salt Lake City, Utah has microfilmed many of the original and published vital records and church registers of New Jersey's cities and counties. They have microfilm copies of the vital records from 1670 to 1900. For details on their holdings please consult your nearest Family History Center.

REG-3
JUL 87

New Jersey State Department of Health

APPLICATION FOR CERTIFIED COPY OF VITAL RECORD

1. *VITAL RECORDS - JUNE, 1878 TO PRESENT*
   When the correct year of the event is supplied, the total fee (payable in advance) for a search is four dollars for each name for which a search must be made. Searches for more than one year cost one dollar for each additional year per name. If found, a certified copy will be forwarded at no additional cost. If not found, the fee will not be refunded. Additional copies may be ordered at this time at a charge of two dollars per copy. Specify the total number of copies requested.
2. *VITAL RECORDS - MAY, 1848 THROUGH MAY, 1878*
   These records have been transferred to the Archives Section, Division of Archives and Records Management, Department of State, CN 307, Trenton, NJ 08625. Information as to fee schedules and how to obtain records from the Archives can be obtained from that Section.

		FOR STATE USE ONLY	
Name of Applicant	Date of Application		
Street Address	Telephone No.		
City State	Zip Code	Certified Copy Completed	

MAKE CHECK OR MONEY ORDER PAYABLE TO "STATE REGISTRAR." DO NOT MAIL CASH OR STAMPS. PLEASE PRINT OR TYPE.

Amount Received

Why is a Certified Copy being requested?

- ☐ School/Sports
- ☐ Social Security ID Card
- ☐ Passport
- ☐ Driver License
- ☐ Genealogy
- ☐ Welfare
- ☐ Soc. Sec. Disability
- ☐ Other Soc. Sec. Benefits
- ☐ Medicare
- ☐ Veteran Benefits
- ☐ Other (specify)
- _____

Method of Payment
- ☐ Check
- ☐ Money Order
- ☐ Cash

Fee Due

▼ **FILL IN ONLY IF YOU WANT A BIRTH RECORD** ▼	No. Copies Requested	Amount Refunded	Date Refunded
Full Name of Child at Time of Birth		Received By	
Place of Birth (City, Town or Township)	County	Enclosures ☐ REG-34 ☐ REG-36 ☐ REG-37 ☐ REG-38 ☐ X ☐ REG-30 ☐ REG-40 ☐ REG-41 ☐ C	
Date of Birth Name of Hospital, If Any			
Father's Name		**SEARCH UNIT**	
Mother's Maiden Name		First Search	
If Child's Name was Changed, Indicate New Name and How it was changed		REG-30	
		Alphabetical Second Check	

▼ **FILL IN IF YOU WANT A MARRIAGE RECORD** ▼	No. Copies Requested	File Date on Record	
Name of Husband		**PROCESSING UNIT**	
Maiden Name of Wife		Places	
Place of Marriage (City, Township)	County	W.W.	
Date of Marriage or Close Approximation		Late Months	

Second Check

FOR ANY DEATH RECORD BEFORE 1901, A SEARCH CANNOT BE MADE UNLESS YOU CAN NAME THE COUNTY WHERE THE EVENT TOOK PLACE.

CORRESPONDENCE/RECEPTION UNIT

▼ **FILL IN ONLY IF YOU WANT A DEATH RECORD** ▼	No. Copies Requested	REG-L7	
Name of Deceased	Date of Death	Hospital Records	
Place of Death (City, Town, Township, County)	Age at Death	REG-28	
Residence if Different from Place of Death		Comments	
Father's Name			
Mother's Maiden Name			

Address your envelope to:

STATE REGISTRAR — SEARCH UNIT
NEW JERSEY STATE DEPARTMENT OF HEALTH
CN 360, TRENTON, NJ 08625-0360
COMPLETE SECTION BELOW - TYPE OR PRINT CLEARLY!
This will be used as a mailing label when we send the results of the search.

Name

Street Address

City   State   Zip Code

Dear Applicant:

The fee you paid is correct unless either block below is checked.

☐ An additional fee of $_____ is due, since either additional years or another name was involved. Send it with this form.

☐ You are entitled to a refund check of $_____ which will be forwarded within 45 days of _____. If you have occasion to write about this matter, return this form with your letter.

—STATE REGISTRAR

H-3618

Send your requests to:

New Mexico Health and Environment Department
Health Services Division
Vital Records Office
P.O. Box 968
Santa Fe, New Mexico 87504-0968

(505) 827-0120

Send your requests for Marriage Certificates and early vital records to:

County Clerk
County Court House
(County where the Marriage License was issued).

Cost for a certified Birth Certificate	$10.00
Cost for a certified Death Certificate	$ 5.00

The New Mexico State Vital Records Office has birth and death records from 1920. The County Clerks have earlier records.

If your request is urgent you may call (505) 827-0598 and charge your certificates to your Visa or MasterCard. There is a $6.00 fee for this service.

Search Application for BIRTH Record

STATE OF NEW MEXICO
ENVIRONMENT Health Services Division

PLEASE PRINT or TYPE

I. BIRTH CERTIFICATE OF

FULL NAME at BIRTH

DATE of BIRTH | SEX

PLACE of BIRTH *(city, county, state)*

II. PARENTS OF PERSON NAMED ON BIRTH CERTIFICATE

FATHER'S FULL NAME

MOTHER'S FULL MAIDEN NAME

ABOVE NAMED PARENTS ARE:
FATHER: ☐ Natural ☐ Adoptive   MOTHER: ☐ Natural ☐ Adoptive

III. PERSON MAKING THIS REQUEST

YOUR NAME: | Last | First | Initial

YOUR ADDRESS: | No. and Street/P.O. Box

Town | State | Zip

IV. NUMBER AND TYPE OF COPIES WANTED and FEE(S)

I am requesting:

_____ full size copy(ies)

Number

_____
Date of Request

I am enclosing the Fee(s) of: $

LEGAL NOTICE: For the protection of the individual, certificates of birth are **NOT** open to public inspection. In order t. comply with this request, State Regulations require Section V below to be completed.

WARNING: False application for a birth certificate is illegal and punishable by fine and/or imprisonment.

V. STATEMENT OF REQUESTOR

Your relationship to person named in Certificate *(e.g. parent, attorney, etc.)* | For what purpose(s) do you need the copy(ies)? | Your signature

VSB 913 Revised 4/81

Search Application for DEATH Record

STATE OF NEW MEXICO

ENVIRONMENT Department

Health Services Division

PLEASE PRINT OR TYPE

I. DEATH CERTIFICATE OF

FULL NAME of DECEASED		FULL NAME of SPOUSE *(Maiden name, if wife)*
DATE of DEATH	SEX	DECEASED's DATE of BIRTH or AGE at TIME of DEATH
PLACE of DEATH *(city, county, state)*		MORTUARY in CHARGE of FINAL ARRANGEMENTS

II. PERSON MAKING THIS REQUEST

YOUR NAME:	Last	First	Initial
YOUR ADDRESS:	No. and Street/P.O. Box		
	Town	State	Zip

III. NUMBER OF COPIES WANTED and FEE(S)

I am requesting: _____ Certified copy(ies)

_____ _____
Number   Date of Request

I am enclosing the Fee(s) of: $ _____

LEGAL NOTICE: For the protection of the individual whose name appears on the death certificate, and surviving family members, certificates of death are **NOT** open to public inspection.

WARNING: False application for a death certificate is illegal and punishable by fine and/or imprisonment.

IV. STATEMENT OF REQUESTOR

Your relationship to person named in certificate *(e.g. spouse, attorney, etc.)*	For what purpose(s) do you need the copy(ies)?	Your signature

VSB 914 Revised 4/81

NEW YORK—
New York City

Send your requests for births from January 1, 1898 and deaths from January 1, 1920 to:

The City of New York Department of Health
Bureau of Vital Records
125 Worth Street
New York, New York 10013-4093

(212) 566-8192

The Municipal Archives has births from July 1847 to 1897, incomplete death records from 1795 to 1929, and incomplete marriage records from 1847 to 1937. See the attached chart. Send your requests to:

Municipal Archives
Department of Records and Information Services
31 Chambers Street
New York, New York 10007-1288

(212) 566-5292

For marriage records from 1908 to the present send your requests to the City Clerk of the Borough where the license was issued. For the address see the attached chart.

Cost for a certified Birth Certificate	$5.00
Cost for a certified Marriage Certificate	$5.00
Cost for a certified Death Certificate	$5.00

If your request is urgent you may call the Bureau of Vital Records and charge your Visa or MasterCard. There is a $5.00 fee for this service. Call (212) 566-6402.

THE CITY OF NEW YORK· DEPARTMENT OF HEALTH

BUREAU OF VITAL RECORDS
125 Worth Street
New York, N.Y. 10013

APPLICATION FOR A BIRTH RECORD

(Print All Items Clearly)

LAST NAME ON BIRTH RECORD	FIRST NAME	☐ FEMALE ☐ MALE

DATE OF BIRTH Month Day Year	PLACE OF BIRTH (NAME OF HOSPITAL, OR IF AT HOME, NO. AND STREET)	BOROUGH OF BIRTH

MOTHER'S MAIDEN NAME (Name Before Marriage) FIRST LAST	CERTIFICATE NUMBER IF KNOWN

FATHER'S NAME FIRST LAST	*For Office Use Only*

NO. OF COPIES	YOUR RELATIONSHIP TO PERSON NAMED ON BIRTH RECORD, IF SELF, STATE "SELF"	
FOR WHAT PURPOSE ARE YOU GOING TO USE THIS BIRTH RECORD		

NOTE: Copy of a birth record can be issued only to persons to whom the record of birth relates, if of age, or a parent or other lawful representative. IF THIS REQUEST IS NOT FOR YOUR OWN BIRTH RECORD OR THAT OF YOUR CHILD, NOTARIZED AUTHORIZATION FROM THE PARENT OR THE PERSON NAMED ON THE CERTIFICATE MUST BE PRESENTED WITH THIS APPLICATION.

Section 3.19, New York City Health Code provides, in part:". . . no person shall make a false, untrue or misleading statement or forge the signature of another on a certificate, application, registration, report or other document required to be prepared pursuant to this Code."
Section 558 (d) of the New York City Charter provides that any violation of the Health Code shall be treated and punished as a misdemeanor.

SIGN YOUR NAME AND ADDRESS BELOW

NAME		
ADDRESS		
CITY	STATE	ZIP CODE

FEES

SEARCH FOR TWO CONSECUTIVE YEARS AND ONE COPY OR A CERTIFIED "NOT FOUND STATEMENT" ....
EACH ADDITIONAL COPY REQUESTED..
EACH EXTRA YEAR SEARCHED (WITH THIS APPLICATION)..
     1. Make check or money order payable to: Department of Health, N.Y.C.
     2. If from a foreign country, send an international money order or a check drawn on a U.S. bank.
     3. Stamps or foreign currency will not be accepted. **CASH NOT ACCEPTED BY MAIL.**

NOTE: PLEASE ATTACH A STAMPED SELF-ADDRESSED ENVELOPE.

FOR OFFICE USE ONLY

SEARCH ► RESULTS►	REPORTED BY ☐ CRT ☐ MANUAL INITIAL ►	CERTIFICATE NUMBER	LAST NAME - 4 LETTERS	DATE OF BIRTH
READING DATE		DATE ISSUED: BY MAIL	DATE ISSUED: IN PERSON	

VR-67 (Rev. 10/82)

THE CITY OF NEW YORK - OFFICE OF THE CITY CLERK
MARRIAGE LICENSE BUREAU

REQUEST FOR A SEARCH OF A MARRIAGE LICENSE ISSUED IN ONE OF THE FIVE BOROUGHS OF THE
CITY OF NEW YORK AND A TRANSCRIPT OF SUCH MARRIAGE LICENSE

NOTE: A search for and or transcript or photocopy of a marriage record will be issued only
to the person to whom the record of marriage relates, parents, children or other lawful
representative. If this record is not for your own marriage, proper written authorization
from the couple whose names appear on the record must be attached to this application.
You must also indicate a reason why a search & transcript is needed. Attorneys, upon your
own stationery, should state which party or parties you represent and the nature of any
pending action.

HOW TO OBTAIN A SEARCH AND MARRIAGE RECORD INFORMATION

1) RECORDS AVAILABLE AND WHERE TO MAIL YOUR REQUEST

Applications should be sent to: (Choose the borough office based on the following)

FOR RECORDS FROM   MAIL TO
May 1943 to present   Borough office where the couple obtained the marriage license
1908 to May 1943   Borough office where the BRIDE resided before marriage
1866 to 1907   Borough office where the couple was married

EXISTING RECORDS AVAILABLE   -   BOROUGH OFFICE ADDRESSES
MANHATTAN- 1866 to present   -   Municipal Building, 1 Centre St. Rm 252, NYC NY 10007
BROOKLYN - 1866 to present   -   Municipal Building, Court St., Rm 205, Brooklyn, NY 11201
QUEENS   - 1881 to present   -   120-55 Queens Blvd, Rm X001, Kew Gardens, NY 11424
BRONX   - 1899 to present   -   1780 Grand Concourse, Rm 201, Bronx, NY 10457
STAT. IS.- 1898 to prensnt   -   Borough Hall-St. George, Rm 311, Staten Island, NY 10301

NOTE: 1) Address envelope to "THE OFFICE OF THE CITY CLERK".
      2) Lower left-hand corner of envelope - Attn: MARRIAGE RECORDS UNIT

2) FEE SCHEDULE: ALL FEES ARE PAYABLE IN ADVANCE. Fee must be paid by certified check,
   postal, bank or international money order, payable to "The City Clerk of New York".
   Checks from foreign countries must be drawn on an american bank. DO NOT SEND CASH
   OR STAMPS. DO NOT SEND PERSONAL CHECKS UNLESS CERTIFIED BY THE BANK.

   SEARCH FEE: $5.00 for the first year or part thereof; $1.00 for the second year;
               $.50 for each additional year.
      with

   TRANSCRIPT OR COPY FEE: $5.00 for each transcript or copy desired

   Total fee for a one year search & one copy is $10.00 (no refunds less than $1.00)

3) VETERANS ONLY: You may obtain verification free upon surrendering and attaching the
   official letter from the Veterans Administration or State Division of Veterans Affairs.
   This letter must be an original and specifically requesting marriage information.
   The letter will not be returned to you.

FOR OFFICE USE ONLY

Form RR1-8/83

Today's Date: _____

Date of Marriage Ceremony: MONTH- DAY- YEAR-	Borough where the license was issued

If uncertain, specify other years you want searched:	

GROOM (man)
Full name:

BRIDE (woman)
Full MAIDEN name:

If woman was previously married,
give LAST NAME of former husband(s):

Reason search & copy are needed:	How Many

Name of person requesting search:	Your relationship to Bride & Groom:

Your Address	City	State	Zip

DO NOT WRITE BELOW - THIS SPACE FOR OFFICE USE

License   Microfilm
Number:_____/_____   Cart No.   _____/_____/_____

Searched by:_____ Type of Cert_____

Receipt No._____ Amount-$_____ Typist_____

Date Mailed_____ Cert No.(s)_____

Date Request
was received_____ Amount of Money Received - $_____

NO RECORD ( ) Amount Refunded-$_____ Receipt No._____Mailed_____

This is to certify that_____

residing at_____Born_____

at_____AND_____

Residing at_____Born_____

at_____Were married on_____

at_____By_____

Groom's Parents_____

Bride's Parents_____

Witnesses_____

Previous Marriages_____

REMARKS _____

THE CITY OF NEW YORK—DEPARTMENT OF HEALTH

BUREAU OF VITAL RECORDS

125 WORTH STREET

NEW YORK, NEW YORK 10013

APPLICATION FOR A COPY OF A DEATH RECORD

PRINT ALL ITEMS CLEARLY

LAST NAME AT TIME OF DEATH	2. FIRST NAME	2A. ☐ FEMALE ☐ MALE

DATE OF DEATH	4. PLACE OF DEATH	5. BOROUGH	6. AGE
onth Day Year			

NO. OF COPIES	8. SPOUSE'S NAME	9. OCCUPATION OF THE DECEASED

FATHER'S NAME	11. SOCIAL SECURITY NUMBER

MOTHER'S NAME (Name Before Marriage)	13. BURIAL PERMIT NUMBER (IF KNOWN)

FOR WHAT PURPOSE ARE YOU GOING TO USE THIS CERTIFICATE	15. YOUR RELATIONSHIP TO DECEDENT

NOTE: Section 205.07 of the Health Code provides, in part:" . . . The confidential medical report of death shall not be subject to subpoena or to inspection." Therefore, copies of the medical report of death cannot be issued.

SIGN YOUR NAME AND ADDRESS BELOW

AME

DDRESS

TY	STATE	ZIP CODE

FORMATION: APPLICATION SHOULD BE MADE IN PERSON OR BY MAIL TO ABOVE BUREAU.

OTE: 1. CASH NOT ACCEPTED BY MAIL

2. PLEASE ATTACH A STAMPED SELF-ADDRESSED ENVELOPE.

(FOR OFFICE USE ONLY)

FEES

ARCH FOR TWO CONSECUTIVE YEARS AND ONE COPY.............................$5.00

CH ADDITIONAL COPY REQUESTED $5.00

CH EXTRA YEAR SEARCHED (WITH THIS APPLICATION) ....:$1.00

RECORD IS NOT ON FILE, A CERTIFIED "NOT FOUND STATEMENT" WILL BE ISSUED.

. Make check or money order payable to: Department of Health, N.Y.C.

. If from a foreign country, send an International money order or a check drawn on a U.S. bank.

3. Stamps or foreign currency will not be accepted.

MUNICIPAL ARCHIVES
Department of Records and Information Services

31 Chambers Street
New York, N.Y. 10007
(212) 566-5292
IDILIO GRACIA PENA, *Director*

APPLICATION FOR A COPY OF A BIRTH RECORD

-Enclose stamped, self-addressed envelope.

-Make check or money order payable to:
      NYC Dep't. of Records.

FEES

$5.00	Search of birth records in one year and one City/Borough for one name and issuance of one certified copy or "not found statement."
$1.00	Per additional year to be searched in one City/Borough for same name.
$1.00	Per additional City/Borough to be searched in one year for same name.
$1.00	Per additional copy of record.

PLEASE PRINT OR TYPE:

Last name on birth record	First name	Female/Male
Date of birth Month Day Year	Certificate number, if known	
Place of birth--if at home, house number and street	City/Borough	
Father's name, if known	Mother's name, if known	
Your relationship to person listed above	Number of copies requested	
Purpose for which this record will be used	Total fee enclosed	
Your name, please print	Signature	
Address		
City	State	Zip Code

MA-22 (3-88)

MUNICIPAL ARCHIVES
Department of Records and Information Services

31 Chambers Street
New York, N.Y. 10007
(212) 566-5292
IDILIO GRACIA PENA, *Director*

APPLICATION FOR A COPY OF A MARRIAGE RECORD

-Enclose stamped, self-addressed envelope.

-Make check or money order payable to:
NYC Dep't. of Records.

FEES

$5.00   Search of marriage records in one year and
        one City/Borough for one Groom and/or Bride
        and issuance of one certified copy or
        "not found" statement.
$1.00   Per additional year to be searched in one
        City/Borough for same names.
$1.00   Per additional City/Borough to be searched
        in one year for same names.
$1.00   Per additional copy of record.

PLEASE PRINT OR TYPE:

Last name of Groom	First name of Groom
Last name of Bride (Maiden name)	First name of Bride

Date of marriage

Month Day Year(s)	
Place of marriage	City/Borough
Your relationship to people named above	Certificate no. if known
Purpose for which this record will be used	Number of copies requested
Your name, please print	Signature

Address

City	State	Zip Code

MA-25 (4-88)

MUNICIPAL ARCHIVES
Department of Records and Information Services

31 Chambers Street
New York, N.Y. 10007
(212) 566-5292
IDILIO GRACIA PENA, *Director*

APPLICATION FOR A COPY OF A DEATH RECORD

-Enclose stamped, self-addressed envelope.

-Make check or money order payable to:
      NYC Dep't. of Records.

FEES

$5.00	Search of death records in one year and one City/Borough for one name and issuance of one certified copy or "not found" statement.
$1.00	Per additional year to be searched in one City/Borough for same name.
$1.00	Per additional City/Borough to be searched in one year for same name.
$1.00	Per additional copy of record.

PLEASE PRINT OR TYPE:

Last name at time of death	First name	Female/Male
Date of death Month Day Year		Occupation
Place of death	City/Borough	Age
Father's name, if known	Mother's name, if known	
Your relationship to decedent	Certificate no. if known	
Purpose for which this record will be used	Number of copies requested	
Your name, please print	Signature	
Address		
City	State	Zip Code

MA-23 (3-88)

THE CITY OF NEW YORK
DEPARTMENT OF RECORDS AND INFORMATION SERVICES
MUNICIPAL ARCHIVES
31 Chambers Street, Room 103
New York, N.Y. 10007
(212) 566-5292

GENEALOGY COLLECTIONS

VITAL RECORDS

Birth, death and marriage records are indexed according to the locality (Borough) in which they were originally filed. The following is a list of existing records for each Borough. Please consult birth, death and marriage application forms for the search and copy fee schedule.

MANHATTAN	Births	July 1847 - 1848; July 1853 - 1897.
	Deaths	1795; 1802 - 1804; 1808; 1812 - 1929.
	Marriages	June 1847 - 1848; July 1853 - 1937*.
BROOKLYN	Births	1866 - 1897.
	Deaths	1847 - 1853; 1857 - 1929.
	Marriages	1866-1937*
BRONX	Deaths	1898 - 1929.

The Bronx did not exist as a separate borough until 1898. Before then, the Bronx was part of Westchester County, except for certain western areas which were annexed by New York (Manhattan) in 1874, and eastern areas annexed in 1895. For vital records in these areas and years, request a search of MANHATTAN.

QUEENS	Deaths	1898 - 1929.
		Scattered Birth, Death and Marriage records, 1880s - 1890s.
RICHMOND (STATEN ISLAND)	Deaths	1898 - 1929.
		Scattered Birth, Death and Marriage records, 1880s - 1890s.

OTHER RECORDS

CENSUS   1890 New York City (Manhattan ONLY) "Police" Census. Listed according to address the census recorded the name, age and sex of each resident, including children.   Please consult Census application form for search and copy fee schedule.

CITY DIRECTORIES MANHATTAN: 1873-1913; 1915-1918; 1920; 1922; 1924; 1931; 1933.
          BROOKLYN: 1796; 1802; 1811; 1822-1826; 1829-1910; 1912-1913; 1933.

Lists alphabetically, by last name, head of household, (male adults primarily; women usually only if widowed), his or her occupation, home address and/or business address. Please consult Directory application form for search and copy fee schedule.

*HEALTH DEPARTMENT MARRIAGE CERTIFICATES ONLY. PLEASE SEE REVERSE FOR IMPORTANT INFORMATION CONCERNING SEARCH AND COPY OF MARRIAGE RECORDS.

September 1988

The Municipal Archives is accessioning marriage records from the Offices of
the City Clerk. It is important to note that for the period 1908 to 1937
there are two sets of marriage records: Health Department certificates and
City Clerk affidavits/licenses. To date, the following has been accessioned
by Municipal Archives:

MANHATTAN: Health Department Marriage certificates and indexes, 1866-1937.

BROOKLYN: Health Department Marriage certificates and indexes, 1866-1937.

These records are being microfilmed. Until the microfilming is complete,
the following procedures are in effect:

Apply to Municipal Archives for:

- SEARCH and COPY of a Brooklyn or Manhattan marriage record prior to
  1908.

- COPY of Health Department Brooklyn or Manhattan marriage certificate
  1908 - 1937 when HEALTH DEPARTMENT CERTIFICATE NUMBER IS PROVIDED.

See Municipal Archives marriage record application form for search and copy
fee information.

Apply to City Clerk for:

- SEARCH and COPY of a Brooklyn or Manhattan marriage record from 1908 to
  the present. (The City Clerk maintains transcripts of the City Clerk
  marriage affidavit/license records which begin in 1908).

See City Clerk marriage record application form for search and copy fee
information.

N.B. If a search of the City Clerk's marriage records for a marriage between
1908 and 1937 is unsuccessful, application may be made to Municipal Archives
for a SEARCH and COPY of a Health Department certificate. Please submit a
copy of the City Clerk "not found" statement along with payment of fee and
request for search.

NEW YORK—
New York State

Send your requests to:

New York State Department of Health
Vital Records Section
Tower Building
Empire State Plaza
Albany, New York 12237-0023

(518) 474-3077

For earlier records send your request to:

Registrar of Vital Statistics
Town or township where the event occurred.

Cost for a certified Birth Certificate	$5.00/$15.00
Cost for a certified Marriage Certificate	$5.00
Cost for a certified Death Certificate	$5.00/$15.00
Cost for a duplicate copy, when ordered at the same time	$5.00

The Vital Records Section has records of births, marriages and deaths from 1880 to the present, except those that occurred in New York City (See NEW YORK—NEW YORK CITY) or those that occurred in Albany, Buffalo or Yonkers prior to 1914. For these three cities write to the Registrar of Vital Statistics of the respective city. The Registrar of Vital Statistics in each town or township generally has records from the early 1800s to the present.

The fee for a Birth or Death Certificate from the Vital Records Section is $15.00. The fee for these same Certificates from the City Registrars of Vital Statistics is $5.00. The fee for Marriage Certificates is $5.00 from both offices.

Application for Copy of Birth Record

Make money order or check payable to New York State Department of Health. Please do not send cash or stamps.

FEE: $5.00 PER COPY

PLEASE PRINT OR TYPE

Name	First	Middle	Last	Date of Birth or Period Covered By Search		
Place of Birth	Hospital (If not hospital, give street & number)			(Village, town or city)		(County)
Father	First	Middle	Last	Maiden Name of Mother	First Middle Last	
Number of Copies Desired	Enter Birth No. if Known			Enter Local Registration No. If known		

Purpose for Which Record is Required Check One

- ☐ Passport
- ☐ Social Security
- ☐ Retirement
- ☐ Employment
- ☐ Working Papers
- ☐ School Entrance
- ☐ Driver's License
- ☐ Marriage License
- ☐ Welfare Assistance
- ☐ Veteran's Benefits
- ☐ Court Proceeding
- ☐ Entrance Into Armed Forces

☐ Other (specify) _____

What is your relationship to person whose record is required?   If self, state "self"

_____

_____

If attorney, give name and relationship of your client to person whose record is required

_____

_____

This office requires written authorization of the person/parents whose record is requested before a search is processed.

Signature of Applicant

Date

Address of Applicant

Please print name and address where record should be sent.

NEW YORK STATE DEPARTMENT OF HEALTH
Bureau of Vital Records
Albany, N.Y. 12237

APPLICATION FOR SEARCH OF MARRIAGE RECORDS

TYPE OF RECORD DESIRED (Check One)

Search and Certification	☐ Fee $5.00 per Copy	Search and Certified Copy	☐ Fee $5.00 per Copy

A Certification, an abstract from the marriage record issued under the seal of the Health Department, includes the names of the contracting parties, their residence at the time the license was issued as well as date and place of birth of the bride and groom.

A Certification may be used as proof that a marriage occurred.

A Certified Transcript includes all of the items of information occurring on the original record of the marriage.

A Certified Transcript may be needed where proof of parentage and certain other detailed information may be required such as: passports, veterans' benefits, court proceedings, or settlement of an estate.

PLEASE COMPLETE FORM AND REMIT FEE

FEES: Make money order or check payable to New York State Department of Health. Please do not send cash or stamps.

There is no fee for a record to be used for eligibility determination for social welfare or veterans' benefits.

PLEASE PRINT OR TYPE

NAME OF GROOM	(First)	(Middle)	(Last)	MAIDEN NAME OF BRIDE	(First)	(Middle)	(Last)
GROOM'S AGE OR DATE OF BIRTH	(Month)	(Day)	(Year)	BRIDE'S AGE OR DATE OF BIRTH	(Month)	(Day)	(Year)
RESIDENCE OF GROOM	(County)		(State)	RESIDENCE OF BRIDE	(County)		(State)
DATE OF MARRIAGE OR PERIOD COVERED BY SEARCH				IF BRIDE PREVIOUSLY MARRIED STATE NAME USED AT THAT TIME			
PLACE WHERE LICENSE WAS ISSUED				PLACE WHERE MARRIAGE WAS PERFORMED			

For what purpose is information required _____

What is your relationship to person whose record is requested? If self, state "self" _____

In what capacity are you acting _____

If attorney: Name and relationship of your client to persons whose marriage record is required _____

Signature of Applicant _____

Address of Applicant _____

Date _____

Please print name and address where record is to be sent.

Name _____

Address _____

City _____ State _____

VS-34M (rev. 6/81)

Application for Search
of Death Record

TYPE OF RECORD DESIRED (check one)

Search and Certification ☐

A Certification, an abstract from the death certificate issued under seal of the Health Department, includes the name, date and place of death.

A Certification may be used as proof that the event occurred.

Search and Certified Copy ☐

A Certified Copy, a photostatic copy of the original death certificate, includes all of the information found on the original death certificate.

A Certified Copy may be required where proof of parentage and certain other detailed information may be necessary such as: veterans' benefits, court proceedings or settlement of an estate.

Fee:/

PLEASE COMPLETE FORM AND REMIT FEE

Make money order or check payable to New York State Department of Health. Please do not send cash or stamps. No fee is charged for a search, certification or certified copy of a record to be used for eligibility determination for social welfare and veterans' benefits.

PLEASE PRINT OR TYPE

Name of Deceased

First   Middle   Last

Date of Death or Period to be Covered by Search

Name of Father of Deceased

First   Middle   Last

Social Security Number of Deceased

Maiden Name of Mother of Deceased

First   Middle   Last

Date of Birth of Deceased

Month   Day   Year

Age at Death

Place of Death

Name of Hospital or Street Address   Village, Town or City   County

Purpose for Which Record is Required

What was your relationship to deceased?_____

In what capacity are you acting?_____

If attorney, name and relationship of your client to deceased_____

Signature of Applicant_____Date_____

Address of Applicant_____

PLEASE PRINT NAME AND ADDRESS WHERE RECORD SHOULD BE SENT

Name_____

Address_____

City_____State_____Zip Code_____

NEW YORK STATE DEPARTMENT OF HEALTH
Vital Records Section, Genealogy Unit
Corning Tower Building, Empire State Plaza
Albany, New York 12237

General Information and Application for Genealogical Services

If the requested record is needed to settle an estate, a letter of authorization is required from the executor, public administrator or attorney for the estate. The relationship of the person of record to the estate must be provided.

VITAL RECORDS COPIES CANNOT BE PROVIDED FOR COMMERCIAL PURPOSES.

1. FEE - _____ per search and copy or _____ per search and notification of no-record for EACH record requested.
2. Original records of births, deaths and marriages for the entire state begin with 1880, EXCEPT for records filed in Albany, Buffalo and Yonkers prior to 1914. Applications for these cities should be made directly to the local office.
3. We do not have ANY records for the city of New York, except for Queens and Richmond Counties between 1880 and 1898.
4. Please read Administrative Rule 35.5 on the reverse side of this sheet which specifies years available for genealogical research.

To insure a complete search, provide as much information as possible. Please complete for type of record requested, birth, death OR marriage.

Birth		**Birth**	
Name at Birth _____		Name at Birth _____	
Date of Birth _____		Date of Birth _____	
Place of Birth _____		Place of Birth _____	
Father's Name _____		Father's Name _____	
Mother's Maiden Name _____		Mother's Maiden Name _____	

Marriage		**Marriage**	
Name of Bride _____		Name of Bride _____	
Name of Groom _____		Name of Groom _____	
Date of Marriage _____		Date of Marriage _____	
Place of Marriage and/or License ____		Place of Marriage and/or License ____	

Death		**Death**	
Name at Death _____		Name at Death _____	
Date at Death _____ Age at Death ____		Date at Death _____ Age at Death ____	
Place of Death _____		Place of Death _____	
Names of Parents _____		Names of Parents _____	
Name of Spouse _____		Name of Spouse _____	

For what purpose is information required? _____

What is your relationship to person whose record is requested? _____

In what capacity are you acting? _____

SIGNATURE OF APPLICANT _____ DATE _____

ADDRESS _____

Send record to: (please print)	If requesting birth and marriage records, please sign the following statement:
Name _____	To the best of my knowledge, the person(s) named in the application are deceased.
Address _____	
City _____ State ____ Zip Code ____	SIGNATURE OF APPLICANT

DOH - 1562 (4/87) Formerly V.S. 34G

NORTH CAROLINA

Send your requests to:

North Carolina Department of Human Resources
Division of Health Services
Vital Records Branch
P.O. Box 2091
Raleigh, North Carolina 27602-2091

(919) 733-3526

Vital records are also maintained by:

County Clerk
County Court House
(County where the event occurred)

Cost for a certified Birth Certificate	$5.00
Cost for a certified Marriage Certificate	$5.00
Cost for a certified Death Certificate	$5.00

The North Carolina Division of Health Services has birth records from October 1, 1913, marriage records from January 1, 1962, and death records from January 1, 1930. County Clerks often have much earlier records.

If your request is urgent you may call and charge your certificates to your Visa or MasterCard. There is a $4.50 charge for this service.

The Family History Library of the Church of Jesus Christ of Latter-day Saints (Mormon Church) in Salt Lake City, Utah has microfilmed many of the original and published vital records and church registers of North Carolina's cities and counties. They have a microfiche copy of the statewide marriage index. For details on their holdings please consult your nearest Family History Center.

REQUEST FOR CERTIFICATE OF BIRTH

	First	Middle	Last	Race
NAME AT BIRTH				

	Month	Day	Year	Age
DATE OF BIRTH				

	City	County	State
PLACE OF BIRTH			

FATHER'S FULL NAME

MOTHER'S FULL MAIDEN NAME

SIGNATURE:

MAILING ADDRESS:

ZIP CODE:

YOUR RELATIONSHIP TO PERSON NAMED:

CERTIFICATE NEEDED FOR

No. Copies: _____

Amount: $ _____

THE FEE FOR EACH COPY OR FOR CONDUCTING A SEARCH WHEN NO RECORD IS FOUND IS1 PLEASE MAKE CHECK OR MONEY ORDER PAYABLE TO VITAL RECORDS BRANCH.

FORWARD APPLICATION AND FEES TO: VITAL RECORDS BRANCH
P. O. BOX 2091
RALEIGH, N. C. 27602,

No. Copies _____

1st Search _____

2nd Search _____

Delays _____

Date Mailed _____

Vol. & Page _____

DHS 1215 (Revised 10/85)
Vital Records

NC Department of Human Resources
Division of Health Services

PLEASE PRINT — DO NOT WRITE

GROOM

FIRST   MIDDLE   LAST

DATE OF MARRIAGE

MONTH   DAY   YEAR

PLACE OF MARRIAGE

CITY   COUNTY   STATE

IF FOR MARRIAGE
FULL MAIDEN NAME OF BRIDE

IF FOR MARRIAGE
NAME OF MINISTER OR MAGISTRATE

IF FOR DIVORCE
FULL NAME OF DEFENDANT

CERTIFICATE
NEEDED FOR

What is your relationship
to the person named on
the certificate?

NAME, ADDRESS
AND ZIP CODE
OF APPLICANT

DHS 2103 - 4/71

NC Department of Human Resources
Division of Health Services

SECTION BELOW
FOR OFFICE USE ONLY

No Copies

1st Search

2nd Search

Date Mailed

Vol. & Page

NAME OF DECEASED — FIRST | MIDDLE | LAST | RACE

DATE OF DEATH — MONTH | DAY | YEAR | AGE

PLACE OF DEATH — CITY | COUNTY | STATE

NAME OF WIFE OR HUSBAND

NAME OF FATHER

NAME OF MOTHER

NAME & ADDRESS OF FUNERAL HOME

What is your relationship to the person named on the certificate?

NAME, ADDRESS AND ZIP CODE OF APPLICANT

DHS FORM 1293 REV. 9/75
VITAL RECORDS

NC Department of Human Resources
Division of Health Services

NORTH DAKOTA

Send your requests to:

North Dakota State Department of Health
Division of Health Statistics and Vital Records
State Capitol
Bismarck, North Dakota 58505

(701) 224-2360

Send your requests for pre-July 1, 1925 Marriage Certificates to:

County Judge
County Court
(County where the Marriage License was issued)

Cost for a certified Birth Certificate	$7.00
Additional copy of Birth Certificate	$4.00
Cost for a certified Marriage Certificate	$5.00
Cost for a certified Death Certificate	$5.00

The North Dakota State Department of Health has birth and death records from July 1, 1893 and marriage records from July 1, 1925. Vital records are also filed in the office of the County Judge of the county where the event occurred; earlier records are often on file.

If your request is urgent you may call and charge your certificates to your Visa or MasterCard. There is a $5.00 fee for this service.

REQUEST FOR COPY OF BIRTH CERTIFICATE

Please Print

FULL NAME AT BIRTH	

DATE OF BIRTH	(month)	(day)	(year)	SEX

PLACE OF BIRTH	(city or township)	(county)

RESIDENCE OF PARENTS AT TIME OF THIS BIRTH	

FULL NAME OF FATHER	(first)	(middle)	(last)

FULL NAME OF MOTHER	(first)	(middle)	(maiden).

ORDER OF BIRTH (1st child, 2nd, etc.)

IS THIS CERTIFICATE FOR AN ADOPTED CHILD? Yes____ No____

FOR WHAT PURPOSE IS THIS COPY REQUESTED?

Enclosed is $___ for ___ certified copies. (See fee schedule below)

IF NOT REQUESTING YOUR OWN CERTIFICATE, WHAT IS YOUR RELATIONSHIP TO THE ABOVE-NAMED PERSON?

Type of Copy Desired
( ) Paper Copy   ( ) Plastic Birth Card

SIGNATURE OF PERSON MAKING THIS REQUEST

PRINTED NAME

ADDRESS

CITY	STATE	ZIP CODE	DAYTIME TELEPHONE NUMBER (area code and seven digits)

IF COPY TO BE MAILED ELSEWHERE

NAME

ADDRESS	CITY	STATE	ZIP CODE

The above information is necessary to properly identify and locate the correct birth certificate. Please enter full information.

Birth certificates are by law confidential. Copies or information are to be furnished only to persons having a direct and tangible interest — the registrant, parent or guardian, legal representative, or on court order.

The fee for one certified copy is ___ Additional copies of the same certificate issued at the same time are ___ each. (Two dollars of this fee is used to support the Children's Trust Fund, a state fund for aiding in the prevention of child abuse and neglect.)

NOTE: Make all checks or money orders payable to "NORTH DAKOTA STATE DEPARTMENT OF HEALTH." Cash is sent at your own risk!

Mail request with fee to:

NORTH DAKOTA STATE DEPARTMENT OF HEALTH
VITAL RECORDS
STATE CAPITOL
BISMARCK, ND 58505

SFN 81?

REQUEST FOR COPY OF MARRIAGE RECORD

Please Print

FULL NAME OF GROOM	FULL MAIDEN NAME OF BRIDE	
RESIDENCE OF GROOM AT MARRIAGE	RESIDENCE OF BRIDE AT MARRIAGE	
DATE OF MARRIAGE (Month) (Day) (Year)	COUNTY WHERE LICENSE ISSUED	
PLACE WHERE MARRIED (City)	(County)	
FOR WHAT PURPOSE IS COPY NEEDED	YOUR RELATIONSHIP TO GROOM/BRIDE (e.g. self, parent, attorney — specify)	
SIGNATURE OF APPLICANT		
STREET ADDRESS OR BOX NUMBER		
CITY AND STATE	ZIP CODE	Enclosed is $_____ for _____ certified copies. (See fee schedule below)

Original Licenses and Certificates of Marriage are filed in the office of the **COUNTY JUDGE** of the **COUNTY WHERE THE LICENSE WAS ISSUED.** It is recommended that requests for certified copies be directed to the custodian of the **original** record as follows: **County Judge** **County Where License Was Issued** **County Seat** See reverse side of this form for a list of the North Dakota counties, respective county seats, and zip codes. • Since July 1, 1925, copies of Licenses and Certificates of Marriage have been forwarded to the State Registrar for statistical purposes and for maintaining a state-wide index. The state office is also authorized to issue certified copies. For marriages which have occurred since July 1, 1925, you may secure copies from the County Judge (as noted above) or from address listed below! **The fee is $5 for one copy** and $2 for each additional copy issued of the same certificate at the same time.	THIS PORTION FOR VITAL RECORD'S OFFICE USE ONLY Date: _____ Telephone ____ Client ____ Mail ____ Searcher: _____ State File No. 133—_____ Number/Type Copies Issued _____ REMARKS:

Mail request with fee to:

NORTH DAKOTA STATE DEPARTMENT OF HEALTH
VITAL RECORDS
STATE CAPITOL
BISMARCK, ND 58505

REQUEST FOR COPY OF DEATH CERTIFICATE

Please Print

FULL NAME OF DECEASED		SEX

DATE OF DEATH (Month)	(Day)	(Year)	SPOUSE'S NAME

PLACE OF DEATH (Hospital)	(City)	(County)

WHAT IS YOUR RELATIONSHIP TO THE DECEASED?	FUNERAL HOME
FOR WHAT PURPOSE IS THIS COPY REQUESTED?	Enclosed is $_____ for_____ certified copies.

SIGNATURE OF PERSON MAKING THIS REQUEST

PRINTED NAME

ADDRESS	CITY	STATE	ZIP CODE

TELEPHONE NO. (area code and seven digits)

IF COPY TO BE MAILED ELSEWHERE

NAME

ADDRESS	CITY	STATE	ZIP CODE

The above information is necessary to properly identify and locate the correct death certificate. Please enter full information.

Death certificates are by law confidential, and copies or information are to be furnished only to persons having a direct and tangible interest — a parent, a member of the immediate family, a legal representative, or on court order. Be sure to state your relationship to the deceased and the purpose for which the copy is needed.

NOTE: Make all checks or money orders payable to the "NORTH DAKOTA STATE DEPARTMENT OF HEALTH." Cash is sent at your own risk!

THIS PORTION FOR VITAL RECORD'S OFFICE USE ONLY

Date: _____

Telephone_____ Client_____ Mail_____

Searcher: _____

State File No. 133—_____

Number/Type Copies Issued_____

REMARKS:

Mail request with fee to:

NORTH DAKOTA STATE DEPARTMENT OF HEALTH
VITAL RECORDS
STATE CAPITOL
BISMARCK, ND 58505

Send your requests to:

Ohio State Department of Health
Division of Vital Statistics
Ohio Departments Building, Room G-20
65 South Front Street
Columbus, Ohio 43266-0333

(614) 466-2533

Send your requests for Marriage Certificates to:

Probate Judge
County Probate Court
(County where the Marriage License was issued)

Cost for a certified Birth Certificate	$7.00
Cost for a certified Death Certificate	$7.00

The Ohio State Department of Health has birth and death records from December 20, 1908. If you simply require an uncertified copy of the birth or death certificate the cost is $1.10 per copy. The County Probate Judges also have vital records on file, often much earlier than the records on file with the Division of Vital Statistics.

STATE OF OHIO

DEPARTMENT OF HEALTH

DIVISION OF VITAL STATISTICS

COLUMBUS, OHIO 43266-0333

APPLICATION FOR CERTIFIED COPY OF BIRTH CERTIFICATE

IMPORTANT

(ENCLOSE CHECK OR MONEY ORDER – DO NOT SEND CASH)

TO BE PRINTED

INFORMATION ABOUT PERSON WHOSE BIRTH CERTIFICATE IS REQUESTED

	FIRST	MIDDLE	LAST	
Full Name at Birth				
	MONTH	DAY	YEAR	AGE (AT LAST BIRTHDAY)
Date of Birth				
	COUNTY	CITY, VILLAGE OR TOWNSHIP		STATE OHIO
Place of Birth				
	FIRST	MIDDLE	LAST	
Full name of Father				
Mother's maiden name (name before marriage)	FIRST	MIDDLE	LAST (MAIDEN)	
Name of person making application		Date	Telephone number	
Present Address - Street and Number or Rural Route			Amount Enclosed $	
City or Village		State	☐ Check ☐ Money Order	
To your knowledge has a copy of this record been obtained before?	☐ Yes	☐ No	☐ Unknown	

DO NOT DETACH

. . . .

Print name and address of person to whom certificate(s) is (are) to be mailed in the space below —— this is a mailing insert and will be used to mail the certified copy which you have requested. When the above application and the name and address in the section below have been completed please send the entire form to:

▼

_____

NAME

_____

STREET NO. & NAME

CITY - - - - - - - STATE   ZIP CODE

OHIO DEPARTMENT OF HEALTH

Division of Vital Statistics

65 South Front Street

Columbus, Ohio 43266-0333

HEA 2709 (Rev. 7/85)   4   5132 06

STATE OF OHIO

DEPARTMENT OF HEALTH

DIVISION OF VITAL STATISTICS

COLUMBUS, OHIO 43266-0333

APPLICATION FOR CERTIFIED COPY OF DEATH CERTIFICATE

IMPORTANT

(ENCLOSE CHECK OR MONEY ORDER — DO NOT SEND CASH)
TO BE PRINTED

INFORMATION ABOUT PERSON WHOSE DEATH CERTIFICATE IS REQUESTED

Name of Deceased _____

Date of Death _____

Place of Death

County _____

City or Village _____

Township _____

Funeral Director _____

Address of Funeral Director

Amount Enclosed $

Applicant's Signature

☐ Check ☐ Money Order

Street and Number   City - - - - - - - State   Zip Code

DO NOT DETACH

Print name and address of person to whom certificate(s) is (are) to be mailed in the space below — — this is a mailing insert and will be used to mail the certified copy which you have requested. When the above application and the name and address in the section below have been completed please send the entire form to:

_____
NAME

_____
STREET NO. & NAME

_____
CITY - - - - - - - STATE   ZIP CODE

OHIO DEPARTMENT OF HEALTH

Division of Vital Statistics

Room G-20

65 South Front Street

Columbus, Ohio 43266-0333

HEA 2712 (Rev. 7/85)

V.S.
5161

OKLAHOMA

Send your requests to:

Oklahoma State Department of Health
Division of Vital Records
1000 Northeast 10th Street
P.O. Box 53551
Oklahoma City, Oklahoma 73152-3551

(405) 271-4040

Send your requests for Marriage Certificates to:

County Clerk
County Court House
(County where the Marriage License was issued)

Cost for a certified Birth Certificate	$5.00
Cost for a certified Death Certificate	$5.00

The Oklahoma State Department of Health has birth and death records from October 1908. Please enclose a self-addressed stamped envelope with your request. The County Clerks also maintain vital records including many records from the 1800s.

Division of Vital Records, Oklahoma State Department of Health

1000 Northeast 10th Street, Post Office Box 53551

Oklahoma City, Oklahoma 73152

APPLICATION FOR SEARCH AND CERTIFIED COPY OF BIRTH CERTIFICATE

Facts Concerning This Birth

Full name of child _____

Date of
birth _____   Place of
birth _____ , OKLAHOMA
     (Mo.)   (Day)   (Year)   (County)   (City)

Full name of father _____

Full Maiden name of mother _____

Signature of person
making this application _____   Date of this
application _____

If both parents names are not indicated on the original certificate of birth and a "full copy" is desired it will be necessary to have the signature of the mother, or the registrant if of legal age, or if certificate is required for "adoption purposes" the signature of the attorney of record and a statement from him to that effect.

The above signature is by ( ) person himself-herself ( ) next-of-kin ( ) authorized agent

Purpose for which this copy is needed
( ) School   ( ) Passport   ( ) Employment   ( ) Adoption   ( ) Other (Please state)_____

Has copy of this person's birth certificate been received before? ( ) ( ) ( )
                                       Yes   No   Unknown

PLEASE PRINT CORRECT MAILING ADDRESS BELOW:

_____
              (Name)

_____
           (Street address)

_____
    (City)   (State)

                          For ... $ _____

                          ... STAMPED,
                          ENVELOPE WITH THIS
                          APPLICATION

Request for a search of the records for a birth certificate of any person born in Oklahoma should be submitted on this blank along with the required fee of $5.00 If the birth record is on file, a certified copy will be mailed. If no record of the birth is found, then blanks and instructions for filing a "delayed" birth certificate will be sent. This fee will be credited on the $10.00 fee required for the first certified copy from the delayed record after it has been placed on file.

The information requested above should be filled in carefully and accurately. It is the minimum needed in the Vital Records office to make a thorough search for any birth record.

Send five dollars ($5.00) in cash, money order or check for each copy desired. Cash is sent at sender's risk. Make checks or money orders payable to the State Department of Health.

A copy required to be submitted to the Veterans Administration or U.S. Commissioner of Pensions, in connection with a claim for military-service-connected benefits may be obtained without fee provided a signed statement is attached which sets forth these facts and requests that the copy be issued without fee. Members of the armed forces and veterans must pay regular fees for copies to be used for all other purposes.

VS 151 10-84

Disvision of Vital Records, Oklahoma State Department of Health

APPLICATION FOR SEARCH AND CERTIFIED COPY OF DEATH CERTIFICATE

Facts Concerning This Death

Full name of deceased _____ Race _____

Date of
death _____ death _____ , OKLAHOMA
      (Mo.)   (Day)   (Year)   (County)   (City)

Place of

Check box if death was stillbirth or fetal death ☐

Funeral director
in charge _____ Address _____

Purpose for which this copy is needed _____

Signature of person   Date of
making this application _____ application _____

PLEASE PRINT CORRECT MAILING ADDRESS BELOW:

Number of copies
wanted _____

_____
(Name)

Fee enclosed $ _____

_____
(Street address)

ENCLOSE A STAMPED,
SELF-ADDRESSED
ENVELOPE WITH THIS
APPLICATION

_____
(City)   (State)

Request for a search of the records for a death certificate of any person who died in the State of Oklahoma should be submitted on this blank along with the required fee of   If the death certificate is on file a certified copy will be mailed.

The information requested above should be filled in carefully and accurately. It is the minimum needed to make a thorough search for a death record.

Send   dollars   in cash, money order or check for each copy desired. Cash is sent at sender's risk. Make checks or money orders payable to the State Department of Health.

A copy required to be submitted to the Veterans Administration or U. S. Commissioner of Pensions, in connection with a claim for military-service-connected benefits may be obtained without fee provided a signed statement is attached which sets forth these facts and requests that the copy be issued without fee. Members of the armed forces and veterans must pay regular fees for copies to be used for all other purposes.

VS 150 10-84

OREGON

Send your requests to:

Oregon State Department of Human Resources
State Health Division
Vital Statistics Section
State Office Building, Room 101
1400 S.W. 5th Avenue
P.O. Box 116
Portland, Oregon 97207-0116

(503) 229-5895

Vital records are also maintained by:

County Clerk
County Court House
(County where the event occurred)

Cost for a certified Birth Certificate	$8.00
Cost for a wallet-size Birth Card	$8.00
Cost for a certified Marriage Certificate	$8.00
Cost for a certified Death Certificate	$8.00

The Oregon Department of Human Resources has birth and death records from January 1, 1903 and marriage records from January 1, 1906. Earlier records are also maintained by the County Clerks.

You may call the office to order copies of certificates and charge them to your Visa or MasterCard. There is an additional $5.00 fee for this service.

The Family History Library of the Church of Jesus Christ of Latter-day Saints (Mormon Church) in Salt Lake City, Utah has microfilmed many of the original and published vital records and church registers of Oregon's cities and counties. They have a microfilm copy of the index to death records from 1903 to 1970. For details on their holdings please consult your nearest Family History Center.

State of Oregon
Department of Human Resources
HEALTH DIVISION

VITAL RECORDS ORDER FORM

Complete the appropriate Block for desired document

BIRTH
$8.00 EACH

Birth in Oregon since 1903

_____ QUANTITY CERTIFIED COPY — Suitable for any purpose

_____ QUANTITY BIRTH CARD — Not accepted by some agencies

1. Name on Record _____
   (First)   (Middle)   (Last)   SEX

2. Date of Birth _____
   (Month)   (Day)   (Year)

3. Place of Birth _____   **OREGON**
   (City)   (County)

4. Father's Name _____

5. Mother's Full
   Maiden Name _____

6. Your Relation- _____   If an adopted child, put X in this square ☐

ship to Line 1
In accordance with law — ORS 432.120, in addition to having one's own record, a birth record can be furnished to the parents, guardian or respective representative. If you do not fall into one of the above categories, we will need written permission from one of the above eligible persons. The written consent must accompany this form.

DO NOT WRITE IN THIS SPACE

OFFICE USE ONLY

CERTIFICATE #:

		1	2
FILM			
FILM (P)			
COMPUTER			
INDEXES			
INDEX (P)			
DF/CO			

REFUND: $

| Excess Fee: | Out/State: |
| No Rec: | Uncompltd: |

CHECK: #

Date _____

DEATH
$8.00 EACH

Death in Oregon since 1903

_____ QUANTITY Certified Copy

1. Name of Deceased _____

2. Spouse of Decedent _____

3. Date of Death _____
   (Month)   (Day)   (Year)

4. Place of Death _____   **OREGON**
   (City)   (County)

OFFICE USE ONLY

File Date	Amendment Fee
NRL/Ref. Issued	Full Issued
Follow Up	Card Issued

Send To:

**OREGON VITAL RECORDS
P.O. Box 116
PORTLAND, OR 97207-0116**

ALL RECORDS ARE $8.00 EACH

If the requested record cannot be found a search fee of at least $8.00 must be retained as prescribed by law — ORS 432.145.

Make checks or money orders payable to:
OREGON STATE HEALTH DIVISION

MARRIAGE
$8.00 EACH

Marriage in Oregon since 1906

_____ QUANTITY Certified Copy

1. Name of Groom _____

2. Bride's Full
   Maiden Name _____

3. Date of Marriage _____
   (Month)   (Day)   (Year)

4. Place License Issued _____   **OREGON**
   (City)   (County)

DIVORCE
$8.00 EACH

Divorce in Oregon since 1925

_____ QUANTITY Certified Copy

1. Name of Husband _____

2. Maiden Name
   Of Wife _____

3. Date of Divorce _____
   (Month)   (Day)   (Year)

4. County Divorce Granted _____   **OREGON**
   (City)   (County)

Your Mailing Address Must Be Entered Here and Below

DAYTIME PHONE NUMBER: (   )

NAME

STREET ADDRESS

CITY   STATE   ZIP

THIS SECTION WILL BE DETACHED AND USED TO MAIL
THE CERTIFIED COPY OF THE CERTIFICATE TO:

Your Mailing Address Must Be Entered Below:

NAME

STREET

CITY, STATE   ZIP

← YOUR MAILING ADDRESS

Thank you for your order.

This is not a bill.

In case yours was an order for more than one person's record, the other parts of your order will be handled and sent separately.

Produced by STATE PRINTING

45-13 (R-8/88)

PENNSYLVANIA

Send your requests to:

Pennsylvania Department of Health
Division of Vital Records
101 South Mercer Street
P.O. Box 1528
New Castle, Pennsylvania 16103-1528

(717) 787-8552

Send your requests for Marriage Certificates to:

County Clerk
County Court House
(County where the Marriage License was issued)

Cost for a certified Birth Certificate	$4.00
Cost for a certified Death Certificate	$3.00

The Pennsylvania Department of Health has birth and death records from January 1903. Include a self-addressed stamped envelope with your request. The County Clerks also maintain vital records. Please note the special addresses on the application form if the birth or death occurred in Erie, Philadelphia, Pittsburgh or Scranton.

The Family History Library of the Church of Jesus Christ of Latter-day Saints (Mormon Church) in Salt Lake City, Utah has microfilmed many of the original and published vital records and church registers of Pennsylvania's cities and counties. They have microfilm copies of births from 1774 to 1873. For details on their holdings please consult your nearest Family History Center.

H105.102 REV 8-85

APPLICATION FOR CERTIFIED COPY OF BIRTH OR DEATH RECORD
RECORDS AVAILABLE FROM 1906 TO THE PRESENT

PRINT OR TYPE　　　　　ALL ITEMS MUST BE COMPLETED　　　　　OFFICE USE ON

INDICATE NUMBER OF COPIES	☐ BIRTH		☐ DEATH		
1. Date of Birth **OR** Date of Death	2. Place of Birth **OR** Place of Death	County	Boro/City/Twp.		File No.
3. Name at Birth **OR** Name at Death				4. Sex / 5. Age	Searched By
6. Father's Full Name	First	Middle	Last		Typed By
7. Mother's Maiden Name	First	Middle	Last		File Date
8. Hospital		Funeral Director			Refund Ck. Nc
9. **REASON FOR REQUEST. THIS ITEM MUST BE COMPLETED**					Date　A
10. **HOW** ARE YOU RELATED TO THIS PERSON?					
11. Signature of Applicant (If Subject Under 18, Parent Must Sign)					
12. Mailing Address					
13. City, State, Zip Code					
14. Daytime Phone Number	Area Code:		Number:		

NOT REFUNDABLE
DO NOT SEND CASH
Make Check or Money Order Payable to VITAL RECORDS

PLEASE ENCLOSE A LEGAL-SIZE SELF-ADDRESSED STAMPED ENVELOPE FOR RETURN OF COPIES

IF ALL ITEMS ARE NOT COMPLETED, APPLICATION MAY BE REJECTED

☐ Prev. Amend.　　☐ Adopt　　☐ Affi

☐ Usage　　☐ Court Order　　☐ Is: Affi

DO NOT REMOVE THIS STUB

If birth or death occured in:　　　　Mail application to:

1) Philadelphia — Division of Vital Records, 402 City Hall Annex, Philadelphia, Pa. 19107
2) Pittsburgh — Division of Vital Records, Room 512, 300 Liberty Ave., Pittsburgh, Pa. 15222
3) Erie — Division of Vital Records, 3832 Liberty St., Erie, Pa. 16509
4) Scranton — Division of Vital Records, 100 Lackawanna Ave., Scranton, Pa. 18503

Print or type your name and address in the space below.

Name
Street
City, State, Zip Code

FOR ALL OTHER AREAS
MAIL COMPLETED APPLICATION TO:

PENNSYLVANIA DEPARTMENT OF HEALTH
DIVISION OF VITAL RECORDS
P.O. BOX 1528
NEW CASTLE, PA. 16103
or visit our public offices at
101 South Mercer Street, New Castle

RHODE ISLAND

Rhode Island Department of Health
Division of Vital Statistics
Cannon Building, Room 101
75 Davis Street
Providence, Rhode Island 02908-5097

(401) 277-2811

Vital records are also maintained by:

Town Clerk
Town Hall
(Town where the event occurred)

Cost for a certified Birth Certificate	$5.00
Cost for a wallet-size Birth Certificate	$5.00
Cost for a certified Marriage Certificate	$5.00
Cost for a certified Death Certificate	$5.00
Cost for a duplicate copy, when ordered at the same time	$3.00

The Rhode Island Division of Vital Statistics has records from 1853. Make your payment payable to "General Treasurer, State of Rhode Island." For early Rhode Island vital records you should consult James Newell Arnold's *Vital Records of Rhode Island 1636-1850* (Providence: Narragansett Historical Publishing Co., 1891-1912. 20 vols.) Vital records are also maintained by Town Clerks.

RHODE ISLAND DEPARTMENT OF HEALTH   DIVISION OF VITAL STATISTICS

APPLICATION FOR A CERTIFIED COPY OF A BIRTH RECORD

1. Please fill in the information below for the individual whose birth record you are requesting:

   FULL NAME AT BIRTH _____

   DATE OF BIRTH _____ CITY/TOWN OF BIRTH _____

   MOTHER'S FULL MAIDEN NAME _____

   FATHER'S FULL NAME _____

2. What is your relationship to the person whose record is being requested?

   _____

3. Why do you need this record? _____

   _____

4. Do you want a FULL COPY of the record or a WALLET-SIZE COPY? (A full copy is good for every purpose; a wallet-size is convenient for carrying, but may not be accepted by every agency).

   (Indicate number of copies) [   ] FULL COPY [   ] WALLET SIZE

5. YOUR SIGNATURE _____ DATE SIGNED _____

   PLEASE ALSO PRINT YOUR NAME HERE _____

   YOUR FULL MAILING ADDRESS _____

   _____

****

BELOW THIS LINE FOR OFFICE USE ONLY _____

| State File Number _____ | Amount Rec'd _____ | Form of Remittance _____ | Date Copy Sent _____ |

Type of Copy Given _____   Initials of Person Issuing _____   Date of Birth _____

No. of Copies ____ First copy   Additional copies of same record at _____

____ Additional years of search at   per year = _____

Delayed birth, correction, paternity, adoption or legitimation at   _____

VS 82B 7/83

RHODE ISLAND DEPARTMENT OF HEALTH   DIVISION OF VITAL STATISTICS

APPLICATION FOR A CERTIFIED COPY OF A MARRIAGE RECORD

1. Please fill in the information below for the persons whose marriage record you
    are requesting:

    FULL NAME OF GROOM _____

    FULL NAME OF BRIDE _____

    FULL MAIDEN NAME OF BRIDE (IF DIFFERENT) _____

    DATE OF MARRIAGE _____ PLACE OF MARRIAGE _____

2. What is your relationship to the persons whose marriage record is being requested

    _____

3. Why do you need this record? _____

    _____

4. YOUR SIGNATURE _____ DATE SIGNED _____

    PLEASE ALSO PRINT YOUR NAME HERE _____

    YOUR FULL MAILING ADDRESS _____

    _____

****

BELOW THIS LINE FOR OFFICE USE ONLY _____

State File   Amount   Form of   Date Copy
Number_____   Rec'd $_____   Remittance_____ Sent_____

Type of copy   Initials of
given_____   person issuing_____ Date of Marriage_____

No. of copies_____First copy   Additional copies of same record at

_____Additional years of search at   per year = _____

VS 82M   7/83

RHODE ISLAND DEPARTMENT OF HEALTH   DIVISION OF VITAL STATISTICS

APPLICATION FOR A CERTIFIED COPY OF A DEATH RECORD

1. Please fill in the information below for the individual whose death record you
    are requesting:

    FULL NAME_____

    DATE OF DEATH_____ PLACE OF DEATH_____

    NAME OF SPOUSE (IF MARRIED)_____

    MOTHER'S FULL MAIDEN NAME_____

    FATHER'S FULL NAME_____

2. What is your relationship to the person whose death record is being requested?

    _____

3. Why do you need this record?_____

    _____

4. YOUR SIGNATURE_____ DATE SIGNED_____

    PLEASE ALSO PRINT YOUR NAME HERE_____

    YOUR FULL MAILING ADDRESS_____

    _____

5. Number of Copies _____
    ☆☆

BELOW THIS LINE FOR OFFICE USE ONLY_____

State File   Amount   Form of   Date Copy
Number_____   Rec'd $_____   Remittance_____   Sent_____

Type of copy   Initials of
given_____   person issuing_____   Date of death_____

No. of copies____ First copy   ____Additional copies of same record at

____Additional years of search at   per year = _____

VS 82D   **7/83**

SOUTH CAROLINA

Send your requests to:

> South Carolina Department of Health
>   and Environmental Control
> Office of Vital Records and Public Health Statistics
> 2600 Bull Street
> Columbia, South Carolina 29201-1797

(803) 734-4830

For pre-July 1, 1950 Marriage Certificates write to:

> Probate Judge
> Probate Court
> (County where the Marriage License was issued)

Cost for a certified Birth Certificate	$5.00
Cost for a wallet-size Birth Certificate	$5.00
Cost for a certified Marriage Certificate	$5.00
Cost for a certified Death Certificate	$5.00
Cost for a duplicate copy, when ordered at the same time	$1.00

The South Carolina Office of Vital Records has birth and death records from January 1, 1915 and marriage records from July 1, 1950. Marriage records before that date are available from the Probate Judge of the county where the license was issued. County Clerks also maintain vital records and in most cases their records are much earlier than those kept by the Office of Vital Records.

If your request is urgent you may call and charge your certificates to your Visa or MasterCard. There is a charge of $19.75 for this service including the postal costs.

The Family History Library of the Church of Jesus Christ of Latter-day Saints (Mormon Church) in Salt Lake City, Utah has microfilmed many of the original and published vital records and church registers of South Carolina's cities and counties. They have microfilm copies of marriage records from 1785 to 1889. For details on their holdings please consult your nearest Family History Center.

APPLICATION FOR CERTIFIED COPY OF BIRTH CERTIFICATE

INFORMATION

1. Only births recorded after **January 1, 1915 in South Carolina** are on file.

2. S. C. Law requires a ____ fee for the search of a birth record. If located, a standard certification of birth will be issued. If not located, search fee is not refundable.

3. **WARNING: FALSE APPLICATION IS PUNISHABLE BY LAW.**
(Section 44-63-161; S. C. Code of Laws, 1976, Amended, July 18, 1978.)

INSTRUCTIONS

1. Complete all of the information sections required on this form. **PLEASE PRINT.**

2. The application must be **signed by registrant, parent/guardian, or their legal representative.**

3. Send completed application and appropriate fee to the address at the top of this form. Checks and money orders should be made payable to Office of Vital Records.

1. FULL NAME	First Name	Middle Name	Last Name	OFFICE USE ONL
2. DATE OF BIRTH	Month	Day	Year	Year — Cert. No.
3. PLACE OF BIRTH	County	Hospital/and or city/town	State South Carolina	1st Search Date
				2nd Date
4. SEX		**5. RACE**		
6. FULL NAME OF FATHER	First Name	Middle Name	Last Name Living ☐ Deceased ☐	Pending Sect. Date C
7. FULL MAIDEN NAME OF MOTHER	First Name	Middle Name	Maiden Name Living ☐ Deceased ☐	D
8. WERE PARENTS MARRIED? Yes ☐ No ☐		**9. NUMBER OF CHILD (1st, 2nd, etc...)**		A
				L
10. NAME OF NEXT OLDER BROTHER OR SISTER, LIVING OR DEAD		DATE OF BIRTH		PR
11. NAME OF NEXT YOUNGER BROTHER OR SISTER LIVING OR DEAD		DATE OF BIRTH		LOC
12. HAS NAME EVER BEEN CHANGED OTHER THAN MARRIAGE? Yes ☐ No ☐		If so, what was the original name?		Final Disposition Issue Date
13. PURPOSE FOR WHICH THIS COPY IS REQUESTED?				Control Number(s)

FEE
14. I am enclosing $ _____ for _____ certificates as follows: **Specify Number and Type Certification**

_____ **Wallet size, short form certification** - Accepted for all purposes except to establish relationship of parent to child. Does not include parents' names. Initial certification - _____ Additional short form certification ordered at same time - each.

_____ **Photocopy certification** - Issued only by the state office and only to registrant if of legal age (18 yrs.) parent/guardian or their legal representative. Initial certification - _____ Additional photocopy certification ordered at same time - each.

15. WRITTEN SIGNATURE OF registrant, parent/guardian or legal representative **DO NOT PRINT**	Your relationship to registrant: Self _____ Parent _____ Guardian _____ Other (specify) _____	☐ Refund Refunded Amount $ _____

ADDRESS

PLEASE PRINT
16. NAME

17. NUMBER, P.O. BOX AND STREET

18. CITY, STATE, AND ZIP CODE

SCDHEC - 612 (Rev. 12-82)

SOUTH CAROLINA DEPARTMENT OF HEALTH AND ENVIRONMENTAL CONTROL

OFFICE OF VITAL RECORDS & PUBLIC HEALTH STATISTICS
2600 BULL STREET
COLUMBIA, S. C. 29201

APPLICATION FOR CERTIFIED COPY OF MARRIAGE RECORD

INFORMATION

1. Only marriage licenses issued **after July, 1950, in South Carolina** are on file.

2. S. C. Law requires a _____ fee for the search of a marriage record. If located, a certified copy of the marriage record will be issued. Additional copies of the same record ordered at the same time are _____ each. If not located, search fee is not refundable.

3. If the marriage occurred prior to July, 1950, or if a copy of the application is required, contact the probate judge of the county where the marriage license was issued.

INSTRUCTIONS

1. Complete all the information sections of the form. **PLEASE PRINT.**

2. An application for a certified copy of a marriage record must be **signed by one of the parties married, their adult child, or the legal representative of one of these persons. Relationship must be stated.**

3. Send completed application and appropriate fee to the address at the top of this form. Checks and money orders should be made payable to the office of Vital Records.

					OFFICE USE ONLY
1. FULL NAME OF GROOM	First	Middle	Last		
2. DATE OF BIRTH	Month	Day	Year	Race	YEAR – CERT. NO.
3. FULL NAME OF BRIDE	First	Middle	Last		
4. DATE OF OF BIRTH	Month	Day	Year	Race	PROC. DATE

5. HAS BRIDE EVER USED ANY OTHER NAME? ☐ Yes ☐ No   If so, please list: _____   DNL.   DATE

6. DATE OF MARRIAGE	Month	Day	Year	FINAL DISPOSITION
7. PLACE LICENSE ISSUED	City	County	State South Carolina	ISSUE DATE

8. FEE   I am enclosing a Fee of $ _____ for _____ CERTIFIED COPIES.   CONTROL NO.

9. WRITTEN SIGNATURE OF ONE OF MARRIED PARTIES, ADULT CHILDREN, OR LEGAL REPRESENTATIVE   Relationship
Self_____ Adult child_____ Legal rep_____

☐ Refund
Refunded
Amount $_____

CERTIFICATE TO BE MAILED TO: (PLEASE PRINT)

10. NAME

11. NUMBER, P. O. BOX AND STREET

12. CITY, STATE, AND ZIP CODE

SCDHEC-678 (Rev. 12-82)

SOUTH CAROLINA DEPARTMENT OF HEALTH AND ENVIRONMENTAL CONTROL

OFFICE OF VITAL RECORDS & PUBLIC HEALTH STATISTICS
2600 BULL STREET
COLUMBIA, S. C. 29201

APPLICATION FOR CERTIFIED COPY OF A DEATH RECORD

INFORMATION

1. Only deaths recorded after January 1, 1915, in South Carolina are on file.

2. S. C. Law requires a _____ fee for the search of a death record. If located, a certified copy of the death record will be issued. Additional copies of the same record ordered at the same time are _____ each. If not located, search fee is not refundable.

3. Verification of date and place of death will be provided if the relationship of the applicant prohibits the issuance of a certified copy. (Regulation 61-19, Section 39, Code of Laws of South Carolina, 1976)

4. **WARNING: FALSE APPLICATION FOR A DEATH CERTIFICATE IS PUNISHABLE BY LAW.** (Section 44-63-161, South Carolina Code of Laws, 1976, Amended, July 18, 1978)

INSTRUCTION

1. Complete all the information sections of the form. **PLEASE PRINT.**

2. An application for a certified copy of a death certificate must be signed by a surviving relative of the deceased person or his legal representative. **Relationship must be stated.**

3. Send completed application and appropriate fee to the address at the top of this form. Checks and money orders should be made payable to the Office of Vital Records.

---

1. **FULL NAME OF DECEASED**	Last Name	First Name	Middle Name and/or Maiden		OFFICE USE ONLY
2. **DATE OF DEATH**	Month	Day	Year		Year — Cert. No.
3. **PLACE OF DEATH**	Hospital/City	County	State SOUTH CAROLINA		DNL. DATE
4. SEX		5. RACE	6. AGE AT TIME OF DEATH		PROC. DATE
7. **SOCIAL SECURITY NO. OF DECEASED (IF KNOWN)**					
8. **NAME OF FUNERAL DIRECTOR**					Final Disposition
9. IF THE DECEASED WAS MARRIED; PLEASE LIST HUSBAND/WIFE			Living ☐ Dead ☐		ISSUE DATE
10. FATHER OF THE DECEASED	Last Name	First Name	Middle Name		CONTROL NO.
11. MOTHER OF THE DECEASED	Last Name	First Name	Middle Name		

12. FEE   I am enclosing a Fee of $ _____ for _____ CERTIFIED COPIES.

13. WRITTEN SIGNATURE OF SURVIVING RELATIVE OR LEGAL REPRESENTATIVE		RELATION TO DECEASED	☐ Refund Refunded Amount $ _____

CERTIFICATE TO BE MAILED TO: (PLEASE PRINT)

14. NAME

15. NUMBER, P. O. BOX AND STREET

16. CITY, STATE, AND ZIP CODE

SCDHEC-677 (Rev. 12-82)

SOUTH DAKOTA

Send your requests to:

> South Dakota Department of Health
> Center for Health Statistics
> Joe Foss Building
> 523 East Capitol
> Pierre, South Dakota 57501-3182

(605) 773-3355

For copies of pre-1905 Marriage Certificates write to:

> County Treasurer
> County Court House
> (County where the Marriage License was issued)

Cost for a certified Birth Certificate	$5.00
Cost for a certified Marriage Certificate	$5.00
Cost for a certified Death Certificate	$5.00

The South Dakota Department of Health has records from July 1905. The County Clerks also maintain vital records and often have records much earlier than the records at the Center for Health Statistics.

If your request is urgent you may call (605) 773-4961 and charge your certificates to your Visa or MasterCard. There is a $5.00 fee for this service.

Department of Health

Center For Health Statistics
523 East Capitol, Joe Foss Bldg.
Pierre, South Dakota 57501-3182
605/773-3355

RECEIPT #_____

DATE_____

We have received your request and fee of $_____ for a certified copy of a vital record.
We require an additional fee of $_____ before we can process your request. THE ADDITIONAL
FEE AND THIS COMPLETED FORM MUST BE RETURNED WITHIN 30 DAYS.

BIRTH	FULL NAME AT BIRTH OR ADOPTIVE NAME_____ DATE OF BIRTH (Month, Day & Year)_____ PLACE OF BIRTH (City & County)_____ FATHER'S FULL NAME_____ MOTHER'S FULL MAIDEN NAME_____ STATE REASON RECORD IS NEEDED_____ (Applies only to out of wedlock births) _____ (Signature of person requesting record)
DEATH	FULL NAME AT TIME OF DEATH_____ DATE OF DEATH (Month, Day & Year)_____ PLACE OF DEATH (City & County)_____
MARRIAGE	FULL NAME OF GROOM_____ FULL NAME OF BRIDE_____ DATE OF MARRIAGE (Month, Day & Year)_____
DIVORCE	FULL NAME OF HUSBAND_____ FULL NAME OF WIFE_____ DATE OF DIVORCE (Month, Day & Year)_____

<u>PRINT OR TYPE</u> NAME AND ADDRESS OF PERSON TO WHOM CERTIFICATE IS TO BE SENT

_____
(Name)

_____
(Street or Box)

_____
(City and State)   ZIP

HAS-0252   REV. 4-85

TENNESSEE

Send your requests to:

Tennessee State Department of Health
    and Environment
Vital Records Office
Cordell Hull Building
Nashville, Tennessee 37219-5402

(615) 741-1763

For early birth, marriage and death records write to:

County Clerk
County Court House
(County where the event occurred)

Cost for a certified Birth Certificate	$10.00
Cost for a short form Birth Certificate	$ 5.00
Cost for a certified Marriage Certificate	$10.00
Cost for a certified Death Certificate	$ 4.00

The Tennessee Office of Vital Records has birth and death records from January 1, 1914 and marriage records from July 1, 1945.

If your request is urgent you may call and charge your certificates to your Visa or MasterCard. There is a $10.00 fee for this service.

The Family History Library of the Church of Jesus Christ of Latter-day Saints (Mormon Church) in Salt Lake City, Utah has microfilmed many of the original and published vital records and church registers of Tennessee's cities and counties. They have microfilm copies of births from 1908 to 1912 and deaths from 1908 to 1912, 1914 to 1925. For details on their holdings please consult your nearest Family History Center.

156

TENNESSEE DEPARTMENT OF HEALTH AND ENVIRONMENT
Vital Records
APPLICATION FOR CERTIFIED COPY OF CERTIFICATE OF BIRTH
Do Not Send Cash. Check Or Money Order Preferred.

DATE: _____

Full Name at Birth_____
             First   Middle   Last

Indicate Any Legal Changes of Names _____

Date of Birth _____ Sex _____
         Month   Day   Year

Place of Birth_____
        City   County   State

Full Name of Father_____ Race _____

Full Maiden Name of Mother_____ Race _____

Last Name of Mother at Time of Birth _____

Name of Doctor or Attendant at Birth (if known)_____

Hospital Where Birth Occurred _____

Next Older Brother or Sister_____ Younger_____

Signature of Person Making Request_____

Relationship _____

Purpose of Copy _____

Telephone number where you may be reached for additional information _____

All items must be completed in order for us to process your request.

Indicate number of each type of Certificate desired and enclose appropriate fee.

For years 1950—Current

☐ —Short Form (a certified transcript that shows Child's Name, Birth Date, Sex, County of Birth, Certificate Number and File Date)

☐ —Long Form (a certified copy showing all information)

Years prior to 1950

☐ Copies

The above fees are charged for the search of our records, and to include one copy, if record is on file in this office.

It is unlawful to willfully and knowingly make any false statement on this application.

PH-1654
VR Rev. 10/85

- -

DO NOT DETACH

This is a mailing insert. PRINT name and address of person to whom the certified copy is to be mailed.

Name: _____

Street or
Route: _____

City or
Town: _____ State: _____ Zip: _____

PH-1654
VR Rev. 10/85

APPLICATION FOR A CERTIFIED COPY OF A CERTIFICATE OF MARRIAGE

Date _____   Number of
                                          Copies Requested _____

Name of Groom _____
                    First   Middle   Last

Name of Bride at Birth _____
                          First   Middle   Last

Place This License Was Issued _____
                                     County   State

Date of Marriage _____
                    Month   Day   Year

Place of Marriage _____
                    City   County   State

Signature of Person Making Request _____

Relationship of Requester _____

Purpose of Copy _____

DO NOT DETACH

IMPORTANT

ENCLOSE FEE OF   FOR EACH COPY REQUESTED
Make check or money order payable to the TENNESSEE DEPARTMENT OF PUBLIC HEALTH
Fee Will Be Charged For Search And Cannot Be Refunded

This is a mailing insert. PRINT name and address of
person to whom the certified copy is to be mailed.

_____

Name _____
Street or
Route _____
City or
Town _____   Zip _____

PH-1670
VR Rev. 8/82

TENNESSEE DEPARTMENT OF HEALTH & ENVIRONMENT
Vital Records

APPLICATION FOR CERTIFIED COPY OF CERTIFICATE OF DEATH
Remit fee of _____ for each copy requested
Make check or money order payable to the TENNESSEE DEPARTMENT OF HEALTH & ENVIRONMENT
Do Not Send Cash. Check or Money Order Preferred.

DATE _____   Number of Copies Requested: _____

Name of Deceased _____
        first   middle   last

Date of Death _____
        month   day   year

Sex _____ Race _____ Age _____

Place of Death_____
        city   county   state

Name of Funeral Home _____

Location of Funeral Home _____
                   city   state

Signature of Person Making Request: _____

Relationship to Deceased: _____

Purpose of Copy: _____

Telephone Number Where You May Be Reached:_____

A fee of _____ is charged for the search of our records even if no record is found, and includes one copy if a record is on file in this office.

(It is unlawful to willfully and knowingly make any false statement on this application.)

PH-1663
VR Rev. 5/85

DO NOT DETACH

Mail Copy To:

This is a mailing insert. PRINT name and address of person to whom the certified copy is to be mailed.

_____

NAME _____
Street or
Route _____
City or
Town _____ State _____ Zip _____

PH-1663
VR Rev. 5/85

Send your requests to:

Texas State Department of Health
Bureau of Vital Statistics
1100 West 49th Street
Austin, Texas 78756-3191

(512) 458-7366

Send your requests for Marriage Certificates to:

County Clerk
County Court House
(County where the Marriage License was issued)

Cost for a certified Birth Certificate	$8.00
Cost for a wallet-size Birth Certificate	$8.00
Cost for the verification of Marriage	$8.00
Cost for a certified Death Certificate	$8.00
Cost for a duplicate copy of a birth or death record, when ordered at the same time	$2.00

The Texas State Department of Health has birth and death records from January 1, 1903. They also have marriage records from January 1, 1966. They will verify marriage information but a certificate can only be issued by the County Clerk. The County Clerks also keep vital records and most of their records are much older than the records kept by the Bureau of Vital Statistics.

TEXAS DEPARTMENT OF HEALTH
BUREAU OF VITAL STATISTICS
1100 WEST 49th STREET
AUSTIN, TEXAS 78756-3191

APPLICATION FOR CERTIFICATION OF BIRTH

INSTRUCTIONS	COPIES REQUESTED	DO NOT WRITE IN THIS SPACE
THE FEE FOR EACH CERTIFICATION MUST BE SUBMITTED WITH THIS APPLICATION.	CERTIFICATION OF BIRTH — HOW MANY [ ]	REQUEST NO. AND DATE
REMITTANCES MUST BE MADE PAYABLE TO THE TEXAS DEPARTMENT OF HEALTH.	CERTIFICATION OF BIRTH (POCKETBOOK SIZE)** — HOW MANY [ ]	AMOUNT
MAIL THIS APPLICATION TO **BUREAU OF VITAL STATISTICS** Texas Department of Health 1100 West 49th St. Austin, Texas 78756-3191	AMOUNT OF MONEY ENCLOSED	CODE

INFORMATION ABOUT PERSON WHOSE BIRTH CERTIFICATE IS REQUESTED (TYPE OR PRINT)

	FIRST NAME	MIDDLE NAME	LAST NAME
1. FULL NAME OF PERSON			
2. DATE OF BIRTH	MONTH	DAY / YEAR	3. SEX
4. PLACE OF BIRTH	CITY OR TOWN	COUNTY	STATE
5. FULL NAME OF FATHER	FIRST NAME	MIDDLE NAME	LAST NAME
6. FULL MAIDEN NAME OF MOTHER	FIRST NAME	MIDDLE NAME	LAST NAME

PERSON REQUESTING CERTIFICATION OF BIRTH

7. DO YOU WANT THE NAMES OF THE PARENTS SHOWN ON THE CERTIFICATION OF BIRTH?   YES [ ]   NO [ ]

8. PURPOSE FOR WHICH CERTIFICATION OF BIRTH IS TO BE USED (School, Employment, Military Service, Passport, Etc.)

9. RELATIONSHIP TO PERSON NAMED IN ITEM 1 ABOVE (Self, Mother, Attorney, Employer, Etc.)

10. SIGNATURE OF APPLICANT	11. DATE SIGNED
12. ADDRESS OF APPLICANT (Type or Print) — STREET ADDRESS	
CITY OR TOWN	STATE ZIP CODE

IF YOU WANT THE CERTIFICATION OF BIRTH MAILED TO SOME OTHER PERSON, COMPLETE THIS SECTION

TYPE OR PRINT	NAME
	STREET ADDRESS
	CITY OR TOWN STATE ZIP CODE

VS-141, REV. 1/82

*THE FEE FOR EACH CERTIFICATION OF BIRTH
IS   REGARDLESS OF SIZE.

**A CERTIFICATION OF BIRTH (POCKETBOOK SIZE) INCLUDES ONLY THE INFORMATION SHOWN IN THE SAMPLE AT RIGHT.

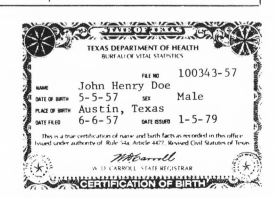

STATE OF TEXAS

TEXAS DEPARTMENT OF HEALTH
BUREAU OF VITAL STATISTICS

FILE NO 100343-57
NAME John Henry Doe
DATE OF BIRTH 5-5-57   SEX Male
PLACE OF BIRTH Austin, Texas
DATE FILED 6-6-57   DATE ISSUED 1-5-79

This is a true certification of name and birth facts as recorded in this office Issued under authority of Rule 54a, Article 4477, Revised Civil Statutes of Texas

W. D. CARROLL STATE REGISTRAR

CERTIFICATION OF BIRTH

ACTUAL SIZE 2½" X 3¾"

Texas Department of Health
Bureau of Vital Statistics
1100 West 49th Street
Austin, Texas 78756-3101

Record #:_____by _____

APPLICATION FOR VERIFICATION OF MARRIAGE OR DIVORCE
PLEASE PRINT

Applicant's Name_____

Street Address_____ Telephone #_____

City_____ State_____ Zip Code_____

Relationship_____ Purpose in obtaining this record_____

Marriage records begin January 1966 — Divorce records begin January 1968 — *THE FEE FOR EACH VERIFICATION IS $2.00
*The verification fee is non-refundable or transferable if a record is not found.

( ) MARRIAGE   ( ) DIVORCE

Husband's Name_____
        Last   First   Middle

Wife's *Maiden Name*_____
        Last   First   Middle

Year of Event 19_____ County of Event_____ _____
                                                            Code

City or Town of Event_____State____ **TX**____

If Verification is to be mailed to some other person, please complete:

Name_____Street Address_____

City_____ State_____ Zip Code_____

WARNING

The penalty for knowingly making a false statement in this form can be 2-10 years in prison and a fine of up to $5,000. (Article 4477c, Revised Civil Statutes of Texas).

_____
Signature of Applicant

_____
Date of Application

VS-141.3 6/87   LTR._____BY_____DATE_____

SPECIAL

TEXAS DEPARTMENT OF HEALTH
BUREAU OF VITAL STATISTICS
1100 WEST 49TH STREET
AUSTIN, TEXAS 78756-3191

APPLICATION FOR CERTIFIED COPY OF DEATH CERTIFICATE

INSTRUCTIONS

The fee for conducting each search and issuing a certified copy of a death certificate is $7.50. If more than one certification of the same record is required at the same time, the fee for the first copy of a death record is $7.50 and $2.00 for each additional copy of the record requested by the applicant in a single request. For any search of the files where a record is not found or a certified copy is not issued, the fee is $7.50.

1. NAME _____ 2. _____
           Given Name(s)   Last Name at Time of Death   Sex

3. SPOUSE _____

4. DATE OF DEATH _____
                Month   Day   Year

    If unknown, show year last known to have been alive _____

5. DATE OF BIRTH/AGE: _____ 6. PLACE OF BIRTH: _____

7. PLACE OF DEATH _____
                City or Town   County

    If unknown, show last city or county of residence _____

8. COLOR/RACE: _____ 9. SOCIAL SECURITY NUMBER: _____

10. FATHER'S NAME: _____

11. MOTHER'S MAIDEN NAME: _____

12. I AM RELATED TO THE DECEASED AS _____

13. MY PURPOSE IN OBTAINING THE COPY IS _____

14. ENCLOSED IS A FEE OF $_____ FOR _____ CERTIFIED COPY OR COPIES.

_____
    DATE OF APPLICATION

_____   _____
SIGNATURE OF APPLICANT   STREET ADDRESS

                             ( )
_____   _____
CITY AND STATE   TELEPHONE # (8 A.M. TO 5 P.M.)

VS-141.1
Rev. 8/88

NOTE: The searching fee is non-refundable nor transferable when a record is not located.

Send your requests to:

Utah State Department of Health
Bureau of Health Statistics
288 North 1460 West
P.O. Box 16700
Salt Lake City, Utah 84116-0700

(801) 538-6380

Send your requests for pre-1978 Marriage Certificates to:

County Clerk
County Court House
(County where the Marriage License was issued)

Cost for a certified Birth Certificate	$11.00
Cost for a certified Marriage Certificate	$ 8.00
Cost for a certified Death Certificate	$ 8.00
Cost for a duplicate copy, when ordered at the same time	$ 4.00

The Utah Bureau of Health Statistics has birth and death records from January 1, 1905 and marriage records from January 1, 1978. There is no form for requesting a marriage certificate. If you do not know the exact date that the event occurred there is a $50.00 fee if a search is undertaken. The County Clerks also keep copies of vital records. Most of their records are much earlier than the records kept at the State Department of Health.

UTAH DEPARTMENT OF HEALTH
APPLICATION FOR CERTIFIED COPY OF A BIRTH CERTIFICATE

INFORMATION

Certificates for births that occurred in Utah since 1905 are on file in this office. Persons who were born in Utah and have no birth certificate on file may make application to file a Delayed Registration of Birth. Application forms for Delayed Registration of Birth must be obtained from this office. It is a violation of Utah State law for any person to obtain, possess, use, sell or furnish for any purpose of deception, a birth certificate or certified copy thereof.

INSTRUCTIONS—FEES ARE EFFECTIVE JULY 1, 1988

1. An application must be completed for each birth certificate requested.

2. If the applicant is not the person whose birth certificate is being requested, the reason for requesting the record must be provided.

3. There is a fee of $11.00 for each search of our files. This includes $3.00 to be used for Child Abuse Prevention programs. The search includes the year the event is reported to have occurred and two years on either side of that year. Each additional five years to be searched requires an additional fee of $11.00. The entire file of birth certificates from 1905 to the present will be searched for the fee of $50.00. One certified copy of the record is issued, or a certificate of search if the record is not found. Additional certified copies of this record ordered at the same time are $4.00 each.

4. Send the completed application and required fee to the Bureau of Vital Records, 288 North 1460 West, P.O. Box 16700, Salt Lake City, Utah 84116-0700.

IDENTIFYING INFORMATION

FULL NAME OF CHILD AT BIRTH _____

DATE OF BIRTH _____

PLACE OF BIRTH (City) _____ (County) _____

FULL NAME OF FATHER _____

BIRTHPLACE OF FATHER _____

FULL MAIDEN NAME OF MOTHER _____

BIRTHPLACE OF MOTHER _____

APPLICANT

Please state your **relationship** and/or the reason for requesting certified copy(s).

_____

Signature of Applicant _____ Date _____

Address of Applicant _____ Telephone Number _____

Number of copies requested   Birth certificate copy ___ $11.00 for first copy
    and amount of fee:
                                  Number of extra copies ___ $ 4.00 each after first copy

                                  Unlaminated Birth Card ___ $ 4.00 each after first copy

If copies are to be mailed to address other than above, specify name and mailing address:

_____

UDH-BVR-1 Revised 6/88

UTAH DEPARTMENT OF HEALTH
APPLICATION FOR CERTIFIED COPY OF A DEATH CERTIFICATE

INFORMATION

Death certificates for deaths that occurred in
Utah since 1905 are on file in this office.

INSTRUCTIONS—FEES ARE EFFECTIVE JULY 1, 1988

1. An application must be completed for each death certificate requested.

2. If the applicant is not a member of the immediate family of the deceased person, the reason for requesting the record must be provided.

3. There is a fee of $8.00 for each search of our files. The search includes the year the event is reported to have occurred and two years on either side of that year. Each additional five years to be searched requires an additional fee of $8.00. The entire file of death certificates from 1905 to the present will be searched for the fee of $50.00. One certified copy of the record is issued, or a certificate of search if the record is not found. Additional certified copies of the same record at the same time are $4.00 each.

4. Send the completed application and required fee to the Bureau of Vital Records, 288 North 1460 West, P.O. Box 16700, Salt Lake City, Utah 84116-0700.

INDENTIFYING INFORMATION

FULL NAME OF DECEASED _____ SOCIAL SECURITY NO. _____

Date of Death _____ (If not known, specity years to be searched) _____

Place of Death (City) _____ (County) _____

Birthplace of Decedent (State or County) _____ Date of Birth of Decedent _____

Usual Residence of Decedent (City & State) _____

Full Name of Father _____

Full Maiden Name of Mother _____

If Deceased was Married, Name of Spouse _____

Reason for Requesting Certified Copy (include your relationship to the person whose certificate is being requested).

APPLICANT

_____

Signature of Applicant _____ Date _____

Address of Applicant _____

_____ Telephone Number _____

Number of copies requested _____ Amount of Fee Attached _____

If copies are to be mailed to address other than above, specify name and mailing address:

_____
| Name | Address |

UDH—BVR—11 Revised 6/88

VERMONT

Send your requests to:

Vermont Department of Health
Vital Records Unit
60 Main Street
P.O. Box 70
Burlington, Vermont 05402-0070

(802) 863-7275
In Vermont call (800) 642-3323, ext. 7275

Send your requests for records from 1760 to December 31, 1954 to:

Vermont Public Records Division
State Administration Building
133 State Street
Montpelier, Vermont 05602

(802) 828-3286

Cost for a certified Birth Certificate	$5.00
Cost for a certified Marriage Certificate	$5.00
Cost for a certified Death Certificate	$5.00

Please make your check payable to the Vermont Department of Health. They do not charge for a verification of a birth, marriage or death record.

The Family History Library of the Church of Jesus Christ of Latter-day Saints (Mormon Church) in Salt Lake City, Utah has microfilmed many of the original and published vital records and church registers of Vermont's cities and counties. They have microfilm copies of the vital records from 1760 to 1908. For details on their holdings please consult your nearest Family History Center.

Application for Vital Record
BIRTH CERTIFICATE

REQUEST FOR (Check one): ____ Certified Copy ____ Verification ____ Record Search

INSTRUCTIONS

NOTE: For records dated prior to 1955, contact:
Public Records, State Administration Building, 133 State Street, Montpelier, VT 05602
(802) 828-3286

Type or print all information clearly.
Sign and date application and return it with your check or money order (made payable to the Vermont Department of Health) to the address shown below. **Do not mall cash.**

Fees:
Certified Copy $5.00
Verification   no charge
Record Search   no charge

Amount enclosed _____

BIRTH INFORMATION

Name on birth certificate _____ Sex _____

Date of birth _____ Town or city of birth _____

Name of father _____

Maiden name of mother _____

APPLICANT INFORMATION

Your name _____

Address _____

_____

Town _____ State _____ Zip _____

Phone number (_____) _____

Your relationship to person on birth certificate _____

Intended use of certificate:

____ Social Security   ____ School Enrollment

____ Passport   ____ Driver's License

____ Family History   ____ Other: Specify: _____

Signature _____ Date _____

Return to: Vermont Department of Health, Vital Records Unit
60 Main Street, Box 70, Burlington, VT 05402

Application for Vital Record
MARRIAGE CERTIFICATE

REQUEST FOR (Check one): _____ Certified Copy _____ Verification _____ Record Search

NOTE: For records dated prior to 1955, contact:
Public Records, State Administration Building, 133 State Street, Montpelier, VT 05602
(802) 828-3286

Type or print all information clearly.
Sign and date application and return it with your check or
money order (made payable to the Vermont Department of
Health) to the address shown below. **Do not mail cash.**

Fees:
Certified Copy $5.00
Verification   no charge
Record Search   no charge

Amount enclosed _____

Date of Marriage _____ Town of Marriage _____

Groom:

Name _____

Date of Birth: _____

Name of Father _____

Name of Mother _____

Bride:

Name _____

Date of Birth: _____

Name of Father _____

Name of Mother _____

Your name _____

Address _____
_____

Town _____ State _____ Zip _____

Phone number (_____) _____

Your relationship to couple on certificate _____

Intended use of certificate:

_____ Proof of Marriage

_____ Family History

_____ Other: Specify: _____

Signature _____ Date _____

Return to: Vermont Department of Health, Vital Records Unit
60 Main Street, Box 70, Burlington, VT 05402

Application for Vital Record
DEATH CERTIFICATE

REQUEST FOR (Check one): ____ Certified Copy ____ Verification ____ Record Search

INSTRUCTIONS

NOTE: For records dated prior to 1955, contact:
Public Records, State Administration Building, 133 State Street, Montpelier, VT 05602
(802) 828-3286

Type or print all information clearly.
Sign and date application and return it with your check or money order (made payable to the Vermont Department of Health) to the address shown below. **Do not mall cash.**

Fees:

Certified Copy	$5.00
Verification	no charge
Record Search	no charge

Amount enclosed _____

DEATH INFORMATION

Name on death certificate _____ Sex _____

Date of death _____ Town or city of death _____

Date of birth _____ City and state of birth _____

Age at death _____ Name of spouse _____

APPLICANT INFORMATION

Your name _____

Address _____

_____

Town _____ State _____ Zip _____

Phone number (_____) _____

Your relationship to person on death certificate _____

Intended use of certificate:

____ Benefits   ____ Family History

____ Settlement of Estate   ____ Other: Specify

Signature _____ Date _____

Return to: Vermont Department of Health, Vital Records Unit
60 Main Street, Box 70, Burlington, VT 05402

VIRGINIA

Send your requests to:

Virginia Department of Health
Division of Vital Records
James Madison Building
P.O. Box 1000
Richmond, Virginia 23208-1000

(804) 786-6221

Vital records are also kept by:

County Clerk
County Court House
(County where the event occurred)

Cost for a certified Birth Certificate	$5.00
Cost for a short form plastic Birth Card	$5.00
Cost for a certified Marriage Certificate	$5.00
Cost for a certified Death Certificate	$5.00

The Virginia Division of Vital Records has records from January 1, 1853. Birth and death records were not routinely filed between 1896 and 1912. County Clerks have vital records that are much earlier than the records of the Division of Vital Records.

VS6-9/85

COMMONWEALTH OF VIRGINIA
APPLICATION FOR A CERTIFICATION OF A BIRTH RECORD

1 FULL NAME AT BIRTH				DO NOT WRITE IN THIS SPACE

2 DATE OF BIRTH		SEX	COLOR OR RACE	

3 PLACE OF BIRTH		**VIRGINIA**	

4 FULL NAME OF FATHER	ENCLOSED IS $ _____	SEARCHED BY _____

5 FULL MAIDEN NAME OF MOTHER	FOR _____ PAPER CERTIFICATIONS ($5.00 EACH)	☐ INDEX ☐ DF ☐ BOOK ☐ HOS

6 NAME OF PHYSICIAN OR MIDWIFE AT BIRTH (IF KNOWN)	**NOTE:** IF SHORT FORM PLASTIC BIRTH CARD DESIRED, CHECK HERE ☐ ($5.00 EACH)	RECHECKED BY _____

7 NAME OF HOSPITAL (IF ANY) WHERE BIRTH OCCURRED		

8 HAS ORIGINAL NAME EVER BEEN CHANGED OTHER THAN BY MARRIAGE?	YES ☐ NO ☐	IF SO, WHAT WAS ORIGINAL NAME?	

9 ARE YOU THE PERSON NAMED IN LINE 1?	YES ☐ NO ☐	IF NOT, WHAT IS YOUR RELATIONSHIP?	I.N.

10 SPECIFIC PURPOSE FOR WHICH THIS CERTIFICATION IS REQUESTED	

11 SIGNATURE OF APPLICANT ▶	

12 STREET ADDRESS	

13 CITY, STATE AND ZIP CODE	ISSUED

DO NOT REMOVE THIS STUB

IMPORTANT

Virginia statutes require a fee of $5.00 be charged for each certification of a vital record or for a search of the files when no certification is made. Make check or money order payable to STATE HEALTH DEPARTMENT.

Birth records were not routinely filed during period 1896-1912. If birth occurred then, or if no record is on file, other types of evidence may be acceptable to using agencies.

Birth records are, by statute, confidential. Certifications may be issued to the individual registrant, members of the registrant's immediate family, the registrant's guardian, their respective legal representative, or by court order.

Warning: Making a false application for a vital record is a felony under state as well as federal law.

NAME
STREET OR ROUTE
CITY OR TOWN, STATE, ZIP CODE

PLEASE NOTE!
PRINT YOUR NAME AND COMPLETE MAILING ADDRESS IN THIS SPACE— THIS IS A MAILING INSERT AND WILL BE USED TO MAIL THE CERTIFICATION TO YOU.

THANK YOU!

Send to:
Division of Vital Records
P.O. Box 1000
Richmond, Virginia 23208-1000

VS 8 7/86

COMMONWEALTH OF VIRGINIA
APPLICATION FOR A CERTIFIED COPY OF A MARRIAGE RECORD

	DO NOT WRITE IN THIS SPACE
1 FULL NAME OF HUSBAND	
2 FULL MAIDEN NAME OF WIFE	
3 DATE OF MARRIAGE — COLOR OR RACE	1st SEARCH BY ☐ INDEX ☐ BOOK ____
4 CITY OR COUNTY IN WHICH MARRIAGE LICENSE WAS ISSUED — VIRGINIA	2nd SEARCH BY ☐ INDEX ☐ BOOK ____
5 SPECIFIC PURPOSE FOR WHICH THIS CERTIFIED COPY IS REQUESTED	CERTIFICATE NUMBER
6 SIGNATURE OF APPLICANT ➤	
7 STREET ADDRESS	
8 CITY, STATE AND ZIP CODE	ISSUED

ENCLOSED IS $_____ FOR _____ CERTIFIED COPIES ($5.00 EACH)

DO NOT REMOVE THIS STUB

IMPORTANT

As required by statute, a fee of $5.00 is charged for each certification of a vital record or for a search of the files when no certification is made. Make check or money order payable to the STATE HEALTH DEPARTMENT. Give all information possible in above application for record. If exact date is unknown, give approximate year of marriage.

Certifications of marriage records may also be obtained from Clerk of Court in city or county in which marriage license was issued.

NAME
STREET OR ROUTE
CITY OR TOWN, STATE, ZIP CODE

PLEASE NOTE!

PRINT YOUR NAME AND COMPLETE MAILING ADDRESS IN THIS SPACE

THIS IS A MAILING INSERT AND WILL BE USED TO MAIL THE CERTIFIED COPY TO YOU.

THANK YOU!

Send To:

Division of Vital Records
P.O. Box 1000
Richmond, Virginia 23208-1000

COMMONWEALTH OF VIRGINIA
APPLICATION FOR A CERTIFIED COPY OF A DEATH RECORD

1 FULL NAME OF DECEASED		**DO NOT WRITE IN THIS SPACE**
2 DATE OF DEATH / SEX / COLOR OR RACE		
3 PLACE OF DEATH — VIRGINIA		
4 NAME OF HOSPITAL (IF ANY, WHERE DEATH OCCURRED)		1st SEARCH BY _____ ☐ INDEX ☐ BOOK ☐ HOSP.
5 IF MARRIED, NAME OF HUSBAND OR WIFE		2nd SEARCH BY _____ ☐ INDEX ☐ BOOK ☐ HOSP.
6 NAME OF FUNERAL DIRECTOR (IF KNOWN)		
7 ADDRESS OF FUNERAL DIRECTOR		CERTIFICATE NUMBER
8 HOW ARE YOU RELATED TO THE PERSON NAMED ON LINE 1?		
9 SPECIFIC PURPOSE FOR WHICH THIS CERTIFIED COPY IS REQUESTED		
10 SIGNATURE OF APPLICANT ➤		
11 STREET ADDRESS		
12 CITY, STATE AND ZIP CODE		
ENCLOSED IS $_____ FOR _____ CERTIFIED COPIES		ISSUED

DO NOT REMOVE THIS STUB

IMPORTANT

Virginia statutes require a fee of $5.00 for a certification of a death record or for a search of the files when no certification is issued. Make check or money order payable to STATE HEALTH DEPARTMENT.

Death records were not routinely filed during period 1896-1912. However, some records are available in the health departments of a few of the larger cities.

Death records are, by statute, confidential. Certifications may be issued to surviving relatives, their legal representatives, an authorized agency acting in their behalf, or by court order.

Warning: Making a false application for a vital record is a felony under state as well as federal law.

NAME
STREET OR ROUTE
CITY OR TOWN, STATE, ZIP CODE

PLEASE NOTE!

PRINT YOUR NAME AND COMPLETE MAILING ADDRESS IN THIS SPACE— THIS IS A MAILING INSERT

THANK YOU!

Send To:
Division of Vital Records
P.O. Box 1000
Richmond, Virginia 23208-1000

WASHINGTON

Send your requests to:

Washington State Department
   of Social and Health Services
Vital Records
P.O. Box 9709, ET-11
Olympia, Washington 98504-9709

(206) 753-5936

Send your requests for pre-1968 Marriage Certificates to:

County Auditor
County Court House
(County where the Marriage License was issued)

Cost for a certified Birth Certificate	$11.00
Cost for an heirloom Birth Certificate	$25.00
Cost for a Birth Card	$11.00
Cost for a certified Marriage Certificate	$11.00
Cost for a certified Death Certificate	$11.00

The Washington Office of Vital Records has birth and death records from July 1, 1907 and marriage records from January 1, 1968. If no record is found $3.00 of the fee will be returned to you. The County Clerks also maintain vital records and have records much earlier than the records at the State Office.

The Family History Library of the Church of Jesus Christ of Latter-day Saints (Mormon Church) in Salt Lake City, Utah has microfilmed many of the original and published vital records and church registers of Washington's cities and counties. They have microfilm copies of birth records and indexes from 1907 to 1959 and death records from 1907 to 1952, with indexes from 1907 to 1949. For details on their holdings please consult your nearest Family History Center.

VITAL RECORDS APPLICATION
Complete the appropriate Block for desired document

☐ **BIRTH**

Quanity _____ CERTIFIED COPY - Suitable for any purpose - $11 Each
Quanity _____ BIRTH CARD - Not accepted by some agencies - $11 Each
Quanity _____ HEIRLOOM - See reverse side - $25 Each

P L E A S E   P R I N T

1. Name on Record _____
   First   Middle   Last

2. Date of Birth _____
   Month   Day   Year

3. Place of Birth _____
   City   County   Name of Hospital

4. Father's Name _____
   First   Middle   Last

5. Mother's Full
   Maiden Name _____
   First   Middle   Maiden Name

Your Relationship
to Line 1 _____

If an adopted child,
put X in this square ☐

Refund _____

Check No. _____

Reason _____
_____

Date _____

Ok to Issue _____

☐ **DEATH**

Quanity _____ CERTIFIED COPY - $11 Each - for each 10-year period searched

P L E A S E   P R I N T

1. Name of Deceased _____
   First   Middle   Last

2. Spouse of Deceased _____
   First   Middle   Last

3. Date of Death _____
   Month   Day   Year (or ten-year time period to be searched)

4. Place of Death _____ WASHINGTON
   City   County

Please Check:

HAVE YOU EVER RECEIVED A COPY OF THIS DOCUMENT BEFORE?

☐ YES   ☐ NO

☐ **MARRIAGE**

Quanity _____ CERTIFIED COPY - $11 Each
Event must have occurred between January 1, 1968 and present

P L E A S E   P R I N T

1. Name of Groom _____
   First   Middle   Last

2. Bride's Full
   Maiden Name _____
   First   Middle   Maiden Name

3. Date of Marriage _____
   Month   Day   Year

4. Place license Issued _____ WASHINGTON
   City   County

Send To:

**VITAL RECORDS
P.O. BOX 9709 MS: ET-11
Olympia, WA 98504-9709**

☐ **DIVORCE**

Quanity _____ CERTIFIED COPY - $11 Each
Event must have occurred between January 1, 1968 and present

P L E A S E   P R I N T

1. Name of Groom _____
   First   Middle   Last

2. Bride's Full
   Maiden Name _____
   First   Middle   Last

3. Date of Dissolution _____
   Month   Day   Year

4. Place Decree Issued _____ WASHINGTON
   City   County

Index No. _____

YOUR MAILING ADDRESS

( )
NAME   PHONE NUMBER

STREET ADDRESS

CITY   STATE   ZIP

SEE REVERSE FOR ADDITIONAL INFORMATION

THIS SECTION WILL BE DETACHED AND USED TO MAIL
THE CERTIFIED COPY OF THE CERTIFICATE TO:

WASHINGTON STATE
DEPARTMENT OF
SOCIAL & HEALTH
SERVICES

| 33 NAME |
| 34 ADDRESS |
| 35 CITY   STATE   ZIP |

VITAL RECORDS

P.O. BOX 9709, MS: ET-11
OLYMPIA, WA 98504-9709

(206) 753-5936

WEST VIRGINIA

Send your requests to:

West Virginia State Health Department
Division of Vital Statistics
Charleston, West Virginia 25305

(304) 348-2931

Vital records are also maintained by:

County Clerk
County Court House
(County where the event occurred)

Cost for a certified Birth Certificate	$5.00
Cost for a certified Marriage Certificate	$5.00
Cost for a certified Death Certificate	$5.00

The West Virginia Division of Vital Statistics has birth and death records from January 1, 1917 and marriage records from January 1, 1964. Make payment payable to "Division of Vital Statistics." The Division does not have a separate form for requesting a copy of a marriage certificate. For records prior to 1964 write to the County Clerk in the county where the marriage took place. The County Clerks have vital records on file much earlier than the records kept at the Division of Vital Statistics.

If your request is urgent you may call and charge your certificates to your Visa or MasterCard. There is a $5.00 fee for this service.

The Family History Library of the Church of Jesus Christ of Latter-day Saints (Mormon Church) in Salt Lake City, Utah has microfilmed many of the original and published vital records and church registers of West Virginia's cities and counties. They have microfilm copies of vital records from 1853 to 1860. For details on their holdings please consult your nearest Family History Center.

APPLICATION FOR CERTIFIED COPY OF CERTIFICATE OF BIRTH OR DEATH
WEST VIRGINIA DEPARTMENT OF HEALTH — DIVISION OF VITAL STATISTICS
CHARLESTON, WEST VIRGINIA 25305

CASH	
CHECK	
MONEY ORD.	
NO. COPIES	
AMOUNT	

HAVE COUNTY RECORDS BEEN SEARCHED? YES ☐ NO ☐

NOTE: FEE OF _____ FOR EACH COPY MUST ACCOMPANY THIS APPLICATION CASH IS SENT AT SENDERS RISK. PLEASE SEND ME _____ COPIES.

BIRTH CERTIF. ◀ **CHECK ONE** ▶ DEATH CERTIF.

BIRTH OR DEATH

NAME— FIRST   MIDDLE   LAST

DATE— MONTH   DAY   YEAR

PLACE— CITY OR POST OFFICE   COUNTY   STATE

ONLY BIRTH

FATHER'S NAME— FIRST   MIDDLE   LAST

MAIDEN NAME OF MOTHER— FIRST   MIDDLE   LAST

ONLY DEATH

NAME OF FUNERAL DIRECTOR—

◁ PLEASE PRINT NAME AND ADDRESS OF PERSON TO WHOM CERTIFICATE IS TO BE MAILED.

WHAT IS YOUR RELATIONSHIP TO THE PERSON NAMED ON THE CERTIFICATE

PLEASE PRINT - DO NOT WRITE

WISCONSIN

Send your requests to:

Wisconsin Department of Health and Social Services
Section of Vital Statistics
1 West Wilson Street
P.O. Box 309
Madison, Wisconsin 53701-0309

(608) 266-0330

Vital records are also kept by:

County Clerk
County Court House
(County where the event occurred)

Cost for a certified Birth Certificate	$8.00
Cost for a certified Marriage Certificate	$5.00
Cost for a certified Death Certificate	$5.00
Cost for a duplicate copy, when ordered at the same time	$2.00

The Wisconsin Department of Health has records as early as 1814, but prior to January 1, 1907 less than half of the records were ever filed. The Department has a list of the earliest records on file arranged by county.

If your request is urgent you may call and charge your certificates to your Visa or MasterCard. There is a $5.00 charge for this service.

The Family History Library of the Church of Jesus Christ of Latter-day Saints (Mormon Church) in Salt Lake City, Utah has microfilmed many of the original and published vital records and church registers of Wisconsin's cities and counties. They have microfilm copies of birth records from 1852 to 1907, delayed birth records from 1937 to 1941, an index to marriage records from 1852 to 1907, and death records from 1862 to 1907. For details on their holdings please consult your nearest Family History Center.

WISCONSIN **BIRTH** CERTIFICATE APPLICATION

Please complete this form and return it to the following address with a self-addressed stamped envelope and appropriate fee. Please make check or money order payable to "CENTER FOR HEALTH STATISTICS"

Division of Health
Section of Vital Statistics
P.O. Box 309
Madison, WI 53701-0309

PENALTIES: Any person who wilfully and knowingly makes false application for a birth certificate shall be fined not more than $10,000, or imprisoned not more than 2 years or both.

APPLICANT INFORMATION

THE FOLLOWING INFORMATION IS ABOUT THE PERSON COMPLETING THIS APPLICATION:

YOUR Name: (Please Print) _____

YOUR Signature: _____ TODAY'S DATE: _____

YOUR Daytime Phone Number: ( ) -

YOUR Address: _____
Street: _____

City: _____ State: _____ Zip: _____

Mail To:
(If Different)

RELATIONSHIP TO PERSON NAMED ON CERTIFICATE

According to Wisconsin State Statute, a **CERTIFIED** copy of a **BIRTH** record is only available to persons with a "Direct and Tangible Interest".

Please complete the box which indicates YOUR RELATIONSHIP to the PERSON NAMED on the record:

☐ A. I AM the PERSON NAMED on the record.

☐ B. I AM the PARENT of the PERSON NAMED on the record, and my parental rights have not been terminated. **NOTE:** In the case of an out-of-wedlock child, the father's rights must have been established by a court or by a paternity affidavit before he may obtain a copy of the record.

☐ C. I AM the Legal Custodian or Guardian of the PERSON NAMED on the record.

☐ D. I AM a member of the immediate family of the PERSON NAMED on the record. *PLEASE CIRCLE ONE:* (Only those listed below qualify as Immediate Family)

  Spouse   Child   Brother   Sister   Grandparent

☐ E. I AM a representative authorized, in writing, by any of the before mentioned (A through D), including an attorney:
Specify who you represent: _____

☐ F. I can demonstrate that the information from the record is necessary for the determination or protection of a personal or property right for myself/my agency/my client.
Specify Interest: _____

☐ G. Other: Non-certified copy only. **NOTE:** Out-of-wedlock births are only available to any of the before mentioned (A through F).

FEES

☐ $8.00 First Copy
☐ $2.00 Each additional copy of the same record issued at the same time.
The fee is for a search and first copy. In the event the record is not found, the fee is not refundable.

BIRTH INFORMATION

FIRST	MIDDLE	LAST (MAIDEN)

SEX	MONTH	DAY	YEAR	CITY	COUNTY

MOTHER'S MAIDEN LAST NAME	FIRST NAME

FATHER'S LAST NAME	FIRST NAME

CERTIFICATE NUMBER IF KNOWN _____

FOR OFFICE USE ONLY

FILE DATE _____ MOTHER'S CO. _____

OH 5281
Rev. 12/86)
hap. 69, Wis Stat.

State of Wisconsi
Division of Healt
Section of Vital Statistic
P.O. Box 30
Madison, WI 53701-030

APPLICATION FOR WISCONSIN **MARRIAGE** CERTIFICATE

Please complete this form and return it to the above address with a self-addressed stamped envelope and appropriate fee.
Please make check or money order payable to:

"CENTER FOR HEALTH STATISTICS"

PENALTIES: Any person who wilfully and knowingly makes false application for a marriage certificate shall be fined not more than $1,000, or imprisoned not more than 90 days or both.

APPLICANT INFORMATION

Applicant Name (Please Print) _____

Applicant Signature _____ Date: _____

Telephone Number: ( ) -

Address: _____

_____

Mail To Address: _____
(If different from above)   **INCLUDE SELF- ADDRESSED STAMPED ENVELOPE**

RELATIONSHIP TO PERSON NAMED ON CERTIFICATE

According to Wisconsin State Statute, a **CERTIFIED** copy of a **MARRIAGE** record is only available to persons with a direct and tangible interest.
Please complete the box which indicates your interest:

☐ A. The registrant (subject) of the record
☐ B. The parent(s) of the registrant.
☐ C. The registrant's legal custodians or guardians.
☐ D. A member of the registrant's immediate family: spouse, children, brothers and sisters, grand-parents. State Relationship: _____
☐ E. A representative authorized by any of the before mentioned (A through D) including an attorney. (Specify) _____
☐ F. Any other person who demonstrates that the information is necessary for the determination or protection of a personal or property right. State Interest: _____
☐ G. Other (non-certified copy only) _____

FEES

☐ $5.00 First Copy
☐ $2.00 Each additional copy of the same record issued at the same time.
    NOTE: The fee is for a search and first copy. In the event the record is not found, the fee is not refundable.

MARRIAGE INFORMATION

FULL NAME OF GROOM

FULL MAIDEN NAME OF BRIDE

PLACE OF MARRIAGE:	CITY, VILLAGE, TOWNSHIP	COUNTY
DATE OF MARRIAGE:		

DOH 5280
(Rev. 01/88)
Chap. 69, Wis Stat.

State of Wiscons
Division of Heal
Section of Vital Statistic
P.O. Box 30
Madison, WI 53701-030

APPLICATION FOR WISCONSIN **DEATH** CERTIFICATE

Please complete this form and return it to the above address with a self-addressed stamped envelope and appropriate fee. Please make check or money order payable to "CENTER FOR HEALTH STATISTICS"

PENALTIES: Any person who wilfully and knowingly makes false application for a death certificate shall be fined not more than $10,000, or imprisoned not more than 2 years or both.

APPLICANT INFORMATION

THE FOLLOWING INFORMATION IS ABOUT THE PERSON **COMPLETING THIS APPLICATION:**

YOUR Name: (Please Print) _____

YOUR Signature: _____ TODAY'S DATE: _____

YOUR Daytime Phone Number: ( ) -

YOUR Address: _____

Mail To:
(If Different)

RELATIONSHIP TO PERSON NAMED ON CERTIFICATE

According to Wisconsin State Statute, a **CERTIFIED** copy of a **DEATH** record is only available to persons with a "Direct and Tangible Interest".

Please complete the box which indicates YOUR RELATIONSHIP to the PERSON NAMED on the record:

☐ A. I AM the PARENT of the PERSON NAMED on the record.

☐ B. I AM the Legal Custodian or Guardian of the PERSON NAMED on the record.

☐ C. I AM a member of the immediate family of the PERSON NAMED on the record. **PLEASE CIRCLE ONE:** (Only those listed below qualify as Immediate Family)
    Spouse   Child   Brother   Sister   Grandparent

☐ D. I AM a representative authorized, in writing, by any of the before mentioned (A through D), including an attorney:
    Specify who you represent: _____

☐ E. I can demonstrate that the information from the record is necessary for the determination or protection of a personal or property right for myself/my agency/my client.
    Specify Interest: _____

☐ F. Other: Non-certified copy only.

FEES

☐ $5.00 First Copy
☐ $2.00 Each additional copy of the same record issued at the same time.
    NOTE: The fee is for a search and first copy. In the event the record is not found, the fee is not refundable.

DEATH INFORMATION

FULL NAME OF DECEDENT		

PLACE OF DEATH:	CITY, VILLAGE, TOWNSHIP	COUNTY

DATE OF DEATH	DECEDENT'S SOCIAL SECURITY NUMBER

DECEDENT'S AGE/BIRTHDATE	DECEDENT'S OCCUPATION

DECEDENT'S SPOUSE	DECEDENT'S PARENTS

WYOMING

Send your requests to:

> Wyoming State Vital Records Services
> Hathaway Building
> Cheyenne, Wyoming 82002

(307) 777-7591

Vital records are also kept by:

> County Clerk
> County Court House
> (County where the event occurred)

Cost for a certified Birth Certificate	$5.00
Cost for a certified Marriage Certificate	$5.00
Cost for a certified Death Certificate	$3.00

The Wyoming State Vital Records Services has birth and death records from July 1909 and marriage records from May 1941. The records kept by the County Clerks are much earlier than those held by the State.

STATE OF WYOMING
APPLICATION FOR CERTIFIED COPY OF BIRTH CERTIFICATE

A request for a certified copy of a birth certificate should be submitted on this form along with the fee of $5.00 per copy. Money orders or personalized checks should be made payable to VITAL RECORDS SERVICES. Please enclose a self-addressed, stamped envelope with this application.

Send to: Vital Records Services
                            Hathaway Building
                            Cheyenne WY 82002

A searching fee of $5.00 is charged for every search of our indexes for a record. If a record is found, you will receive a certified copy with no additional charge. If no record is found, instructions for filing a Delayed Birth Certificate will be sent.

Enclosed is $_____ for _____ certified copy(s).

FULL NAME
AT BIRTH _____
                  First   Middle   Last

DATE OF BIRTH _____ SEX _____

PLACE OF BIRTH _____

FATHER'S NAME _____
                         First   Middle   Last

MOTHER'S MAIDEN NAME _____
                         First   Middle   Last

SIGNATURE OF PERSON WHOSE
CERTIFICATE IS BEING
REQUESTED OR PARENT _____
If under 19 years of age, signature of parent or legal guardian required. Legal guardian must submit a copy of guardianship papers.

Address to which copy is to be mailed:

             _____

             _____

             _____

VR 1 - 3
5/88 5,000

APPLICATION FOR A CERTIFIED COPY
OF A RECORD OF MARRIAGE OR DIVORCE

Vital Records Services
Hathaway Building
Cheyenne, WY 82002

Certified copies of marriage or divorce records may be released only to the husband or wife named on the certificate or their legal representative.

Certified copies are $5.00 each. Money orders or personalized checks should be made payable to VITAL RECORDS SERVICES.

Type of record requested: Marriage _____ Divorce _____

Enclosed is $_____ for _____ certified copy(s).

NAME OF HUSBAND _____

NAME OF WIFE _____

DATE OF EVENT _____

PLACE OF EVENT _____

SIGNATURE OF PERSON
NAMED ON CERTIFICATE _____

ADDRESS _____

If certificate is to be mailed to a different address, enclose a stamped, addressed envelope.

Mail to: _____

              _____

              _____

VR 3-A
6/86 1,000

STATE OF WYOMING
APPLICATION FOR CERTIFIED COPY OF DEATH CERTIFICATE

VITAL RECORDS SERVICES
HATHAWAY BUILDING
CHEYENNE, WY 82002

Certified copies of death certificates should be requested with the information below along with a fee of $3.00 per copy. Money orders or checks should be made payable to VITAL RECORDS SERVICES. Please enclose a self-addressed, stamped envelope with this application.

If the date of death is unknown, a searching fee of $5.00 for every five years searched is charged. You will receive either a certified copy or a verification at no additional charge.

Enclosed is $_____ for _____ certified copies.

FULL NAME
OF DECEASED _____
First   Middle   Last

PLACE OF DEATH _____,WYOMING
City   County

DATE OF DEATH _____

SURVIVING SPOUSE _____

SIGNATURE OF
PERSON MAKING APPLICATION _____

Relationship to Deceased _____

Purpose for which Copy is Needed _____

Mailing Address of Applicant _____

_____

Enclose an addressed, stamped envelope if copies are to be mailed to a different address. Indicate below that address is:

_____

_____

_____

VR 2-3
7/86 3,000

AMERICAN SAMOA

Send your requests to:

Registrar of Vital Statistics
Vital Statistics Section
Health Services Department
LBJ Tropical Medical Center
Pago Pago, American Samoa 96799

(684) 633-1222

Cost for a certified Birth Certificate	$2.00
Cost for a certified Marriage Certificate	$2.00
Cost for a certified Death Certificate	$2.00

The Registrar has records from 1900. The Registrar, at this time, only issues an application form for birth certificates.

TO: _____

_____

_____

REFERENCE: _____

I REQUEST A CERTIFIED COPY OF MY BIRTH CERTIFICATE BE SENT TO THE
ABOVE ADDRESS TO ESTABLISH BIRTH IN THE UNITED STATES. THIS BIRTH
CERTIFICATE MUST HAVE A RAISED OR MULTI-COLORED STATE SEAL ON IT.
THE FOLLOWING INFORMATION IS PROVIDED TO ASSIST YOUR OFFICE IN
LOCATING MY BIRTH CERTIFICATE.

_____
SIGNATURE

NAME I WAS BORN UNDER:_____
　　　　　　　　　　　　　FIRST　　　　　MIDDLE　　　　MAIDEN　　　　LAST

PLACE OF BIRTH:_____
　　　　　　　　　CITY OR TOWN　　　　COUNTY　　　　　　STATE

DATE OF BIRTH:_____
　　　　　　　　　MONTH　　　　　　DAY　　　　　YEAR

SEX:_____ RACE:_____

FATHER'S NAME:_____
　　　　　　　　　FIRST　　　　　　　　MIDDLE　　　　　LAST

MOTHER'S MAIDEN NAME:_____
　　　　　　　　　　　　FIRST　　　　　　　MIDDLE　　　　LAST

NAME OF HOSPITAL:_____

ENCLOSED FIND A MONEY ORDER IN THE AMMOUNT OF $_____

Send your requests to:

Office of Vital Statistics
Department of Public Health and Social Services
P.O. Box 2816
Agana, Guam 96910

(011) (671) 734-2931

Cost for a certified Birth Certificate	$2.00
Cost for a certified Marriage Certificate	$2.00
Cost for a certified Death Certificate	$2.00

The Office of Vital Statistics has birth, marriage and death records from October 26, 1901.

OFFICE OF VITAL STATISTICS
Department of Public Health and Social Services
P.O. Box 2816
Agana, Guam 96910

APPLICATION FOR A COPY OF Birth ☐ Death ☐ Marriage ☐

INFORMATION FOR APPLICANT: It is absolutely essential that the name be accurately spelled and that the exact date - month, day and year - the exact place of birth, name of hospital be fully given in every application.

PRINT ALL ITEMS CLEARLY

1. NAME _____
   (First name)   (Middle)   (Last name at time of birth)

2. DATE OF BIRTH _____ DATE OF DEATH _____
   (Month) (Day) (Year)   DATE OF MARRIAGE _____

3. PLACE OF BIRTH _____ PLACE OF DEATH _____
   (Name of Hospital or village)

4. FATHER'S NAME _____
   (First)   (Middle)   (Last)

5. MOTHER'S MAIDEN NAME _____
   (First)   (Middle)   (Last)

6. NUMBER OF COPIES DESIRED _____Certificate. NUMBER, IF KNOWN _____

7. _____
   Relationship to person named in Item one above. If self, state "SELF"

NOTE: Copy of a birth or death record can be issued only to persons to whom the record relates, if of age, or a parent or other lawful representative.

IF THIS REQUEST IS NOT FOR YOUR OWN BIRTH RECORD OR THAT OF YOUR CHILD, PROPER WRITTEN AUTHORIZATION FROM THE PERSON MUST BE PRESENTED WITH THIS APPLICATION.

SIGN YOUR NAME AND ADDRESS BELOW

NAME _____

ADDRESS _____

CITY _____ STATE _____ ZIP CODE _____

FEE

PURSUANT TO PUBLIC LAW 10-44, Section 9324, a fee of   is now being charged for each certified copy issued.

APPLICANTS ARE ADVISED NOT TO SEND CASH BY MAIL. Fees must be paid at time application is made.   Money order should be made payable to the Treasurer of Guam. Stamps and foreign currency cannot be accepted.

PANAMA CANAL ZONE

Send your requests to:

Vital Statistics Unit
Panama Canal Commission
APO Miami 34011-5000

Cost for a certified Birth Certificate	$2.00
Cost for a certified Marriage Certificate	$2.00
Cost for a certified Death Certificate	$2.00

The Panama Canal Commission maintains and issues certificates for births, marriages, and deaths that occurred in the former Canal Zone from 1904 to September 30, 1979 when the Panama Canal Treaty became effective and the Canal Zone Government ceased to exist.

PANAMA CANAL COMMISSION

The Panama Canal Commission requires the payment of   for each copy issued of a birth, death or marriage certificate. Please complete this application and return it to the address below with the necessary amount. Money order should be made payable to the TREASURER, Panama Canal Commission, in U.S. currency.

This office maintains certificates ONLY for births, deaths or marriages that occurred in the former Canal Zone. For births, deaths or marriages that occurred in the Republic of Panama, write to: El Registro Civil, Apartado 5281, Panama 5, Republic of Panama.

....
(Date)

Vital Statistics Unit
Panama Canal Commission
Administrative Services Division
APO Miami   34011-5000

REGISTRAR:

Please issue...............copy (copies) in ☐ English ☐ Spanish of the ☐ birth ☐ death ☐ marriage certificate requested below. I have attached $........................ (money order).

For Birth Certificate:

Name on Certificate ....

Date of Birth ....

Place of Birth..

Full Name of Father...

Mother's Maiden Name ....

For Death Certificate:

Name of Deceased..

Date of Death ....

Place of Death..

For Marriage Certificate:

Name of parties: Male .... Female..

Date of Marriage .... Marriage License No. ....

Location of Marriage .... Balboa.............................. Cristobal.............

....
Signature of person applying for certificate

....
Relationship to person on certificate

Purpose desired ....

....
Mailing address (complete only if certificate is to be mailed).

PUERTO RICO

Send your requests to:

Puerto Rico Department of Health
Demographic Registry
P.O. Box 9342
San Juan, Puerto Rico 00908

(809) 728-7980

Cost for a certified Birth Certificate	$2.00
Cost for a certified Marriage Certificate	$2.00
Cost for a certified Death Certificate	$2.00

The Puerto Rico Department of Health has vital records from June 22, 1931.

DEMOGRAPHIC REGISTRY AREA

BIRTH CERTIFICATE APPLICATION

Name at Birth: _____
          Father's last name   Mother's last name   Name

Date of Birth: _____
          Month   Day   Year

Place of Birth: _____
                          Town

Father's Name: _____

Mother's maiden Name: _____

Name of the Hospital: _____

Are you the person named in line #1? _____Yes _____No. If not,

what is your relationship with her or him _____.

Specific purpose for which this certification is requested: _____

_____

Signature of Applicant: _____

Address where you want the certificate to be sent: _____

_____

Address of Applicant: _____

_____

Number of copies: _____.

Applicant IDENTIFICATION: _____Driving License _____Work

_____Passport _____Other DATE: _____

IMPORTANT:

If event occurred from June 22, 1931 to present, you can apply with us to
the following address: Department of Health, Demographic Registry, P.O.
Box 9342, San Juan, Puerto Rico 00908.

If event occurred from 1885 to June 21, 1931 you must write to the municipality where the event occurred.

Please send a photocopy of an IDENTIFICATION with photography of applicant.

Applicant in Puerto Rico, please send a   Internal Revenue Stamp for
each copy requested.

Applicant out of Puerto Rico, please send a   money order for each
copy you need payable to "SECRETARY OF THE TREASURY" for each copy requested.

Please send us a pre-addressed envelope to mail your certificate.

_____
Direct Interest-Registrant, parents, their sons or legal representatives.

DEMOGRAPHIC REGISTRY AREA

MARRIAGE CERTIFICATE APPLICATION

Husband's Name: _____

              Father's last name   Mother's last name   Name

Spouse's maiden Name: _____

              Father's last name   Mother's last name   Name

Date of Marriage: _____

          Month   Day   Year

Place of Marriage: _____

                  Town

Are you the person named in line #1? _____Yes _____No. If not,

what is your relationship with this person: _____.

Specific purpose for which this certification is requested: _____

_____.

Signature of Applicant: _____.

Applicant's address: _____

_____.

Address you want the certificate to be sent: _____

_____.

Number of copies: _____.

Applicant's IDENTIFICATION: _____Driving License _____Work

_____Passport _____Other DATE: _____

IMPORTANT:

If event occurred from June 22, 1931 to present you can apply with us to the following address: Department of Health, Demographic Registry, P.O. Box 9342, San Juan, Puerto Rico 00908.

If event occurred from 1885 to June 21, 1931 you must write to the municipality where the event occurred.

Please send a photocopy of an IDENTIFICATION with photography of applicant.

Applicant in Puerto Rico, please send Internal Revenue Stamp for each copy requested.

Applicant out of state, please send a money order payable to "SECRETARY OF THE TREASURY" for each copy requested.

Please send us a self addressed envelope to mail your certificate.

_____

Applicant's definition—contracting parties, parents, child or legal representative.

_____

COPY EXPEDITION'S

DEPARTMENT OF HEALTH
DEMOGRAPHIC REGISTRY AREA

DEATH CERTIFICATED APPLICATION

Deceased Name: _____

                Father's last name   Mother's last name   Name

Date of Death: _____

            Month   Day   Year

Place of Death: _____

                       Town

Name of the Hospital: _____

Relationship with deceased: _____

Specific purpose for which this certification is requested: _____

_____

Applicant's signature: _____

Aplicant's address: _____

_____

Address where you want the certificate to be sent: _____

_____

Number of copies: _____

Applicant IDENTIFICATION: _____Driving License _____Work

_____Passport _____Other DATE: _____

IMPORTANT:

If event occurred from June 22, 1931 to present, you can apply with us to the following address: Department of Health, Demographic Registry, P.O. Box 9342, San Juan, Puerto Rico 00908.

If event occurred from 1885 to June 21, 1931 you must write to the munici- pality where the event occurred.

Please send a photocopy of an IDENTIFICATION with photography of applicant.

Applicant in Puerto Rico please send a   Internal Revenue Stamp for each copy requested.

Applicant out of Puerto Rico send a   money order payable to "SE- CRETARY OF THE TREASURY" for each copy requested.

Please send us a self addressed envelope to mail your certificate

_____

Applicant's definition-The funeral home, parents, child or legal repre- sentative of the deceased.

_____

COPY EXPEDITION'S

TRUST TERRITORY OF THE PACIFIC ISLANDS—

Mariana Islands

Send your requests to:

Commonwealth Courts
Commonwealth Governments
Saipan, CM 96950

For additional help contact:

Director of Health Services
Trust Territory of the Pacific Islands
Saipan, Northern Mariana Islands 96950

Cost for a certified Birth Certificate	$2.50
Cost for a certified Marriage Certificate	Varies
Cost for a certified Death Certificate	$2.50

The Court has records from 12 November 1952. Some records are at the Hawaii State Bureau of Vital Statistics. Personal checks are not accepted.

TRUST TERRITORY OF THE PACIFIC ISLANDS—

Marshall Islands

Send your requests to:

Chief Clerk of Supreme Courts
Republic of the Marshall Islands
Majuro, Marshall Islands 96960

For additional help contact:

Director of Health Services
Trust Territory of the Pacific Islands
Saipan, Northern Mariana Islands 96950

Cost for a certified Birth Certificate	$ .25
Cost for a certified Marriage Certificate	Varies
Cost for a certified Death Certificate	$ .25

The Court has records from 12 November 1952. Some records are at the Hawaii State Bureau of Vital Statistics. Personal checks are not accepted. There is also a typing charge of $.10 for every 100 words.

TRUST TERRITORY OF THE PACIFIC ISLANDS—
Federation of Micronesia
(Losrae, Ponape, Truk, Yap)

Send your requests to:

Clerk of Courts
State of Losrae, FSM
Lelu, Losrae, ECI 96944

Clerk of Courts
State of Ponape, FSM
Kolonia, Ponape, ECI 96941

Clerk of Courts
State of Truk, FSM
Moen, Truk, ECI 96942

Clerk of Courts
State of Yap, FSM
Colonia, Yap WCI 96943

For additional help contact:

Director of Health Services
Trust Territory of the Pacific Islands
Saipan, Northern Mariana Islands 96950

Cost for a certified Birth Certificate	$ .25
Cost for a certified Marriage Certificate	Varies
Cost for a certified Death Certificate	$.25

The courts have records from 12 November 1952. Some records are at the Hawaii Bureau of Vital Statistics. Personal checks are not accepted. There is also a typing charge of $ .10 for every 100 words.

TRUST TERRITORY OF THE PACIFIC ISLANDS—

Republic of Palau

Send your requests to:

Chief Clerk of Supreme Courts
Republic of Palau
Koror, Palau, WCI 96940

For additional help contact:

Director of Health Services
Trust Territory of the Pacific Islands
Saipan, Northern Mariana Islands 96950

Cost for a certified Birth Certificate	$ .25
Cost for a certified Marriage Certificate	Varies
Cost for a certified Death Certificate	$ .25

The Court has records from 12 November 1952. Some records are at the Hawaii State Bureau of Vital Statistics. Personal checks are not accepted. There is also a typing charge of $.10 for every 100 words.

VIRGIN ISLANDS—
St. Croix

Send your requests to:

Virgin Islands Department of Health
Office of the Registrar of Vital Statistics
Charles Harwood Memorial Hospital
P.O. Box 520
Christiansted, St. Croix, Virgin Islands 00820

(809) 773-4050

Send your requests for Marriage Certificates to:

Chief Deputy Clerk
Territorial Court of the Virgin Islands
P.O. Box 929
St. Croix, Virgin Islands 00820

(809) 778-3350

Cost for a certified Birth Certificate	$5.00
Cost for a short form Birth Certificate	$3.00
Cost for a certified Death Certificate	$5.00

The Office has birth and death records from 1919.

VIRGIN ISLANDS OF THE UNITED STATES

DEPARTMENT OF HEALTH
OFFICE OF THE REGISTRAR OF VITAL STATISTICS

HD-ve   St. –––––––––––––––––, Virgin Islands

APPLICATION FOR BIRTH RECORD

PLEASE PRINT OR TYPE: FAILURE TO COMPLETE THIS FORM PROPERLY MAY DELAY SERVICE TO YOU.

TYPE OF RECORD DESIRED (Check one)

VERIFICATION

A verification is a statement as to the date of birth and name of the child. A verification is used when it is necessary to prove age only.

CERTIFIED COPY

A certified copy is an abstract from the original birth certificate. It gives the name, sex, date and place of birth, certificate number, as well as the names of the parents.

An application for a certified copy of birth must be signed by the person named in the original certificate if 18 years or more or by a parent or legal representative of that person.

FEES: Send money order or check payable to the VIRGIN ISLANDS DEPARTMENT OF HEALTH.

(Please do not send cash)

FULL NAME	DATE OF BIRTH Or period to be searched.
PLACE OF BIRTH (City and Island)	
NAME FATHER	MAIDEN NAME MOTHER
AGE AT BIRTH	AGE AT BIRTH
BIRTHPLACE	BIRTHPLACE
ADDRESS (At time of birth)	ADDRESS (At time of birth)
PURPOSE FOR WHICH RECORD IS REQUIRED	SOCIAL SECURITY NUMBER

Your relationship to person whose record is required? If self, state "SELF" _____

If attorney give name and relationship of your client to person whose record is required. _____

TO WHOM SHALL RECORD BE SENT?

Name _____

Address _____

City _____ State _____

Signature of Applicant _____

Address of Applicant _____

_____

Date _____

Sworn to and subscribed before me this _____ day of _____ 19 _____ .

_____
(Signature and Seal of Notary Public)

VIRGIN ISLANDS OF THE UNITED STATES

DEPARTMENT OF HEALTH

OFFICE OF THE REGISTRAR OF VITAL STATISTICS

St. — — — — — — — — — — — — — —, Virgin Islands

HD-vf

●

APPLICATION FOR DEATH RECORD

PLEASE PRINT OR TYPE: FAILURE TO COMPLETE THIS FORM PROPERLY MAY DELAY SERVICE TO YOU.

TYPE OF RECORD DESIRED (Check one)

VERIFICATION	CERTIFIED COPY ☐ Fee
A verification is a statement as to the date of death and name of decedent. A verification is used as proof that the event occurred.	A certified copy is a replica of the original death certificate.
Anyone may apply for a verification of death.	Anyone who can establish that the record is needed for proof of parentage, social security and other benefits, settlement of estate, or for judicial or other proper purpose may apply for a certified copy.

FEES: Send money order or check payable to the VIRGIN ISLANDS DEPARTMENT OF HEALTH.
(PLEASE DO NOT SEND CASH)

No fee is charged when the certificate is required by a local, state or federal government agency.

NAME OF DECEDENT	DATE OF DEATH OR PERIOD TO BE SEARCHED
PLACE OF DEATH (CITY AND ISLAND)	
NAME OF FATHER OF DECEDENT	MAIDEN NAME OF MOTHER OF DECEDENT
NUMBER OF COPIES DESIRED	CERTIFICATE NUMBER, IF KNOWN
PURPOSE FOR WHICH RECORD IS REQUIRED	

What is your relationship to decedent? _____

In what capacity are you acting? _____

If attorney, give name and relationship of your client to decedent. _____

TO WHOM SHALL RECORD BE SENT?	Signature of Applicant _____
Name _____	Address of Applicant _____
Address _____	_____
City _____ State _____	Date _____

VIRGIN ISLANDS—
St. Thomas and St. John

Send your requests to:

Virgin Islands Department of Health
Office of the Registrar of Vital Statistics
St. Thomas, Virgin Islands 00802

(809) 774-1734

Send your requests for Marriage Certificates to:

Court Clerk
Territorial Court of the Virgin Islands
P.O. Box 70
Charlotte Amalie, St. Thomas, Virgin Islands 00801

(809) 774-6680

Cost for a certified Birth Certificate	$5.00
Cost for a short form Birth Certificate	$3.00
Cost for a certified Marriage Certificate	$2.00
Cost for a certified Death Certificate	$5.00

The Office has birth records from July 1, 1906 and death records from January 1, 1906.

VIRGIN ISLANDS OF THE UNITED STATES

DEPARTMENT OF HEALTH
OFFICE OF THE REGISTRAR OF VITAL STATISTICS

HD-ve   St. ———————————, Virgin Islands

APPLICATION FOR BIRTH RECORD

PLEASE PRINT OR TYPE: FAILURE TO COMPLETE THIS FORM PROPERLY MAY DELAY SERVICE TO YOU.

TYPE OF RECORD DESIRED (Check one)

VERIFICATION

A verification is a statement as to the date of birth and name of the child. A verification is used when it is necessary to prove age only.

CERTIFIED COPY

A certified copy is an abstract from the original birth certificate. It gives the name, sex, date and place of birth, certificate number, as well as the names of the parents.

An application for a certified copy of birth must be signed by the person named in the original certificate if 18 years or more or by a parent or legal representative of that person.

FEES: Send money order or check payable to the VIRGIN ISLANDS DEPARTMENT OF HEALTH.
(Please do not send cash)

FULL NAME	DATE OF BIRTH Or period to be searched.
PLACE OF BIRTH (City and Island)	
NAME FATHER	MAIDEN NAME MOTHER
AGE AT BIRTH	AGE AT BIRTH
BIRTHPLACE	BIRTHPLACE
ADDRESS (At time of birth)	ADDRESS (At time of birth)
PURPOSE FOR WHICH RECORD IS REQUIRED	SOCIAL SECURITY NUMBER

Your relationship to person whose record is required? If self, state "SELF". _____

If attorney give name and relationship of your client to person whose record is required. _____

TO WHOM SHALL RECORD BE SENT?

Name_____

Address_____

City_____State_____

Signature of Applicant_____

Address of Applicant_____

_____

Date _____

Sworn to and subscribed before me this _____ day of _____ 19 _____.

_____
(Signature and Seal of Notary Public)

VIRGIN ISLANDS OF THE UNITED STATES

DEPARTMENT OF HEALTH

OFFICE OF THE REGISTRAR OF VITAL STATISTICS

St. — — — — — — — — — — — — — —, Virgin Islands

HD-vf

●

APPLICATION FOR DEATH RECORD

PLEASE PRINT OR TYPE: FAILURE TO COMPLETE THIS FORM PROPERLY MAY DELAY SERVICE TO YOU.

TYPE OF RECORD DESIRED (Check one)

VERIFICATION	CERTIFIED COPY ☐ Fee
A verification is a statement as to the date of death and name of decedent. A verification is used as proof that the event occurred. Anyone may apply for a verification of death.	A certified copy is a replica of the original death certificate. Anyone who can establish that the record is needed for proof of parentage, social security and other benefits, settlement of estate, or for judicial or other proper purpose may apply for a certified copy.

FEES: Send money order or check payable to the VIRGIN ISLANDS DEPARTMENT OF HEALTH. **(PLEASE DO NOT SEND CASH)**

No fee is charged when the certificate is required by a local, state or federal government agency.

NAME OF DECEDENT	DATE OF DEATH OR PERIOD TO BE SEARCHED
PLACE OF DEATH (CITY AND ISLAND)	
NAME OF FATHER OF DECEDENT	MAIDEN NAME OF MOTHER OF DECEDENT
NUMBER OF COPIES DESIRED	CERTIFICATE NUMBER, IF KNOWN
PURPOSE FOR WHICH RECORD IS REQUIRED	

What is your relationship to decedent? _____

In what capacity are you acting? _____

If attorney, give name and relationship of your client to decedent. _____

TO WHOM SHALL RECORD BE SENT?	Signature of Applicant _____
Name _____	Address of Applicant _____
Address _____	_____
City _____ State _____	Date _____

CANADA—
Alberta

Send your requests to:

Health
Division of Vital Statistics
Texaco Building
10130, 112th Street
Edmonton, Alberta, Canada T5K 2P2

(403) 427-2683

FAX (403) 422-9117

Cost for a certified Birth Certificate	Can $10.00
Cost for a wallet-size Birth Certificate	Can $10.00
Cost for a certified Marriage Certificate	Can $10.00
Cost for a wallet-size Marriage Certificate	Can $10.00
Cost for a certified Death Certificate	Can $10.00

The Alberta Division of Vital Statistics has birth records from 1853, marriage records from 1898, and death records from 1893. Make check payable to "Provincial Treasurer."

VITAL STATISTICS
APPLICATION FOR
CERTIFICATE OR SEARCH

Alberta

~~COMMUNITY AND OCCUPATIONAL~~ HEALTH
DIVISION OF VITAL STATISTIC
TEXACO BUILDING, 10130 - 112 STREE
EDMONTON, ALBERTA T5K 2P
PHONE: 427-268

CERTIFICATES ARE $10.00 EACH PAYABLE TO: PROVINCIAL TREASURER. Indicate quantity and size.

IF BIRTH CERTIFICATE(S) REQUIRED COMPLETE THIS SECTION (please print)

				Quantity	Size
Surname (if married woman MAIDEN surname)	(Given Names)		Sex ☐ M ☐ F		☐ Wallet
Date of Birth: Month by Name / Day / Year	Place of Birth (city, town, or village): ALBERTA	Name of Hospital Where Birth Occurred:			☐ Framing
					* RESTRICTED COPY
Surname of Father:	(Given Names)	Birthplace of Father:			☐ certified copy * see note 4A
Maiden Surname of Mother:	Any other surname mother known by	Given Names	Birthplace of Mother:		☐ genealogical * see note 4B
Date of Registration:	Place of Registration:	Amendment Number:	Registration Number:	Searched/Verified:	

IF MARRIAGE CERTIFICATE(S) REQUIRED COMPLETE THIS SECTION (please print)

			Quantity	Size
Surname of Groom:	(Given Names)	Birthplace of Groom:		☐ Wallet
				☐ Framing
Surname of Bride (prior to this marriage)	(Given Names)	Birthplace of Bride:		* RESTRICTED COPY
				☐ certified copy * see note 4A
Date of Marriage: Month by Name / Day / Year	Place of Marriage (city, town, or village): ALBERTA			☐ genealogical * see note 4B
Date of Registration:	Place of Registration:	Amendment Number:	Registration Number:	Searched/Verified:

ONE SIZE ONLY

IF DEATH CERTIFICATE(S) REQUIRED COMPLETE THIS SECTION (please print)

				Quantity	Size
Surname of Deceased:	(Given Names)	Age:	Sex ☐ M ☐ F		☐ Framing
Date of Death: Month by Name / Day / Year	Place of Death (city, town, or village): ALBERTA	Date of Birth: Month by Name / Day / Year			* RESTRICTED COPY
Usual Residence of Deceased Prior to Death:		Marital Status:			☐ certified copy * see note 4A
					☐ genealogical * see note 4B
Date of Registration:	Place of Registration:	Amendment Number:	Registration Number:	Searched/Verified:	

COMPLETE THIS SECTION (please print)

I require these certificates for the following purpose
(give date of departure if for passport):

State your Relationship to person named on certificate:

Signature of Applicant:

X

Telephone Number:

Your Reference No. (if applicable)

Fee Enclosed:
$

PRINT CLEARLY, THIS IS YOUR MAILING ADDRESS

Name:

If Company, Attention:

Apt. No. | Street Address:

City: | Province: | Postal Code:

FOR OFFICE USE ONLY

CASH/CHEQUE

Amount $ . . . .

Mail Clerk: . . . .

Cashier: . . . .

Remarks:

DVS - 32 88/06

CANADA—
British Columbia

Send your requests to:

Province of British Columbia
Ministry of Health
Division of Vital Statistics
1515 Blanshard Street
Victoria, British Columbia, Canada V8W 3C8

(604) 387-0041

Cost for a certified Birth Certificate	Can $15.00
Cost for a wallet-size Birth Certificate	Can $15.00
Cost for a certified Marriage Certificate	Can $15.00
Cost for a wallet-size Marriage Certificate	Can $15.00
Cost for a certified Death Certificate	Can $15.00

The British Columbia Ministry of Health has vital records from 1872 and some baptismal registers from 1849.

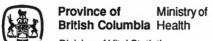

Province of British Columbia **Ministry of Health**
Division of Vital Statistics

APPLICATION FOR SERVICE

YOUR FILE _____

MAILING ADDRESS:
PLEASE **PRINT** YOUR NAME AND ADDRESS
CLEARLY INCLUDING **POSTAL CODE**

NAME _____

ADDRESS _____

CITY & PROV. _____

POSTAL CODE _____

IF COMPANY,
ATTENTION _____

TELEPHONE No. _____ TODAY'S DATE _____ 19 _____

REFUND $

PLEASE INDICATE TYPE AND NUMBER
OF CERTIFICATE(S) REQUIRED _____

IF BIRTH CERTIFICATE(S) REQUIRED COMPLETE THIS SECTION (PLEASE PRINT)

SURNAME (IF FOR MARRIED WOMAN GIVEN MAIDEN SURNAME)	(GIVEN NAMES)	SEX	SMALL 9.5 cm x 6.4 cm

DATE OF BIRTH — MONTH	DAY	YEAR	PLACE OF BIRTH (CITY, TOWN OR VILLAGE)	BRITISH COLUMBIA

SURNAME OF FATHER	(GIVEN NAMES)	BIRTHPLACE OF FATHER	

MAIDEN SURNAME OF MOTHER	(GIVEN NAMES)	BIRTHPLACE OF MOTHER	LARGE 21.6 cm x 17.8 cm

REGISTRATION NUMBER	REGISTRATION DATE	AMENDMENT No.	S _____ D _____ V

IF MARRIAGE CERTIFICATE(S) REQUIRED COMPLETE THIS SECTION (PLEASE PRINT)

SURNAME OF GROOM	(GIVEN NAMES)	BIRTHPLACE OF GROOM	SMALL 9.5 cm x 6.4 cm

SURNAME OF BRIDE PRIOR TO MARRIAGE	(GIVEN NAMES)	BIRTHPLACE OF BRIDE	LARGE 21.6 cm x 17.8 cm

DATE OF MARRIAGE — MONTH	DAY	YEAR	PLACE OF MARRIAGE (CITY, TOWN OR VILLAGE)	BRITISH COLUMBIA	CERTIFIED PHOTOCOPY SEE NOTE 3

REGISTRATION NUMBER	REGISTRATION DATE	AMENDMENT No.	SEARCHED _____ VERIFIED _____

IF DEATH CERTIFICATE(S) REQUIRED COMPLETE THIS SECTION (PLEASE PRINT)

SURNAME OF DECEASED	(GIVEN NAMES)	AGE	SEX	

DATE OF DEATH — MONTH	DAY	YEAR	PLACE OF DEATH (CITY, TOWN OR VILLAGE)	BRITISH COLUMBIA	LARGE 21.6 cm x 17.8 cm

PERMANENT RESIDENCE OF DECEASED PRIOR TO DEATH	PLACE OF BIRTH	

REGISTRATION NUMBER	REGISTRATION DATE	AMENDMENT No.	SEARCHED _____ VERIFIED _____

STATE **YOUR** RELATIONSHIP TO THE PERSON NAMED IN APPLICATION

FEE ENCLOSED

STATE **SPECIFIC REASON** WHY CERTIFICATION IS REQUIRED

X _____
(WRITTEN SIGNATURE OF APPLICANT) (DO NOT PRINT)

$ _____

HLTH 430 REV. 88/04   W-1449

CANADA—
Manitoba

Send your requests to:

Manitoba Community Services
Vital Statistics
Norquay Building, Room 104
401 York Avenue
Winnipeg, Manitoba, Canada R3C OP8

(204) 945-3701

Cost for a certified Birth Certificate	Can $15.00
Cost for a certified Marriage Certificate	Can $15.00
Cost for a certified Death Certificate	Can $15.00

The Manitoba Office of Vital Statistics has records from 1882.

If your request is urgent there is a Can $50.00 fee for a 24-hour rush service.

Application Form /
Formule de demande

Manitoba
Community
Services
Vital Statistics

Services
communautaires
Manitoba
État civil

MAILING ADDRESS

PLEASE **PRINT** YOUR NAME AND ADDRESS CLEARLY. THIS PORTION WILL BE USED WHEN MAILING YOUR CERTIFICATE.

ADRESSE POSTALE

PRIÈRE D'ÉCRIRE VOS NOM ET ADRESSE CLAIREMENT EN LETTRES MOULÉES. CETTE PARTIE SERVIRA À L'ENVOI DE VOTRE CERTIFICAT.

NAME / NOM

ADDRESS / ADRESSE

CITY / VILLE | PROVINCE | POSTAL CODE / CODE POSTAL

PLEASE PRINT ALL INFORMATION CLEARLY/ÉCRIRE CLAIREMENT EN LETTRES MOULÉES

BIRTH / NAISSANCE

SURNAME / NOM DE FAMILLE | GIVEN NAME(S) / PRÉNOM(S) | SEX / SEXE

DATE OF BIRTH / DATE DE NAISSANCE — month/mois — day/jour — year/année | PLACE OF BIRTH/LIEU DE NAISSANCE

NAME OF FATHER (SURNAME) / PÈRE: NOM DE FAMILLE | GIVEN NAME(S) / PRÉNOM(S) | MAIDEN NAME OF MOTHER (SURNAME) / MÈRE: NOM DE JEUNE FILLE | GIVEN NAME(S) / PRÉNOM(S)

DEATH / DÉCÈS

SURNAME OF DECEASED/NOM DE FAMILLE DU DÉFUNT | GIVEN NAME(S)/PRÉNOM(S) | MARITAL STATUS/ÉTAT MATRIMONIAL

DATE OF DEATH / DATE DU DÉCÈS — month/mois — day/jour — year/année | PLACE OF DEATH/LIEU DU DÉCÈS | AGE/ÂGE | SEX/SEXE

MARRIAGE / MARIAGE

NAME OF BRIDEGROOM (SURNAME) / NOM DE FAMILLE DE L'ÉPOUX | GIVEN NAME(S) / PRÉNOM(S)

MAIDEN SURNAME OF BRIDE/NOM DE JEUNE FILLE DE L'EPOUSE | GIVEN NAME(S) / PRÉNOM(S)

DATE OF MARRIAGE / DATE DU MARIAGE — month/mois — day/jour — year/année | PLACE OF MARRIAGE/LIEU DU MARIAGE

FATHER OF BRIDEGROOM/PÈRE DE L'ÉPOUX GIVEN NAME(S)/PRÉNOM(S) | FATHER OF BRIDE/PÈRE DE L'ÉPOUSE GIVEN NAME(S)/PRÉNOM(S)

MAIDEN SURNAME OF MOTHER MÈRE: NOM DE JEUNE FILLE | GIVEN NAME(S)/PRÉNOM(S) | MAIDEN SURNAME OF MOTHER MÈRE: NOM DE JEUNE FILLE | GIVEN NAME(S)/PRÉNOM(S)

INDICATE TYPE AND NUMBER OF CERTIFICATES REQUIRED / INDIQUER LE GENRE ET LE NOMBRE DE CERTIFICATS VOULUS	ENGLISH/ ANGLAIS FRENCH/ FRANÇAIS	BIRTH / NAISSANCE			DEATH / DÉCÈS	MARRIAGE / MARIAGE			FEE ENCLOSED/ MONTANT INCLUS
		Wallet/Format portefeuille	Long/Format Long	Restricted/ Usage limité	Long/Format Long	Wallet/Format portefeuille	Long/Format Long	Restricted/ Usage limité	
									$

RELATIONSHIP TO APPLICANT/ PARENTÉ AVEC LE REQUÉRANT. | SIGNATURE OF APPLICANT / SIGNATURE DU REQUÉRANT X | PHONE NO. / N° DE TÉL.

PLEASE INDICATE THE REASON FOR APPLICATION/ PRIÈRE D'INDIQUER LA RAISON DE CETTE DEMANDE

MG-1607 (Rev. 88)   RETURN ALL COPIES

NUMERICAL COPY / COPIE NUMÉRIQUE

CANADA—
New Brunswick

Send your requests to:

Registrar General
Department of Health and Community Services
Division of Vital Statistics
P.O. Box 6000
Fredericton, New Brunswick, Canada E3B 5H1

(506) 453-2311

Cost for a certified Birth Certificate	Can $15.00
Cost for a wallet-size Birth Certificate	Can $10.00
Cost for a certified Marriage Certificate	Can $15.00
Cost for a certified Death Certificate	Can $15.00

The Registrar has records from January 1888.

The Family History Library of Salt Lake City, Utah has microfilmed many of the original and published vital records and church registers of New Brunswick's cities. They have microfilm copies of the Provincial marriage records from 1806 to 1888. For details on their holdings please consult your nearest Family History Center.

APPLICATION FOR CERTIFICATE OF BIRTH, MARRIAGE OR DEATH

35-2262 (5/88)

**DEPARTMENT OF HEALTH
AND COMMUNITY SERVICES
VITAL STATISTICS
P.O. BOX 6000, FREDERICTON, N.B.
E3B 5H1**

DEMANDE DE CERTIFICAT DE NAISSANCE, DE MARIAGE OU DE DÉCÈS

**MINISTÈRE DE LA SANTÉ
ET DES SERVICES COMMUNAUTAIRES
STATISTIQUES DE L'ÉTAT CIVIL
C.P. 6000, FREDERICTON (N.-B.)
E3B 5H1**

*Please print all information clearly.
Complete in full and return to the office above*

*Prière d'écrire clairement en lettres moulées
Veuillez remplir en entier et renvoyer à l'adresse ci-dessus*

Name And Address Of Applicant / Nom et adresse du demandeur

Surname / Nom de famille

Given Names / Prénoms

Street / Rue

Mailing Address, if different than usual residence

Indiquez l'adresse postale si elle diffère de celle du domicile principal

Street / Rue

City / Ville

City / Ville

Province   Postal Code postal

Province   Postal Code postal

OFFICE USE ONLY

À L'USAGE DU BUREAU SEULEMENT

If Birth Certificates Required, Complete This Section / Pour obtenir un (des) certificat(s) de naissance, veuillez remplir cette partie

Surname (if married woman, maiden surname) / Nom de famille ou nom de jeune fille si vous êtes mariée

Given Names / Prénoms

Sex / Sexe

Birth Date / Date de naissance
Yr. / Année   Month / mois   Day / Jour

Place of Birth / Lieu de naissance

County / Comté

NB

Surname of Father / Nom de famille du père

Given Names / Prénoms

Maiden Surname of Mother / Nom de jeune fille de la mère

Given Names / Prénoms

Registration Number / Numéro d'enregistrement

Date Issued / Date d'émission

Issued By / Émis par

If Marriage Certificates Required, Complete This Section / Pour obtenir un (des) certificat(s) de mariage, veuillez remplir cette partie

Surname of Bridegroom / Nom de famille de l'époux

Given Names / Prénoms

Maiden Surname of Bride / Nom de jeune fille de l'épouse

Given Names / Prénoms

Date of Marriage / Date du mariage
Yr. / Année   Month / mois   Day / Jour

Place of Marriage / Lieu du mariage

NB

Registration Number / Numéro d'enregistrement

Date Issued / Date d'émission

Issued By / Émis par

If Death Certificates Required, Complete This Section / Pour obtenir un (des) certificat(s) de décès, veuillez remplir cette partie

Surname of Deceased / Nom de famille du défunt

Given Names / Prénoms

Sex / Sexe

Date of Death / Date du décès
Yr. / Année   Month / mois   Day / Jour

Place of Death / Lieu du décès

NB

If deceased was married give name of spouse / Si le défunt était marié, indiquez le nom du conjoint

Name of Father of Deceased / Nom de famille du père du défunt

Maiden Name of Mother of Deceased / Nom de jeune fille de la mère du défunt

Registration Number / Numéro d'enregistrement

Date Issued / Date d'émission

Issued By / Émis par

Indicate the Type and Number of Certificates Required / Indiquez le genre et le nombre de certificats requis

	Certified Certifié	Wallet Size Format-poche	Photographic Print Épreuve photographique
Birth Naissance			
Marriage Mariage			
Death Décès			

☐ In English en anglais
☐ In French en français

Fee Enclosed
$
Montant inclus

Relationship to Person Named / Liens de parenté avec la personne nommée

Reason for Application / Raison de la demande

Telephone / Téléphone

Signature of Applicant / Signature du demandeur

Checked By / Vérifié par

Refund / Remboursement
$

Cheque No / N° du chèque

CANADA—
Newfoundland

Send your requests to:

Department of Health
Vital Statistics Division
Confederation Building
St. John's, Newfoundland, Canada A1C 5T7

(709) 576-3308

Cost for a certified Birth Certificate	Can $10.00
Cost for a certified Marriage Certificate	Can $10.00
Cost for a certified Death Certificate	Can $10.00

The Newfoundland Department of Health has records from 1892.

Vital Statistics Division, Department of Health

APPLICATION FOR BIRTH CERTIFICATE

Last Name ....

....
first name   middle name

Date of birth ....

Place of birth ....

Name of Parish or Mission ....

Names of parents ....

| The fee is for every certificate | Certificates required:
PAPER .... or WALLET SIZE .... |

Signature of Applicant ....

Address ....

Relationship to Applicant ....

PLEASE DO NOT WRITE BELOW THIS LINE!

This is an extract from the registration:

Name

Sex

Date   Father

Place   Mother

Record Number   Date of Registration

Baptized on   By Rev.

		Amt.	Cash Book No.
Search by	Date	rec'd.	Receipt No.
Certificate No.	Counter-signed by		Date

H-623
15-623-0515

H-703

APPLICATION FOR SEARCH AND CERTIFICATE—MARRIAGE

TO: Department of Health
Vital Statistics Division
St. John's, Newfoundland

File No. ....

I hereby apply for Search of the Records and Certificate of Marriage of..

.... and ....
<small>(name of bridegroom)</small>   <small>(name of bride)</small>

Month, day and year of marriage..

Place of Marriage..

Marriage was solemnized by the Rev. ....

in the .... Church.
       <small>(denomination)</small>

I enclose $............................in payment of fee for .... certificates.

Signature of applicant ....

ADDRESS..

The fee is   for every certificate

REPORT ON SEARCH

_____

_____

PLEASE DO NOT WRITE BELOW THIS LINE!

Bridegroom		Bride	
Age	Bachelor, Widower	Age	Spinster, Widow

Date of Marriage

Place of Marriage

Marriage solemnized by

Date of Registration		Record Number	

Search by	Date	Amount Received	

Certificate No.	Typed by	Cash Book	

APPLICATION FOR SEARCH AND CERTIFICATE—DEATH

To the Department of Health,

  Vital Statistics Division,

    St. John's, Newfoundland.

File No. _____

I hereby apply for Search of the Records and Certificate of Death of _____

_____

(name of deceased)

Month, day and year of death _____

Place of Death _____

Place of burial _____

I enclose $_____ in payment of fee for _____ certificates.

Signature of applicant _____

ADDRESS _____

The fee is   for every certificate

Report on Search

_____

_____

_____

PLEASE DO NOT WRITE BELOW THIS LINE!

Name of deceased

Age	Sex	Date of Death
Marital Status		Place of Death
Religion		Place of Burial
Record Number		Date of Registration

Search by	Date	Amount Received
Certificate No.	Typed by	Cash Book

CANADA—
Northwest Territories

Send your requests to:

Registrar General
Vital Statistics
Government of the Northwest Territories
P.O. Box 1320
Yellowknife, Northwest Territories, Canada X1A 2L9

(403) 873-7404

Cost for a certified Birth Certificate	Can $5.00
Cost for a certified Marriage Certificate	Can $5.00
Cost for a certified Death Certificate	Can $5.00

The Northwest Territories Registrar General has records from 1925.

Northwest
Territories

APPLICATION FOR CERTIFICATE

REGISTRAR GENERAL, VITAL STATISTICS
GOVERNMENT OF THE NORTHWEST TERRITORIES
YELLOWKNIFE, N.W.T. X1A 2L9

SHADED AREA
FOR OFFICE
USE ONLY

IF BIRTH
CERTIFICATE(S)
REQUIRED,
COMPLETE
THIS SECTION.

NAME (SURNAME, IF MARRIED WOMAN, MAIDEN SURNAME)	SEX	WALLET SIZE

DATE OF BIRTH
YR   MO   DAY

PLACE OF BIRTH (CITY, TOWN OR VILLAGE)

PAPER
(21.5 cm X 28 cm)

NAME OF FATHER (SURNAME)   (GIVEN NAMES)

RESTRICTED PHOTO-
COPY, SEE NOTES

MAIDEN NAME OF MOTHER (SURNAME)   (GIVEN NAMES)

REGISTRATION DATE: REGISTRATON NUMBER:

IF MARRIAGE
CERTIFICATE(S)
REQUIRED,
COMPLETE
THIS SECTION.

NAME OF BRIDEGROOM (SURNAME)   (GIVEN NAMES)   WALLET SIZE

MAIDEN NAME OF BRIDE (SURNAME)   (GIVEN NAMES)

PAPER
(21.5 cm X 28 cm)

RESTRICTED PHOTO-
COPY, SEE NOTES

DATE OF MARRIAGE
YR   MO   DAY

PLACE OF MARRIAGE (CITY, TOWN OR VILLAGE)

REGISTRATION DATE: REGISTRATION NUMBER:

IF DEATH
CERTIFICATE(S)
REQUIRED,
COMPLETE
THIS SECTION.

NAME OF DECEASED (SURNAME)   (GIVEN NAMES)   SEX   DEATH CERTIFICATE

DATE OF DEATH
YR   MO   DAY

PLACE OF DEATH (CITY, TOWN OR VILLAGE)

PERMANENT RESIDENCE OF DECEASED PRIOR TO DEATH

AGE	MARITAL STATUS	IF DECEASED MARRIED, GIVE NAME OF SPOUSE.

NAME OF FATHER OF DECEASED   MAIDEN NAME OF MOTHER OF DECEASED

REGISTRATION DATE: REGISTRATION NUMBER:

DO NOT DETACH. PLEASE RETURN COMPLETE SET INTACT

I REQUIRE THESE CERTIFICATE(S) FOR THE FOLLOWING REASON(S). _____

RELATIONSHIP TO PERSON NAMED _____

SIGNATURE OF APPLICANT	PHONE NUMBER BUSINESS	RESIDENCE	DATE YR MO DAY	FEE ENCLOSED WITH THIS APPLICATION $

NAME

FOR OFFICE USE ONLY.

STREET ADDRESS

AMOUNT RECEIVED:

CITY   PROVINCE

REFUND/RETURN:

CANADA—
Nova Scotia

Send your requests to:

Deputy Registrar General
Nova Scotia Department of Health
1723 Hollis Street
P.O. Box 157
Halifax, Nova Scotia, Canada B3J 2M9

(902) 424-8381

Cost for a certified Birth Certificate	Can $10.00
Cost for a wallet-size Birth Certificate	Can $ 5.00
Cost for a certified Marriage Certificate	Can $10.00
Cost for a wallet-size Marriage Certificate	Can $ 5.00
Cost for a certified Death Certificate	Can $10.00
Cost for a short form Death Certificate	Can $ 5.00

The Nova Scotia Department of Health has birth and death records from October 1, 1908 and marriage records from 1907 to 1918 (depending on the county).

The Family History Library of Salt Lake City, Utah has microfilmed many of the original and published vital records and church registers of Nova Scotia's cities. They have microfilm copies of the birth, marriage and death indexes from 1864 to 1918, birth and death records from 1864 to 1877, and marriage records from 1849 to 1919. For details on their holdings please consult your nearest Family History Center.

Department of Health and Fitness

APPLICANT'S NAME:

FULL ADDRESS:

POSTAL CODE:

Signature of Applicant: _____

I HEREBY APPLY FOR CERTIFICATE(S) AS INDICATED BELOW:

PLEASE ADDRESS ALL COMMUNICATIONS TO:

Deputy Registrar General
P. O. Box 157
Halifax, Nova Scotia   B3J 2M9

NOTE: Please complete full information under appropriate section below,

---

IF BIRTH CERTIFICATE(S) REQUIRED COMPLETE THIS SECTION (Please Print) | (Please ✔)

Full Name -------------------- .... | Wallet-size [ ]

Full Date of Birth ---------- ....

Full Place of Birth --------- .... | Long-form (Restricted – Subject to the Vital Statistics Act) [ ]

Father's Full Name ---------- ....

Mother's Full Maiden Name --- ....

Specific Reason for Request ....

IF MARRIAGE CERTIFICATE(S) REQUIRED COMPLETE THIS SECTION (Please Print) | (Please ✔)

Full Name of Groom ------- .... | Wallet-size [ ]

Full Maiden Name of Bride- ....

Full Date of Marriage ---- .... | Long-form (Restricted – Subject to the Vital Statistics Act) [ ]

Full Place of Marriage --- ....

Specific Reason for Request..

IF DEATH CERTIFICATE(S) REQUIRED COMPLETE THIS SECTION (Please Print) | (Please ✔)

Full Name of Person Deceased .... | Short-form [ ]

Full Date of Death --------- ....

Full Place of Death -------- .... | Long-form (Restricted – Subject to the Vital Statistics Act) [ ]

Permanent Residence of Deceased Prior to Death ---- ....

Specific Reason for Request- ....

FEES: – Payable in advance, by money order or personalized cheque to the Deputy Registrar Genera
          P. O. Box 157, Halifax, Nova Scotia, B3J 2M9:

(a) Wallet-size – $5.00 each   (b) Restricted (long-form) – $10.00

(c) Each search of records (confirmation of event only), without certificate issued – $2.00

Responsibility cannot be accepted by this Department for remittances by cash, or for remittances which are not received in this office.

CANADA—
Ontario

Send your requests to:

Office of the Registrar General
MacDonald Block
Parliament Buildings
Toronto, Ontario, Canada M7A 1Y5

(416) 965-1687

Cost for a Birth Certificate	Can $10.00
Cost for a wallet-size Birth Certificate	Can $10.00
Cost for a Marriage Certificate	Can $10.00
Cost for a wallet-size Marriage Certificate	Can $10.00
Cost for a Death Certificate	Can $10.00

The Registrar General has records from 1869. The Registrar also issues a certified copy of birth, marriage and death certificates for specific purposes such as litigation. These certificates cost Can $15.00 and must be approved by the Deputy Registrar General.

The Registrar will issue certificates to the individual, the individual's parents or children, or to an attorney. Any other requests are considered genealogical searches and the charge is Can $15.00 per certificate.

The Family History Library of Salt Lake City, Utah has microfilmed many of the original and published vital records and church registers of Ontario's cities. They have microfilm copies of marriage bonds from 1803 to 1845 and 1865, and marriage registers from 1801 to 1944. For details on their holdings please consult your nearest Family History Center.

Office of the Registrar General
Bureau du registraire général
Ontario

Application for Certificate or Search
Demande de certificat ou de recherche

*Please read notes on reverse of this form
*Veuillez lire les remarques au verso

Mail Certificate to:
Poster le certificat à:

Name / Nom		Apt. No. / N° d'app.
Street and No. / Rue et N°		
City Zone Prov. / Ville Zone Prov.		Postal Code postal

Applicant - Address - If different to mailing address
Adresse du demandeur si c'est une autre personne

Name / Nom		Apt. No. / N° d'app.
Street and No. / Rue et N°		
City Zone Prov. / Ville Zone Prov.		Postal Code postal

| Today's Date / Date d'aujourd'hui | Telephone No. - Home / N° de téléphone - Domicile | Telephone No. - Business / N° de téléphone - Bureau | Fee enclosed $ / Frais inclus $ |

| State relationship to person named on certificate/solicitors see on reverse / Lien de parenté avec la personne nommée sur le certificat/avocats voir au verso | Signature of Applicant / Signature du demandeur | State reason certificate required / Motif de la demande de certificat |

*Please indicate type and number of certificates required
*Prière d'indiquer le genre et le nombre de certificats requis

Complete this part for birth certificate   **Remplir cette section pour un certificat de naissance**

BIRTH 0 NAISSANCE

- Wallet Size / Format Poche — 0
- File Size / Format Dossier — 1
- Extended / Détaillé — 3
- Certified / Certifié — 2
- Genealogical (See Reverse) / Généalogique (Voir verso) — 4

Last Name / Nom	First Name/Other Names / Prénoms	Sex / Sexe
Date of Birth D/J M/M Y/A / Date de naissance	Place of Birth (city, town or village) / Lieu de naissance (ville ou village)	Hospital where event ocurred - if known / Si connu, nom de l'hôpital.
Last Name of Father / Nom du père	First Name / Prénoms	Father's Birthplace / Lieu de naissance du père	Age at time of birth / Âge à la naissance
Birth Name of Mother (Last Name) / Nom de jeune fille de la mère	First Name / Prénoms	Mother's Birthplace / Lieu de naissance de la mère	Age at time of birth / Âge à la naissance

For Office Use Only
Registration Number / Numero d'enregistrement

Registration Date / Date d'enregistrement

Complete this part for marriage certificate   **01**   **Remplir cette section pour un certificat de mariage**

MARRIAGE 01 MARIAGE

- Wallet Size / Format Poche — 0
- File Size / Format Dossier — 1
- Certified / Certifié — 2
- Genealogical (See Reverse) / Généalogique (voir verso) — 4

Last Name of Groom / Nom du marié	First Name/Other Names / Prénoms	Age at time of Marriage / Âge le jour du mariage	Groom's Father's Name / Nom du père du marié	Mother's Birth Name / Nom de jeune fille de la mère
Last Name of Bride / Nom de la mariée	First Name / Prénoms	Age at time of Marriage / Âge le jour du mariage	Bride's Father's Name / Nom du père de la mariée	Mother's Birth Name / Nom de jeune fille de la mère
Date of Marriage D/J M/M Y/A / Date du mariage	Place of marriage (City, Town or Village) / Lieu du mariage (ville ou village)			
Bridegroom's Place of Birth / Lieu de naissance du marié	Bride's Place of Birth / Lieu de naissance de la mariée			

For Office Use Only
Registration Number / Numéro d'enregistrement

Registration Date / Date d'enregistrement

Complete this part for death certificate   **02**   **Remplir cette section pour un certificat de décès**

DEATH 02 DÉCÈS

- File Size / Format dossier — 1
- Certified / certifie — 2
- Genealogical (See Reverse) / Genea logique (Voir Verso) — 4

Last Name of deceased / Nom du défunt	First Name/Other Names / Prénoms	Sex / Sexe
Date of Death D/J M/M Y/A / Date du décès	Place of Death (city, town or village) / Lieu de décès (ville ou village)	Hospital / Hôpital	Marital status / État matrimonial	Occupation / Profession
Permanent residence of deceased prior to death / Domicile permanent du défunt avant le décès	Age upon death / Âge eu décès	Birthplace / Lieu de naissance		
Father's Name / Nom du père	Father's Place of Birth / Lieu de naissance du père	Mother's Name / Nom de la mère	Mother's Place of Birth / Lieu de naissance de la mère	

For Office Use Only
Registration Number / Numéro d'enregistrement
Registration Date / Date d'enregistrement

11076 (10/86)

CANADA—
Prince Edward Island

Send your requests to:

Prince Edward Island
   Department of Health & Social Services
Director of Vital Statistics
P.O. Box 2000
Charlottetown, Prince Edward Island
Canada C1A 7N8

(902) 892-1001

Cost for a certified Birth Certificate	Can $10.00
Cost for a wallet-size Birth Certificate	Can $ 5.00
Cost for a plastic wallet-size Birth Certificate	Can $ 5.50
Cost for a certified Marriage Certificate	Can $10.00
Cost for a plastic wallet-size Marriage Certificate	Can $ 5.50
Cost for a certified Death Certificate	Can $10.00

The Division of Vital Statistics has records from 1906. Make your fee payable to The Minister of Finance.

V.S. 8 - **APPLICATION FORM (BIRTH)**   Regulations 28-1

TO:
Director of Vital Statistics
P.O. Box 2000
Charlottetown, P.E.I.
C1A 7N8   Date _____

Print Full   SURNAME _____
   Name
of Person   GIVEN NAMES _____

DATE OF BIRTH _____

PLACE OF BIRTH _____

FULL NAME OF FATHER _____ HIS BIRTHPLACE _____

FULL NAME OF MOTHER _____ HER BIRTHPLACE _____
   (Before Marriage)

REGISTRATION NUMBER, IF KNOWN _____

PLEASE NOTE:

If there is any possibility that this birth was registered under a different surname or a different spelling of the surname, indicate all names or spellings that might have been used on the following line:

_____

I hereby make application for a search, if necessary, and the following:

Indicate what is required and number	_____ Wallet Size Certificate	Please read notes on reverse of this form.
	_____ Short Form Certificate	
	_____ Certified copy or Long Form Certificate	

STATE REASON CERTIFICATE REQUIRED _____

Signature of Applicant _____

Address _____

(Space Below This Line for Vital Statistics Only)

Full Name of Person _____ Sex _____

Date of Birth _____ Place of Birth _____

Name of Father _____ His Birthplace _____

Name of Mother _____ Her Birthplace _____
   before Marriage

Registration Date _____ Registration Number _____

Date Issued _____ Certificate typed by _____

Form 8A   Province of Prince Edward Island   Reg. 28-1

DIVISION OF VITAL STATISTICS
THE VITAL STATISTICS ACT

MARRIAGE

Date _____

☐ Wallet Size Certificate

I hereby make
    APPLICATION FOR SEARCH and _____

☐ Short Form Paper Certificate

☐ Certified Copy of Original Marriage

Full Name of Bridegroom _____

Birthplace of Bridegroom _____

Full Name of Bride _____

Birthplace of Bride _____

Date of Marriage _____

Place of Marriage _____

State Reason Certificate Required _____

Signature of Applicant _____

Address _____

PLEASE READ NOTES ON REVERSE OF THIS FORM

(Space Below This Line for Vital Statistics Office Use Only)

Full Name of Bridegroom _____

Birthplace of Bridegroom _____

Full Name of Bride _____

Birthplace of Bride _____

Date of Marriage _____

Place of Marriage _____

Registration Date _____   Registration No. _____

Date Issued _____   Certificate typed by _____

Form 8A　　　　　　　Province of Prince Edward Island　　　　　　　Reg. 28-1

DIVISION OF VITAL STATISTICS
THE VITAL STATISTICS ACT

Date _____

I hereby make APPLICATION FOR SEARCH and _____ DEATH CERTIFICATE(S) of

Full Name of Person _____

Date of Death _____

Place of Death _____

Marital Status _____ Sex _____ Age _____

Regular Residence _____

State Reason Certificate Required _____

Signature of Applicant _____

Address _____

PLEASE READ NOTES ON REVERSE OF THIS FORM

(Space Below This Line for Vital Statistics Office Use Only)

Full Name of Deceased _____

Date of Death _____ Sex _____ Age _____

Place of Death _____

Marital Status _____

Regular Residence _____

Date of Registration _____ Registration No. _____

Date Issued _____ Certificate typed by _____

CANADA—
Quebec

Send your requests to:

Ministere de la Justice
Registre de Reference
300, boul. Jean Lesage, RC 20
Quebec (Quebec) Canada G1K 8K6

(418) 649-3527

Cost for a certified Birth Certificate	Can $8.00
Cost for a certified Marriage Certificate	Can $8.00
Cost for a certified Death Certificate	Can $8.00

Vital records from January 1, 1926 to the present are now available from the Ministry of Justice. Locally, records are kept by the parish church and at the town hall. Annually, copies of these records are transferred to the Superior Court of the respective Judicial District. Records before 1888 are at the Regional Offices of the Quebec National Archives. See the attached list for the addresses of these offices. The Ministry of Justice does not provide application forms for requesting copies of vital records.

Gouvernement du Québec
Ministère de la Justice
Registre de référence à l'état civil

Any person wishing to make genealogical searches may apply to one or other (as the case may be) of the following sources:

A - CHURCH SOURCE

Persons born and baptized (in most religions) in Québec have their births entered in the registers of the archives of the Church of their baptism. The same applies to Church marriages and burials. To obtain extracts of these, application must be made to the Church where the event was registered. The date (or at least the year) of the event must be known. The fees vary from one Church to another (from $2 to $5).

B - MUNICIPAL SOURCE (births only)

Persons whose birth was registered at the City or Town Hall may obtain extracts of birth registration by applying to the particular City or Town Clerk in question. The date (or at least the year) of the registration must be known. The fees also vary (from $2 to $5).

C - GOVERNMENT SOURCE (Office of the Superior Court - Civil Archives)

At the end of each year, a copy of the registers of births (baptisms), marriages and burials which occurred during that year (Source A) is deposited at the Office of the Superior Court in the judicial district to which the parish belongs. It is from these registers that the prothonotary issues extracts of the acts of birth, marriage and burial (certificates). The registers of birth kept by the municipalities (Sources B) are subject to same regulation.

To obtain an extract from an act of birth, marriage or burial from that source, application must be made to the Office of the Superior Court in question. If that Office is not known, the application should be addressed to the most likely Office with a request that it be forwarded to the proper place if necessary. The name of the Church (or the City or Town Hall, Source B) must be known as well as the date (or at least the year) of the event. The fee is $8 per copy. It should be noted that the registers prior to 1885 have been withdrawn and are kept in the National Archives (Source D). The list of Offices of the Civil Archives (or Offices of the Superior Court) is as follows:

D - GOVERNMENT SOURCE (National Archives)

The registers prior to 1885 have been transferred to the regional Offices of the Québec National Archives by most of the judicial districts (Source C) and, in accordance with the regulation, all registers 100 years old or over are also to be so transferred this will eventually be done systematically.

MINISTERE DE LA JUSTICE
ARCHIVES CIVILES

ALMA - 725, rue Harvey ouest, G8B 1P5
AMOS - 891, 3e Rue ouest, J9T 2T4
ARTHABASKA - 800, boul. Bois-Francs sud, G6F 5W5
BAIE-COMEAU - 71, avenue Mance, G4Z 1N2
CAMPBELL'S BAY, rue John, C.P.159, JOX 1KO
CHIBOUGAMAU - 329, 3e Rue, G8P 1N4
CHICOUTIMI - 227, rue Racine, G7H 1S2
COWANSVILLE - 920, rue Principale, J2X 1K2
DRUMMONDVILLE - 1680, boul. St-Joseph, J2C 2G3
HAVRE-AUBERT - Québec, GOB 1JO
HULL - 17, rue Laurier, J8X 4C1
JOLIETTE - 450, rue Saint-Louis, J6E 2Y9
LAC MEGANTIC - 5527, rue Frontenac #316, G6B 1H6
LA MALBAIE - 30, chemin de la Vallée, C.P.1090, GOT 1JO
LA SARRE - 651, 2e Rue est, J9Z 2Y9
LA TUQUE - 290, Saint-Joseph, C.P.7, G9X 3P1
LONGUEUIL - 1111, boul. Jacques-Cartier e. R.C.24, J4M 2J6
MONT-LAURIER - 645, de la Madone, J9L 3G9
MONTMAGNY - 24, rue Palais de Justice, C.P.482, G5V 1P6
MONTREAL - 1, rue Notre-Dame e. ch.1-140, H2Y 1B6
NEW-CARLISLE - ROUTE NATIONALE, C.P.517, GOC 1ZO
PERCE - Route Nationale, C.P.188, GOC 2LO
QUEBEC - 300, boul. Jean-Lesage, ch.SS-38, G1K 8K6
RIMOUSKI - 183, de la Cathédrale, C.P.800, G5L 5J1
RIVIERE-DU-LOUP - 33, de la Cour, G5R 1J1
ROBERVAL - 750, boul. St-Joseph, G8H 2L5
ROUYN-NORANDA - 2, avenue du Palais, J9X 2N9
ST-HYACINTHE - 1550, rue Dessaulles, J2S 2S8
SAINT-JEAN - 109, St-Charles, J3B 2C2
SAINT-JEROME - 400, rue Laviolette, J7Y 2T6
ST-JOSEPH-DE-BEAUCE - 795, avenue du Palais, GOS 2VO
SEPT-ILES - 425, Laure, G4R 1X6
SHAWINIGAN - 212, 6e Rue, G9N 8B6
SHERBROOKE - 375, King ouest, J1H 6B9
SOREL - 46, rue Charlotte, J3P 6N5
THETFORD-MINES - 693, St-Alphonse o. C.P.579, G6G 5T6
TROIS-RIVIERES, 250 Laviolette, G9A 1T9
VAL D'OR - 900, 7e Rue, J9P 4P8
VALLEYFIELD - 180, Salaberry, J6T 2J2
VILLE-MARIE - 8, rue St-Gabriel nord, JOZ 2WO

The registers kept in the centres may be consulted at the local Office. Office hours are from 8h30 to 16h30 and visitors make their own searches in a room set aside for that purpose (most Offices being so equiped). A search consultant is there to assist you (1).

Service by mail is also available if the pertinent search details are known These details are: the date of the event and name of the Church (or Town Hall) where the registration would have taken place (ex.: 15 August 1791 , St.Patrick's Church, Montréal). A photocopy (not certified) of the document in question will then be furnished. There is a fee of 25 cents per copy, with a minimum of $2 per order. Application is made to the Office nearest to the area in question with a place if necessary. The following is a list of these Offices:

MINISTERE DES AFFAIRES CULTURELLES
ARCHIVES NATIONALES DU QUEBEC

CHICOUTIMI (Québec) 930, rue Jacques-Cartier est, G7H 2A9
HULL (Québec) 170, Hôtel de Ville, J8X 4C2
MONTREAL (Québec) 1945, rue Mullins, H3K 1N9
QUEBEC (Québec) 1210, avenue du Séminaire, G1V 4N1
RIMOUSKI (Québec) 337, rue Moreault, ss., G5L 1P4
ROUYN (Québec) 200, 9e Rue, Noranda, J9X 2B9
SEPT-ILES (Québec) 649, Laure, G4R 1X8
SHERBROOKE (Québec) 740, Galt ouest, J1H 1Z3
TROIS-RIVIERES (Québec) 225, des Forges, G9A 2G7

(see overleaf)

— GOVERNMENT SOURCE   (Reference to events from 1926)

Since January 1st 1926, all births, marriages and deaths occurring in Québec are reported to the government for demographic statistical purposes. The reports are microfilmed and information retrieval is readily obtained when certain data are known.

To obtain information from these reports, the following must be known: the date of the event (or at least the year), and confirmatory material such as, the mother's name in the case of a birth; the name of the spouse in the case of a marriage; the name of the spouse (or the father if the person was unmarried) of the deceased in the case of a death. Searches are also made when the exact year is unknown. However, the event must have taken place within a stated period of years within which the search will be concentrated. Here is a list of the periods to be advised according to the event:

```
FOR A BIRTH    - 5 years (ex., from 1940 to 1945)
FOR A MARRIAGE - Period from 1926 to 1974; period from 1975 to 1985 and from 1986 to present
FOR A DEATH    - Period from 1926 to 1970; period from 1971 to 1985 and from 1986 to the present.
```

Applications for information concerning these events must be sent to the address which follows. When the information is traced, a written attestation of the event is furnished. There is a fee of $8.00 for each attestation.

> Ministère de la Justice
> Registre de référence
> 300, boul. Jean Lesage, RC 20
> QUEBEC (Québec) G1K 8K6

— SPECIALIST IN GENEALOGICAL SEARCHES

If the event searched cannot be traced, or the searches have provided uncessfull upon application to the afore-mentioned sources, recourse may be had to a specialist in genealogical searches.

There are genealogical societies in Québec and some of their members will undertake to do your genealogical searches for a fee. To obtain the assistance of such a qualified person, send your request together with a return stamped-addressed envelope to the society located in the area of interest to you. The following are the addresses of the genealogical societies mentioned above:

CHICOUTIMI - (Québec) Société généalogique du Saguenay, C.P.814, G7H 5E8
HULL - (Québec) Société de généalogie de l'Outaouais, C.P.2025, succ.B, J8X 3Z2
JOLIETTE - (Québec) Société de généalogie de Lanaudière, C.P.221, J6E 3Z2
MONTREAL - (Québec) Société généalogique canadienne-française, C.P.335, Place d'Armes, H2Y 3H1
POINTE-CLAIRE (Québec) Québec Family Society, 164, chemin Lakeshore, C.P.1026, H9S 4H9
RIMOUSKI (Québec) Société de généalogie de l'Est du Québec, C.P.253, G5L 7C1
SAINTE-FOY (Québec) Société de généalogie de Québec, C.P.9066, G1V 4A8
SAINT-JEROME (Québec) Société de généalogie des Laurentides, C.P.31, J7Z 5T7
SALABERRY-DE-VALLEYFIELD (Québec) Société de généalogie de Salaberry-de-Val.,75, St-Jean-Baptiste, J6T 1Z6
SHERBROOKE (Québec) Société de généalogie des Cantons de l'Est, C.P.635, J1H 5K5
TROIS-PISTOLES (Québec) Société généalogique et historique de Trois-Pistoles, C.P.1478, G0L 4X0
TROIS-RIVIERES (Québec) Société de généalogie de la Mauricie, C.P.901, G9A 5K2

— OTHER SOURCES

There are also many books that have been published on the subject of Québec genealogy. For full information on these works, consult your local library or bookstore or any of the above Societies.

MESSAGE

(1) The registers kept in the Civil Archives Offices (Offices of the Superior Court) may also be consulted, but on appointment only.

French version available at the address given in source "E"   Québec, February 26, 1988

CANADA—
Saskatchewan

Send your requests to:

Province of Saskatchewan
Department of Health
Division of Vital Statistics
3475 Albert Street, Room 123
Regina, Saskatchewan, Canada S4S 6X6

(306) 787-3092

Cost for a certified Birth Certificate	Can $15.00
Cost for a certified Marriage Certificate	Can $15.00
Cost for a certified Death Certificate	Can $15.00

The Saskatchewan Department of Health has records from 1878.

| | Saskatchewan Health | 3475 Albert Street | **Application for Certificate** | **($15.00 Each)** |

Vital Statistics   Regina, Saskatchewan

S4S 6X6   Phone (306) 787-3092

Payment must accompany Application

Birth Certificate(s) - Please See Reverse Before Completing

Please Read Reverse Side For Details on Certificate Type

Surname (If Married Woman, **Maiden** Surname)	Given Names	Sex	Quantity	Type
Birth Date (Month by Name, Day, Year)	Birthplace (City, Town or Village) _____, SASKATCHEWAN			Wallet
Father - Surname and Given Names				Intermediate
Mother - **Maiden** Surname and Given Names				Extended with Parental Information
Birth Registration Number, If Known				Restricted Copy
				Genealogical Copy

For Office Use Only

Marriage Certificate(s) - Please See Reverse Before Completing

Please Read Reverse Side For Details on Certificate Type

		Quantity	Type
Groom - Surname and Given Names	Date of Marriage (Month by Name, Day, Year)		Wallet
			Intermediate
Bride - **Maiden** Surname and Given Names	Place of Marriage (City, Town, or Village) _____. SASKATCHEWAN		Restricted Copy
			Genealogical Copy

For Office Use Only

Death Certificate(s) - Please See Reverse Before Completing

Please Read Reverse Side For Details on Certificate Type

Surname and Given Names of Deceased	Date of Death (Month by Name, Day, Year)	Sex	Quantity	Type
Place of Death _____, SASKATCHEWAN	Age	Marital Status		Intermediate
Residence Prior to Death	Spouse's Name, if Applicable			Restricted Copy
Father - Surname and Given Names	Mother - **Maiden** Surname and Given Names			Genealogical Copy

For Office Use Only

§ **Southam Paragon** (306) 949-7880

Please do not separate this form - this portion will be used as your mailing label and receipt▶

Saskatchewan Health   Vital Statistics

Vital Statistics Reference No., If Any

Your Reference No., If Any

Certificate(s) will be ☐ Picked Up, or   **($15.00 Each)**
☐ Mailed

Reason for Requiring the Certificate(s) Ordered

Date _____ , 19 ____ Phone No. Work _____ Home _____

X Signature of Applicant _____

This is your mailing label. Please enter your name, address and postal code.
Please print clearly - include your postal code on the last line of your address

Your Relationship to Person Named on Certificate(s) Requested

Place Of Residence, If Different From Mailing Address

For Office Use Only

V S 17 (1/89)

CANADA—
Yukon

Yukon Health and Human Resources
Division of Vital Statistics
P.O. Box 2703
Whitehorse, Yukon, Canada Y1A 2C6

(403) 667-5207

Cost for a certified or a wallet-size Birth Certificate	Can $10.00
Cost for a certified or a wallet-size Marriage Certificate	Can $10.00
Cost for a photocopy of the original Marriage Certificate	Can $10.00
Cost for a certified Death Certificate	Can $10.00

The Division has birth records from 1898 and complete records from 1925. Birth and marriage certificates are issued in a wallet size and framing size. The framing size is a more complete document. A photocopy of the original birth or marriage certificate is also available but it is a restricted document.

If your request is urgent please enclose an additional fee of Can $2.00.

APPLICATION FOR
CERTIFICATE OR SEARCH

Yukon
Health and Human Resources
DIVISION OF VITAL STATISTICS
BOX 2703
WHITEHORSE, YUKON Y1A 2C6
PH. (403) 667-5207

PLEASE INDICATE
TYPE & NUMBER
OF CERTIFICATES
REQUIRED ↓

IF BIRTH CERTIFICATE(S) REQUIRED COMPLETE THIS SECTION (PLEASE PRINT)

QUANTITY/SIZE

B I R T H

| SURNAME (IF MARRIED SURNAME AT BIRTH) | (GIVEN NAMES) | SEX |

WALLET

| YEAR | MONTH BY NAME | DAY | PLACE OF BIRTH (CITY, TOWN OR VILLAGE) | PROVINCE/TERRITORY |

FRAMING

| SURNAME OF FATHER | (GIVEN NAMES) | BIRTHPLACE OF FATHER |

CERTIFIED TRUE COPY

| SURNAME OF MOTHER AT BIRTH | (GIVEN NAMES) | BIRTHPLACE OF MOTHER |

| DATE OF REGISTRATION | PLACE OF REGISTRATION | REGISTRATION NUMBER |
| SEARCHED | RESEARCHED | VERIFIED | CERT. NO. | AMENDMENT NO. |

IF MARRIAGE CERTIFICATE(S) REQUIRED COMPLETE THIS SECTION (PLEASE PRINT)

QUANTITY/SIZE
WALLET

M A R R I A G E

| SURNAME OF GROOM | (GIVEN NAMES) | BIRTHPLACE OF GROOM |

FRAMING

| SURNAME OF BRIDE AT BIRTH | (GIVEN NAMES) | BIRTHPLACE OF BRIDE |

CERTIFIED TRUE COPY

| YEAR | MONTH BY NAME | DAY | PLACE OF MARRIAGE (CITY, TOWN OR VILLAGE) | PROVINCE/TERRITORY |

| DATE OF REGISTRATION | PLACE OF REGISTRATION | REGISTRATION NUMBER |
| SEARCHED | RESEARCHED | VERIFIED | CERT. NO. | AMENDMENT NO. |

IF DEATH CERTIFICATE(S) REQUIRED COMPLETE THIS SECTION (PLEASE PRINT)

QUANTITY/SIZE

D E A T H

| SURNAME OF DECEASED | (GIVEN NAMES) | AGE | SEX |

| YEAR | MONTH BY NAME | DAY | PLACE OF DEATH (CITY, TOWN OR VILLAGE) | PROVINCE/TERRITORY |

FRAMING

| PERMANENT RESIDENCE OF DECEASED PRIOR TO DEATH | MARITAL STATUS |

| DATE OF REGISTRATION | PLACE OF REGISTRATION | REGISTRATION NUMBER |
| SEARCHED | RESEARCHED | VERIFIED | CERT. NO. | AMENDMENT NO. |

PLEASE INDICATE THE REASON FOR APPLICATION:

STATE RELATIONSHIP TO PERSON NAMED:

SIGNATURE OF APPLICANT:

FOR OFFICE USE ONLY

REMARKS

X

| DATE YR. | MO. | DAY | FEE ENCLOSED WITH THIS APPLICATION $ |

M A I L I N G   A D D R E S S

NAME

STREET ADDRESS

| CITY | PROVINCE | POSTAL CODE |

REFUND

DATE MAILED

YG (3385) NC2

w

ANTIGUA

Send your requests to:

Registrar General's Office
St. John's, Antigua

(809) 462-0609

Cost for a certified Birth Certificate	US $2.00
Cost for a certified Marriage Certificate	US $2.00
Cost for a certified Death Certificate	US $2.00

The Registrar General has records from August 1, 1856. The local churches also have their own records. No application forms are provided by this office.

BAHAMAS

Send your requests to:

Registrar General's Office
P.O. Box N532
Nassau, Bahamas

(809) 322-3316

Cost for a certified Birth Certificate	$2.50
Cost for a certified Marriage Certificate	$5.00
Cost for a certified Death Certificate	$2.50
Cost for a duplicate copy, when ordered at the same time	$2.00

The Registrar has birth and death records from January 1, 1850 and marriage records from January 1, 1799. The Registrar does not provide application forms for marriage and death certificates.

REGISTRAR GENERAL'S OFFICE

P. O. Box N532   Nassau, Bahamas

To: Registrar General
Nassau, Bahamas

APPLICATION FOR BIRTH CERTIFICATE

I desire to have a search made for and* _____ copy/ies supplied
of the Register of Birth of

_____
(Enter All Names)

A.

Born at _____

on the Island of _____

Date of Birth _____

Father's full name _____

Mother's full name _____

Mother's maiden name _____

Signature of Applicant _____

*
  Insert number of copies required.

OFFICE USE ONLY

B.

Period searched _____ By _____

Period checked _____ By _____

Certified copies made _____ By _____

Examined by _____

Copies received by _____

Registration found in year _____ At page _____

C.

_____ (a) No record of Birth can be found on file.

_____ (b) Birth Record shows information given above to be correct.

_____ (c) Birth of male/female child recorded without name.

_____ (d) Father's name not recorded.

Indicate with (   ) where appropriate at (a), (b), (c) or (d).

BARBADOS

Send your requests to:

Registrar
Registration Office
Supreme Court of Barbados
Law Courts
Coleridge Street
Bridgetown, Barbados, WI

(809) 426-3461

Cost for a certified Birth Certificate	BD $5.00
Cost for a certified Marriage Certificate	BD $5.00
Cost for a certified Death Certificate	BD $5.00

The Registrar has births from 1890, marriages from 1637, and deaths from 1925. The Registrar does not provide application forms for requesting copies of vital records. For people over 60 years of age the cost is BD $1.00.

The Family History Library of Salt Lake City, Utah has microfilmed many of the original and published vital records and church registers of Barbados. They have microfilmed the vital records and church registers from 1637 to 1887. For details on their holdings please consult your nearest Family History Center.

BERMUDA

Send your requests to:

Registry General
Ministry of Labour and Home Affairs
Government Administration Building
30 Parliament Street
Hamilton, 5-24, Bermuda

(809) 295-5151

Cost for a certified Birth Certificate	US $18.00
Cost for a certified short form Birth Certificate	US $14.00
Cost for a certified Marriage Certificate	US $21.00
Cost for a certified Death Certificate	US $18.00

The Registry has birth and marriage records from 1866 and death records from 1865 to the present. The Registry provides no forms for requesting copies of vital records. You may send payment by a money order payable in U.S. currency.

CAYMAN ISLANDS

Send your requests to:

Registrar General
Tower Building
George Town
Grand Cayman, Cayman Islands, BWI

(809) 949-7900

Cost for a certified Birth Certificate	US $3.75
Cost for a certified Marriage Certificate	US $8.75
Cost for a certified Death Certificate	US $3.75

Payment should be made by certified check payable to the Government of the Cayman Islands. No forms are required to apply for copies of vital records.

DOMINICA

Send your requests to:

Registrar General's Office
Registry
Bay Front
Roseau, Commonwealth of Dominica

(809) 448-2401

Cost for a certified Birth Certificate	US $2.00
Cost for a certified Marriage Certificate	US $2.00
Cost for a certified Death Certificate	US $2.00

The Registrar General has records from April 2, 1861. The local churches also have their own records. No application forms are provided by this office.

242

GRENADA

Send your requests to:

Registrar General's Office
Church Street
St. George's, Grenada

(809) 440-2030

Cost for a certified Birth Certificate	US $1.75
Cost for a certified Marriage Certificate	US $1.75
Cost for a certified Death Certificate	US $1.75

The Registrar General has records from January 1, 1866. The local churches also have their own records. No application forms are provided by this office.

JAMAICA

Send your requests to:

Registrar General's Office
Spanish Town, Jamaica

(809) 984-3041

Cost for a certified Birth Certificate	Jamaica $.45
Cost for a certified Marriage Certificate	Jamaica $.45
Cost for a certified Death Certificate	Jamaica $.45

The fee must also include postage. The Office provides no form for requesting copies of death certificates.

The Family History Library of Salt Lake City, Utah has microfilmed many of the original and published vital records and church registers of Jamaica. They have microfilmed the Church of England registers from 1664 to 1880 that are at the Registrar General's Office. For details on their holdings please consult your nearest Family History Center.

APPLICATION FOR BIRTH CERTIFICATE

NUMBER OF COPIES REQUIRED: ....

NAME OF CHILD..
DATE AND YEAR OF BIRTH...
PLACE AND PARISH OF BIRTH..
FATHER'S FULL NAME ....
MOTHER'S FULL NAME ....
MOTHER'S MAIDEN SURNAME..
ENTRY NUMBER.....................................

FULL NAME AND ADDRESS OF APPLICANT:

....
....
....
....

APPLICATION FOR MARRIAGE CERTIFICATE

NUMBER OF COPIES REQUIRED..................

HUSBAND'S FULL NAME...

WIFE'S FULL NAME..

WIFE'S MAIDEN SURNAME...

DATE AND YEAR OF MARRIAGE ....

PLACE AND PARISH OF MARRIAGE..

MARRIAGE OFFICER'S NAME ....

ENTRY NUMBER...................................

FULL NAME AND ADDRESS OF APPLICANT:

....

....

....

....

MONTSERRAT

Send your requests to:

Registrar General's Office
P.O. Box 22
Plymouth, Montserrat

(809) 491-2129

Cost for a certified Birth Certificate	US $5.50
Cost for a certified Marriage Certificate	US $5.50
Cost for a certified Death Certificate	US $5.50

The Registrar General has records from February 12, 1862. The local churches also have their own records. No application forms are provided by this office but they request that you give complete details and indicate in which of the three districts of Montserrat the event occurred.

There is an additional charge of US $1.15 for postage to mail the certificates to the United States.

ST. KITTS/NEVIS

Send your requests to:

Registrar General's Office
P.O. Box 236
Basseterre, St. Kitts

(809) 465-2521

Cost for a certified Birth Certificate	US $2.00
Cost for a certified Marriage Certificate	US $2.00
Cost for a certified Death Certificate	US $2.00

The Registrar General has records from January 1, 1859. The local churches also have their own records. No application forms are provided by this office.

ST. LUCIA

Send your requests to:

Registrar General's Office
Castries, St. Lucia

(809) 452-1257

Cost for a certified Birth Certificate	US $2.55
Cost for a certified Marriage Certificate	US $2.55
Cost for a certified Death Certificate	US $2.55

The Registrar General has records from January 1, 1869. The local churches also have their own records. No application forms are provided by this office.

ST. VINCENT
and THE GRENADINES

Send your requests to:

Registrar General's Office
Kingstown, St. Vincent

(809) 457-1424

Cost for a certified Birth Certificate	US $1.75
Cost for a certified Marriage Certificate	US $1.75
Cost for a certified Death Certificate	US $1.75

The Registrar General has records from July 1, 1874. The local churches also have their own records. No application forms are provided by this office.

TRINIDAD and TOBAGO

Send your requests to:

Registrar General's Office
Port of Spain, Trinidad and Tobago

(809) 623-5793

Cost for a certified Birth Certificate   US $1.75

Cost for a certified Marriage Certificate   US $1.75

Cost for a certified Death Certificate   US $1.75

The Registrar General has records for Trinidad from January 1, 1848 and for Tobago from January 30, 1868. Trinidad and Tobago were united in 1889. The local churches also have their own records. No application forms are provided by this office.

TURKS and CAICOS

Send your requests to:

Registrar General's Office
Front Street
Grand Turk, Turks and Caicos

(809) 946-2114

Cost for a certified Birth Certificate	US $1.68
Cost for a certified Marriage Certificate	US $1.68
Cost for a certified Death Certificate	US $1.68

The Registrar General has records from January 2, 1863. The local churches also have their own records. No application forms are provided by this office.

2. British Isles
and Related Countries

UNITED KINGDOM—
England and Wales

Personal inquiries to:

> General Register Office
> St. Catherine's House
> 10 Kingsway
> London WC2B 6JP, England

(011)-(44) 1-242-0262

Mail requests to:

> General Register Office
> Smedley Hydro
> Southport
> Merseyside PR8 2HH, England

Cost for a certified Birth Certificate	£13.00
Cost for a short form Birth Certificate	£11.00
Cost for a certified Marriage Certificate	£13.00
Cost for a certified Death Certificate	£13.00

The General Register Office has records from July 1, 1837. All requests by mail are now handled by the Southport office. Make checks payable to "The Registrar General."

The Family History Library of Salt Lake City, Utah has microfilmed many of the original and published vital records and church registers of England and Wales's cities and counties. They have the microfilm index to births, marriages, and deaths from 1 July 1837 to 1980. For details on their holdings please consult your nearest Family History Center.

APPLICATION FOR BIRTH CERTIFICATE

General Register Office, St. Catherines House, 10 Kingsway, London WC2B 6JP

Please allow   days for despatch of certificates

Requirements

.... Full certificate(s) at   each

.... Short certificate(s) at   each   £_____

amount received

Please tick appropriate box:

☐ Birth Register

☐ Adoption Register

Particulars of the person whose certificate is required. Remember, we need full details to ensure a positive search.

Surname	
Forenames	
Date of birth	
Place of birth	
Fathers surname	
Fathers forenames	
Mothers maiden surname	
Mothers forenames	

Applicant

Mr/Mrs/Miss

Full postal address

Notes

This Office holds records of births registered in England and Wales since 1st July 1837.

If you attend St Catherines House, and make the search personally the certificate is then usually ready after 48 hours. The fees are   for a full certificate or   for a short certificate.

You can also obtain certificates at the same fee on application in person or by post to the Superintendent Registrar for the district where the birth occurred.

Short Certificate - shows only the name, sex, date of birth and place of birth.

Full Certificate - This is a full copy of the birth entry, and includes particulars of parentage and registration.

Adoption Certificate - the full certificate is a copy of the entry with the date of birth, particulars of the adoption and the adoptive parent or parents; a short certificate bears no reference to adoption.

Cheques, postal orders, etc should be made payable to **"The Registrar General".** Payment from abroad may be made by cheque, international money order, or draft, in favour of the Registrar General. Orders, cheques and drafts should always be expressed in Sterling.

If we cannot find the entry, after a two year search either side of the date given, a fee of £6.00 will be retained, whether the application is for a full or short certificate, and the balance returned.

FOR OFFICE USE ONLY

CAS	
Amount received	
Fees Certificates	
Full	
Total charge	
Refund	
Desp'd	

Qtr/Year	Vol	Restricted to			
		D/S			
Page	Entry	Year	M J S D		
		Year	M J S D		
District		Year	M J S D		
Sub-District		Year	M J S D		
LB MB CB MD City of County of		Year	M J S D		

Address label (please use BLOCK LETTERS)
Enter in this space the name and full postal address to which the certificate should be sent

APPLICATION FOR MARRIAGE CERTIFICATE

General Register Office, St. Catherines House, 10 Kingsway, London WC2B 6JP

Please allow   days for despatch of certificates

Requirements

..... certificate(s) at   each.

	amount received
	£_____

Particulars of the person(s) whose certificate is required. Remember, we need full details to ensure a positive search.

Man's	Surname
	Forenames
Woman's	Surname
	Forenames
Date of marriage	
Place of marriage	
Name of man's father	
Name of woman's father	

Applicant

Mr/Mrs/Miss	
Full	
postal	
address	

Notes

This Office holds records of marriages registered in England and Wales since 1st July 1837.

If you attend St Catherines House, and make the search personally the certificate is then usually ready after 48 hours. The fee is

You can also obtain certificates at the same fee on application in person or by post to the Officiating minister of the church where the marriage took place or to the Superintendent Registrar of the same district.

Cheques, postal orders, etc should be made payable to **"The Registrar General"**. Payment from abroad may be made by cheque, international money order, or draft, in favour of the Registrar General. Orders, cheques and drafts should always be expressed in Sterling.

If we cannot find the entry, after a two year search either side of the date given, a fee of £6.00 will be retained.

FOR OFFICE USE ONLY

CAS	
Amount received	
Fees	Certificates
	Full
Total charge	
Refund	
Desp'd	

Qtr/Year	Vol	Restricted to			
		D/S			
Page	Entry	Year	M	J	S	D
		Year	M	J	S	D
District		Year	M	J	S	D
		Year	M	J	S	D
LB MB CB MD City of County of		Year	M	J	S	D

Address label (please use BLOCK LETTERS)
Enter in this space the name and full postal address to which the certificate should be sent

APPLICATION FOR DEATH CERTIFICATE

General Register Office, St. Catherines House, 10 Kingsway, London WC2B 6JP

Please allow   **days for despatch of certificates**

Requirements

.... certificate(s) at   each

amount received

£_____

Particulars of the person whose certificate is required. Remember, we need full details to ensure a positive search.

Surname	
Forename(s)	
Date of death	
Place of death	
Age at death	
Occupation of Deceased	
Marital status of Deceased (if female)	

Applicant

Mr/Mrs/Miss	
Full postal address	

Notes

This Office holds records of deaths registered in England and Wales since 1st July 1837.

If you attend St Catherines House, and make the search personally the certificate is then usually ready after 48 hours. The fee is

You can also obtain certificates at the same fee on application in person or by post to the Superintendent Registrar of the district where the death occurred.

Cheques, postal orders, etc should be made payable to **"The Registrar General"**. Payment from abroad may be made by cheque, international money order, or draft, in favour of the Registrar General. Orders, cheques and drafts should always be expressed in Sterling.

If we cannot find the entry, after a two year search either side of the date given, a fee of £6.00 will be retained.

FOR OFFICE USE ONLY

CAS	
Amount received	
Fees Certificates	
Full	
Total charge	
Refund	
Desp'd	

Qtr/Year	Vol	Restricted to				
		D/S				
Page	Entry	Year	M	J	S	D
		Year	M	J	S	D
District		Year	M	J	S	D
Sub-District		Year	M	J	S	D
		Year	M	J	S	D
LB MB CB MD City of County of						

Address label (please use BLOCK LETTERS)
Enter in this space the name and full postal address to which the certificate should be sent

UNITED KINGDOM—
Scotland

Send your requests to:

General Register Office for Scotland
New Register House
Edinburgh EH1 3YT, Scotland

(011)-(44) 31-556-3952

Cost for a certified Birth Certificate	£8.00
Cost for a short form Birth Certificate	£7.00
Cost for a duplicate Birth Certificate (short form)	£2.50
Cost for a certified Marriage Certificate	£8.00
Cost for a certified Death Certificate	£8.00
Cost for a duplicate copy, when ordered at the same time	£3.50

The Registrar General has records from 1855.

The Family History Library of Salt Lake City, Utah has microfilmed many of the original and published vital records and church registers of Scotland's cities and counties. They have microfilm copies of the index and registrations of birth, marriage, and death from 1855 to 1952. For details on their holdings please consult your nearest Family History Center.

GENERAL REGISTER OFFICE FOR SCOTLAND

Records Section

New Register House Edinburgh EH1 3YT

Telephone 031-556 3952

To:

Date

Dear

Your letter has been returned to you for the following reason(s):-

There was not enough information to trace the entry. Please complete the application overleaf and return it to this office; and/or

No/insufficient money was enclosed to cover the cost.

Please indicate in the appropriate box(es) below the number of extracts or certificates required.

1. ☐ Abbreviated certificate of birth. This shows the person's name, surname, sex, date and place of birth. Not applicable to records before 1855.   Cost £

2. ☐ Extract of Birth. This is a full copy of the entry in the birth register and is used for all purposes.   Cost £

3. ☐ Extract of Death   Cost £

4. ☐ Extract of Marriage   Cost £

5. ☐ Extract of Divorce   Cost £

If more than one copy of the same entry is ordered at the same time, the fee for the second and subsequent extract is £

Cheques and postal orders should be crossed and made payable to "The Registrar General". Overseas applicants should include airmail postage. International Reply Coupons are not acceptable as payment.

All refunds will be made by sterling cheque. It is uneconomic to refund small amounts, and amounts under   will not therefore be refunded.

Yours sincerely

Note:

When a decree of divorce was granted by the Court of Session, it was formerly the practice to enter a note on the marriage entry to show that the marriage had ended in divorce. This practice was discontinued on 1 May 1984. Where a divorce was notified to the Registrar General on or after that date, there will be no note regarding divorce on the corresponding marriage entry or on any extract of the entry.

Evidence of divorce is obtainable either from the Court where the decree was granted or from the General Register Office, New Register House, Edinburgh EH1 3YT.

*Delete as appropriate

*BIRTH

*Surname at Birth/Adoption

Forenames

*MALE/FEMALE

Place (town or parish) in which Birth occurred (adopted persons please state date of adoption, if known)

*PARENTS/ADOPTIVE PARENTS

Father's surname

Father's forenames

Mother's maiden surname

Mother's forenames

Date of Birth
DAY   MONTH   YEAR

Date of application ....

Signature ....

R.D. No.	Year	Entry No.

RCE

*MARRIAGE/DIVORCE

Groom's surname

Forenames

Bride's surname

Forenames

Place (town or parish) in which Marriage occurred

Widow or Divorcee please state former married name

Date of Marriage
DAY   MONTH   YEAR

Date of Divorce (if applicable)
DAY   MONTH   YEAR

Date of application ....

Signature ....

FOR OFFICE USE

R.D. No.	Year	Entry No.

RCE

*DEATH

Surname

Forenames

Age at Death

Place (town or parish) in which Death occurred

*PARENTS/ADOPTIVE PARENTS

Father's surname

Father's forenames

Mother's maiden surname

Mother's forenames

Date of Death
DAY   MONTH   YEAR

Date of application ....

Signature ....

R.D. No.	Year	Entry No.

RCE

UNITED KINGDOM—
Northern Ireland

Send your requests to:

General Register Office
Department of Health and Social Services
Oxford House
49-55 Chichester Street
Belfast BT1 4HL, Northern Ireland

(011)-(44) 232-235211

Cost for a certified Birth Certificate	£3.75
Cost for a short form Birth Certificate	£2.25
Cost for a certified Marriage Certificate	£3.75
Cost for a certified Death Certificate	£3.75
Cost for a duplicate copy, when ordered at the same time	£2.50

The General Register Office has birth and death records from January 1, 1864 and marriages from 1922. Marriage records from April 1, 1845 (with Roman Catholic marriage records from January 1, 1864) are on file in Dublin at the General Register Office.

The Family History Library of Salt Lake City, Utah has microfilmed many of the original and published vital records and church registers of Northern Ireland's cities and counties. They have microfilm copies of the indexes and the registers to births, marriages, and deaths from 1922 to 1959. For details on their holdings please consult your nearest Family History Center.

APPLICATION FOR A
SEARCH/BIRTH CERTIFICATE

To: The Registrar General,
Oxford House, 49 - 55 Chichester Street,
Belfast BT1 4HL. (Tel. No. 235211)

FIRST COMPLETE PART A THEN FILL IN WHICHEVER OTHER PART REFERS TO THE TYPE OF CERTIFICATE YOU REQUIRE

A

PLEASE USE BLOCK CAPITALS

Name of Applicant Mr.
Mrs. ....
Miss. (STATE NAME IN FULL)

Full postal address ....

.... Tele. No ....

I enclose cheque/postal order for £...........................

Date .... Signature ....

PARTICULARS OF THE PERSON WHOSE CERTIFICATE IS REQUIRED

1. BIRTH REGISTER	Full Name at Birth	Father's Full Name	Mother's Full Name
USE PART 2 INSTEAD IF A CERTIFICATE FROM THE ADOPTED CHILD-REN REGISTER IS REQUIRED	Christian or Forenames / Surname / Date of Birth / Place of Birth	Christian or Forenames / Surname	Christian or Forenames / Surname / Maiden Surname / Mother's Residence at time of Birth

2. ADOPTED CHILD-REN REGISTER	Particulars of Adopted Person	Name(s) of Adopter(s)	Particulars of Adoption Order
THIS DATES FROM 1 JULY 1930 ONLY	Christian or Forenames / Surname / Date of Birth	Christian or Forenames / Surname	Name of Court which made the Adoption Order / Date of the Order

B

Full Certificate

I require .... full certificate(s).
(Number)

C

Short Certificate

I require .... short certificate(s).
(Number)

D

Certificate for the Purposes of the Friendly Societies Acts

I require .... certificate(s) for the following Registered Friendly Society:
(Number)

....

E

Certificate for certain other statutory purposes

I require a certificate for each undermentioned purpose against which I have placed a cross.

STATUTORY PURPOSE OF CERTIFICATE	INSERT X IF REQD	STATUTORY PURPOSE OF CERTIFICATE	INSERT X IF REQD
Child Benefit Order		Government Annuities	
Education & Libraries Order		National Savings Bank	
Electoral Law Act		Premium Savings Bonds	
Factories Act		Savings Contract	
Shops Act		Trustee Savings Bank	
Social Security Act		Ulster Savings Certificates	
		War & National Savings Certificates	

G.R.O. 40

FIRST SEARCH

Result ....
....

Date .... Searched by ....

CHECK SEARCH

Result ....
....

Date .... Searched by ....

Notes

....
....
....
....
....

Entry to be Offered	Action Taken
....	....
....	....
....	....
....	....
....	....
....	....

Fees Payable

Number   £   p

...........Full @ ....

...........Short @...   ....

...........Stat Purposes @.............................   ....

Total

Checked by ....

Date ....

Stamped by ....

Date ....

In	£	p.
	:	
	:	

Out		
	:	
	:	
	:	

By ....

Recd. ....

Cashier ....

Date ....

By ....

Receipt

Dmd. 8873099 10/85 80M TPC 7336 Gp. 173

APPLICATION FOR A
SEARCH/MARRIAGE CERTIFICATE

To: The Registrar General,
Oxford House, 49 - 55 Chichester Street,
Belfast BT1 4HL. (Tel. No. 235211)

PLEASE COMPLETE PARTS A & B

A

PLEASE USE BLOCK CAPITALS

Name of Applicant
Mr.
Mrs. ....
Miss.   (STATE NAME IN FULL)

Full postal address ....

.... Tele. No ....

I enclose cheque/postal order for ....

Date .... *Signature* ....

MAN	WOMAN	Any other surname before this marriage
Surname	Maiden Surname	
Christian or Forenames	Christian or Forenames	

PLACE OF MARRIAGE	DATE OF MARRIAGE		
Full Address	Day	Month	Year

B

I require .... certificate(s).
            (Number)

GRO 42

FIRST SEARCH   Result ....
                               ....
                               Date ....Searched by...

CHECK SEARCH

                               Result ....
                               ....
                               Date ....Searched by ....

Notes

....
....
....
....
....

Entry to be Offered	Action Taken
....	....
....	....
....	....
....	....
....	....
....	....

Fees Payable

Number   £   p   Checked by ....

.................Full @...   Date ....

                                                                               Stamped by ....

                              Total _____   Date ....

	£	p.
In	:	
	:	

Out	:	
	:	
	:	

By ....

Recd. ....

Cashier ....

Date ....

By ....

Receipt

APPLICATION FOR A
SEARCH/DEATH CERTIFICATE

To: The Registrar General,
Oxford House, 49 - 55 Chichester Street,
Belfast BT1 4HL. (Tel. No. 235211)

FIRST COMPLETE PART A THEN FILL IN WHICHEVER OTHER PART REFERS TO THE TYPE OF CERTIFICATE YOU REQUIRE

A

PLEASE USE BLOCK CAPITALS

Name of Applicant

Mr.
Mrs. ....
Miss.   (STATE NAME IN FULL)

Full postal address .... Tele. No............................

I enclose cheque/postal order for ....

Date .... Signature ....

PARTICULARS OF THE PERSON WHOSE CERTIFICATE IS REQUIRED

Christian or Forenames

Surname

Date of Death

Place of Death	Usual Residence

Date of Birth, or age at Death

If person was married or widowed at time of death - Name of Spouse

If Death occured in last three years,
was Death reported to Coroner?

B

Full Certificate

I require .... full cerificate(s).
                (Number)

C

Certificate for purposes of Friendly Societies Acts

I require .... certificate(s) for the following Registered Friendly Society:

....

D

CERTIFICATE FOR CERTAIN OTHER STATUTORY PURPOSES

I require a certificate for each undermentioned purpose against which I have placed a cross.

STATUTORY PURPOSE OF CERTIFICATE	INSERT X IF REQD.	STATUTORY PURPOSE OF CERTIFICATE	INSERT X IF REQD.
Child Benefit Order		National Savings Bank	
Social Security Act		Premuim Savings Bonds	
Government Annuities		Trustee Savings Bank	
Saving Contracts		Ulster Savings Certificates	
		War & National Savings Certificates	

G.R.O. 41

FIRST SEARCH

Result ....

....

Date ....Searched by.......................................

CHECK SEARCH

Result ....

....

Date ....Searched by.....................................

Notes

....

....

....

....

....

Entry to be Offered	Action Taken
....	....
....	....
....	....
....	....
....	....
....	....

Fees Payable

Number	£	p	
..................Full @..............	....		Checked by ....
	....		Date ....
.................Stat Purposes @	....		Stamped by ....
Total	_____		Date ....

	£	p.
In	:	
	:	
Out	:	
	:	
	:	

By ....

Recd. ....

Cashier ....

Date ....

By ....

Receipt

Dmd. 8372439 1182 20M TPC 5880 Gp.173

IRELAND (Eire)

Send your requests to:

Registrar General
General Register Office
Joyce House
8-11 Lombard Street East
Dublin 2, Ireland

(011)-(353) 1-711-000

Cost for a certified Birth Certificate	Ire £5.50
Cost for a short form Birth Certificate	Ire £3.50
Cost for a certified Marriage Certificate	Ire £5.50
Cost for a certified Death Certificate	Ire £5.50
Cost for a duplicate copy, when ordered at the same time	Ire £4.00

The Registrar General has records from 1864 and Protestant (Church of Ireland) marriages from 1845. For births, marriages, and deaths that occurred in Dublin address your requests to the Superintendent Registrar (same address as above).

The Family History Library of Salt Lake City, Utah has microfilmed many of the original and published vital records and church registers of Ireland's cities and counties. They have microfilm copies of the indexes to births and deaths from 1864 to 1921 and marriages from 1845 to 1921; microfilm copies of the registers of births from 1864 to March 1955, marriages from 1845 to 1870, and deaths from 1864 to 1870. For details on their holdings please consult your nearest Family History Center.

Seol aon fhreagra chun:—
Address any reply to:—
AN tARD CHLÁRAITHEOIR
fé'n uimhir seo:—
(quoting:—)

....19....

A Chara

With reference to your application for a birth certificate the information requested below should be provided as accurately as possible and the form returned to this Office with the necessary fee. All Cheques, Postal or Money Orders should be made payable to "The Registrar General".

Mise le meas.

Ard-Chláraitheoir

———————————

FEES

Full Birth Certificate (including search fee)..

Short Birth Certificate (including search fee)...

If more than one certificate relating to the birth of the same person is required an additional fee of   should be forwarded for each extra full certificate or   for each extra short certificate.

All Cheques and Postal Orders to be made payable to An tArd Chláraitheoir.

SURNAME of PERSON whose Birth Certificate is required
_____

FIRST NAME(S) in full
_____

Date of Birth
_____

Place of Birth
(If in a town, name of street to be given)
_____

Father's Name
_____

Father's Occupation
_____

Mother's First Name(s) and Maiden Surname
_____

Has the Person whose Birth record is required been legally adopted?   Yes/No
_____

Signature of Applicant..

Address..

....

Date...19.....

26B.

OIFIG AN ARD—CHLÁRAITHEORA,
8-11 SRÁID LOMBAIRD THOIR,
(8-11 Lombard Street East),
BAILE ÁTHA CLIATH, 2.
(Dublin 2).

Seol aon fhreagra chun:—
Address any reply to:—
AN tARD CHLÁRAITHEOIR
fé'n uimhir seo:—
(quoting:—)

....19....

A Chara

With reference to your application for a marriage certificate the information requested below should be provided as accurately as possible and the form returned to this Office with the necessary fee. All Cheques, Postal or Money Orders should be made payable to "THE REGISTRAR GENERAL".

Mise le meas.

Ard-Chláraitheoir

FEES

Marriage Certificate (including search fee)...

If more than one certificate relating to the marriage of the same person is required an additional fee of should be forwarded for each extra certificate.

NAME and ADDRESS of the Parties Married   '(a)..
(to be written in full in each case).

(b)..

Date of Marriage

Where Married

Signature of Applicant...

Address...

....

Date...19.....

26M.

150244 Gr. 10.01 3m 4/85 Fodhla H340 GRO 75

Seol aon fhreagra chun:—
Address any reply to:—
AN tARD CHLÁRAITHEOIR
fé'n uimhir seo:—
(quoting:—)

....19....

A Chara

With reference to your application for a death certificate the information requested below should be provided as accurately as possible and the form returned to this Office with the necessary fee. All Cheques, Postal or Money Orders should be made payable to "THE REGISTRAR GENERAL".

Mise le meas.

Ard-Chláraitheoir

FEES

Death Certificate (including search fee)..

If more than one certificate relating to the death of the same person is required an additional fee of should be forwarded for each extra certificate.

SURNAME of DECEASED _____

FIRST NAME(S) in full _____

Date of Death _____

Place of Death
(If in a town, name of street to be given) _____

Age of Deceased _____

Occupation of Deceased _____

State whether Single, Married, Widow, Widower _____

Signature of Applicant..

Address..

....

Date..19....

150243 Gr. 10.01 3m 4/85 Fodhla H339 CRO 75

AUSTRALIA—
Australian Capital Territory

Send your requests to:

Office of the Registrar General
  of Births, Deaths & Marriages
National Mutual Centre, 4th Floor
Darwin Place
P.O. Box 788
Canberra City, ACT, Australia 2601

(011) (6162) 758-686

Cost for a certified Birth Certificate	Au $12.00
Cost for a short form Birth Certificate	Au $12.00
Cost for a certified Marriage Certificate	Au $12.00
Cost for a certified Death Certificate	Au $12.00

The Registrar General holds records from January 1, 1930.

Australian Capital Territory

OFFICE OF THE REGISTRAR BIRTHS, DEATHS, AND MARRIAGES

APPLICATION FOR BIRTH CERTIFICATE

RECORD OF FEES PAID

PARTICULARS OF BIRTH
(Please use block letters)

Given (Christian) Names

Surname

Date of Birth

Age last Birthday (if applicable)

Place of Birth

A.C.T.

Father's full Given (Christian) Names

Mother's full Given (Christian) Names

Mother's full MAIDEN Surname

FOR OFFICE USE ONLY

Reg. No. ....

No. of Certified Copies ....

No. of Extracts ....

Total No. of Certificates ....

No. to be posted ....

No. to be collected ....

Date for Collection ....

Date Posted ....

Date Collected ....

Purpose for which certificate is required ....

Name of Applicant *(Block Letters)* Mr
Mrs ....
Miss

....

Relationship to person registered ....

Address in full ....

.... Postcode ....

Telephone No. .... Date of Application ....

Signature ....

Post to — The Registrar,
Births, Deaths & Marriages,
P.O. Box 788
CANBERRA CITY. 2601

Deliver to — Births, Deaths & Marriages Office,
4th Floor, National Mutual Centre,
Darwin Place,
CANBERRA CITY. A.C.T.

Australian Capital Territory
OFFICE OF THE REGISTRAR BIRTHS, DEATHS, AND MARRIAGES

APPLICATION FOR MARRIAGE CERTIFICATE

RECORD OF FEES PAID

APPLICANT TO FURNISH PARTICULARS OF MARRIAGE
(Please use block letters)

Bridegroom's given names	
Surname	
Bride's given names	
Surname before Marriage	
Date of Marriage	/ /19
Place of Marriage	A.C.T.

FOR OFFICE USE ONLY

Reg. No. ....

No. of Certified Copies ....

No. of Extracts ....

Total No. of Certificates ....

No. to be posted ....

No. to be collected ....

Date for Collection ....

Date Posted ....

Date Collected ....

Purpose for which certificate is required ....

Name of Applicant *(Block Letters)* Mr Mrs Miss ....

....

Relationship to bride/groom ....

Address in full ....

.... Postcode ....

Telephone No. .... Date of Application ....

Signature ....

Post to — The Registrar,
Births, Deaths & Marriages,
P.O. Box 788
CANBERRA CITY. 2601

Deliver to — Births, Deaths & Marriages Office,
4th Floor, National Mutual Centre,
Darwin Place,
CANBERRA CITY. A.C.T.

BDM

Australian Capital Territory
OFFICE OF THE REGISTRAR BIRTHS, DEATHS, AND MARRIAGES

APPLICATION FOR DEATH CERTIFICATE

RECORD OF FEES PAID

APPLICANT TO FURNISH PARTICULARS OF DECEASED
(Please use block letters)

Given (Christian) Names	
Surname	
Husband/Wife of	
Date of Death	
Place of Death	A.C.T.
Age last Birthday	years
Father's full Names (including Surname)	
Mother's full Given (Christian) Names and Maiden Surname	

FOR OFFICE USE ONLY

Reg. No. ....

No. of Certified Copies ....

No. of Extracts ....

Total No. of Certificates ....

No. to be posted ....

No. to be collected ....

Date for Collection ....

Date Posted ....

Date Collected ....

Purpose for which certificate is required ....

Mr
Mrs
Name of Applicant *(Block Letters)* Miss ....

....

Relationship to deceased ....

Address in full ....

.... Postcode ....

Telephone No. .... Date of Application ....

Signature ....

Post to — The Registrar,
Births, Deaths & Marriages,
P.O. Box 788
CANBERRA CITY. 2601

Deliver to — Births, Deaths & Marriages Office,
4th Floor, National Mutual Centre,
Darwin Place,
CANBERRA CITY. A.C.T.

AUSTRALIA—
New South Wales

Send your requests to:

Office of the Registrar General
   of Births, Deaths & Marriages
P.O. Box 30 G.P.O.
Sydney, New South Wales
Australia 2001

(011) (612) 228-8988

Cost for a certified Birth Certificate	Au $14.00
Cost for a certified Marriage Certificate	Au $14.00
Cost for a certified Death Certificate	Au $14.00

The Registrar General has records from March 1, 1856.

The Family History Library of Salt Lake City, Utah has microfilmed many of the original and published vital records and church registers of New South Wales's cities. They have microfilm copies of births from 1856 to 1909, baptisms early to 1856, marriages early to 1905, deaths 1856 to 1905, and burials early to 1856. For details on their holdings please consult your nearest Family History Center.

N.S.W. BIRTH

Application for Search and/or Certified Copy or Extract

THIS RECEIPT MUST BE PRODUCED AT THE DELIVERY COUNTER IF CALLING FOR DOCUMENTS

Registry of Births, Deaths and Marriages,
Box 30, G.P.O., Sydney 2001

THIS RECEIPT IS ISSUED SUBJECT ONLY TO THE CHEQUE ON ACCOUNT OF WHICH IT IS GIVEN BEING DULY CLEARED

If any enquiry is necessary please quote

FEE $

I hereby apply for a search and / or
of the Registration of the undermentioned Birth.

☐ Certified Copy
☐ Short Extract

PARTICULARS OF BIRTH

1	Surname (if married woman maiden surname)			
	Christian Names in Full			**OFFICE USE ONLY**
2	Date and Year of Birth or Period of Years to be Searched if Date of Birth is Unknown		PRESENT AGE	FULL ☐ EXTRACT ☐
3	Place of Birth		N.S.W.	NUMBER IN REGISTER
4	Father's Name in full			SEARCHED BY / INITIALS AND DATE
5	Mother's Maiden Name in full			
6	Applicant's Relationship to person described in Item 1			CERTIFICATE EXAMINED / INITIALS AND DATE
7	Reason for which Certificate is Required			

If insufficient space, use back of form

ADDITIONAL FEE TO BE PAID

ISSUED OR POSTED

(Signature of Applicant) _____

(Address) _____

_____ Phone: _____

IF CERTIFICATE IS TO BE POSTED PLEASE COMPLETE THIS SECTION
PLEASE USE BLOCK LETTERS

Your Office Reference _____

Name

Address
and
Postcode

PR 190 **N.S.W. MARRIAGE**

Application for Search and/or Certified Copy or Extract

Registry of Births, Deaths and Marriages,
Box 30. G.P.O., Sydney 2001.

THIS RECEIPT IS ISSUED SUBJECT ONLY
TO THE CHEQUE ON ACCOUNT OF WHICH
IT IS GIVEN BEING DULY CLEARED

THIS RECEIPT MUST BE PRODUCED AT THE DELIVERY COUNTER IF CALLING FOR DOCUMENTS

If any enquiry is necessary please quote

FEE $

I hereby apply for a search for and/or
of the Registration of the undermentioned Marriage.

☐ Certified Copy
☐ Short Extract

PARTICULARS OF MARRIAGE

1	BRIDE GROOM	Surname		
		Christian or other Names in Full		OFFICE USE ONLY
2	BRIDE	Surname Before Marriage		FULL ☐ EXTRACT ☐
		Christian or other Names in Full		NUMBER IN REGISTER
3	Date and Year Of Marriage or Period of Years to be Searched if Date of Marriage is Unknown			SEARCHED BY / INITIALS AND DATE
4	Place of Marriage	N.S.W.		CERTIFICATE EXAMINED / INITIALS AND DATE
5	Applicant's Relationship to person described in Item 1 or 2			
6	Reason for which Certificate is Required	If insufficient space, use back of form		ADDITIONAL FEE TO BE PAID

(Signature of Applicant) . . . .

(Address) . . . .

ISSUED OR POSTED

. . . . .Phone . . . .

IF CERTIFICATE IS TO BE POSTED PLEASE COMPLETE THIS SECTION

PLEASE USE BLOCK LETTERS

Your Office Reference _____

Name

Address and Postcode

PR 189

N.S.W. DEATH
Application for Search and/or Certified Copy or Extract

Registry of Births, Deaths and Marriages, Box 30, G.P.O., Sydney 2001.

THIS RECEIPT IS ISSUED SUBJECT ONLY TO THE CHEQUE ON ACCOUNT OF WHICH IT IS GIVEN BEING DULY CLEARED

THIS RECEIPT MUST BE PRODUCED AT THE DELIVERY COUNTER IF CALLING FOR DOCUMENTS

If any enquiry is necessary please quote

FEE $

I hereby apply for a search for and/or
of the Registration of the undermentioned Death.

☐ Certified Copy
☐ Short Extract

PARTICULARS OF DEATH

1	Surname of Deceased	
	Christian or Given Names in Full	
2	Date and Year of Death or Period of Years to be Searched if Date of Death is Unknown	
3	Place of death	N.S.W.
4	Father's Name in Full	
5	Mother's Maiden Name in Full	
6	Applicant's Relationship to person described in Item 1	
7	Reason for which Certificate is Required	

If insufficient space, use back of form.

(Signature of Applicant) _____

(Address) _____

Phone: _____

OFFICE USE ONLY

FULL ☐   EXTRACT ☐

Number in Register	
Searched By	Initials and Date
Certificate Examined	Initials and Date
Additional Fee to be Paid	
Issued or Posted	

IF CERTIFICATE IS TO BE POSTED PLEASE COMPLETE THIS SECTION
PLEASE USE BLOCK LETTERS

Your Office Reference ....

Name

Address
and
Postcode

ST4431

PROUDLY PRINTED IN AUSTRALIA

AUSTRALIA—
Northern Territory

Send your requests to:

Office of the Registrar General
    of Births, Deaths & Marriages
G.P.O. Box 3094
Darwin, Northern Territory
Australia 5794

(011) (6189) 6119

Cost for a certified Birth Certificate	Au $8.00
Cost for a certified Marriage Certificate	Au $8.00
Cost for a certified Death Certificate	Au $8.00

The Registrar General has records from August 24, 1870.

NORTHERN TERRITORY OF AUSTRALIA
OFFICE OF THE REGISTRAR BIRTHS, DEATHS, AND MARRIAGES

APPLICATION FOR BIRTH CERTIFICATE

FEES — to be prepaid: Search in Register & issue of SHORT EXTRACT from entry containing name,
date & place of birth of person
Search in Register & issue of LONG EXTRACT from entry containing name,
date & place of birth of person & names of parents
Search in Register & issue of CERTIFIED COPY.
Additional Search Fee where insufficient or inaccurate details are stated.

APPLICANT TO FURNISH PARTICULARS OF BIRTH (Please use block letters)		FOR OFFICE USE ONLY
(Registered) SURNAME		Receipt No. ....
Given (Christian) Names		Amount .... Date ....
Date of Birth		Reg. No. ....
Age last Birthday (if applicable)		No. of Certified Copies .... No. of Extracts ....
Place of Birth	N.T.	Total No. of Certificates .... No. to be posted .... No. to be collected .... Date for Collection .... Certificate Nos. ....
Father's full name		
Mother's full given names (Christian Names)		Date Posted ....
Mother's full MAIDEN Surname		Date Collected .... Received ....

Purpose for which certificate is required ⟶
(Registration of Births, Deaths & Marriages Act— S.50) _____

Name of Applicant
(Block Letters) _____   Mr Mrs Ms Miss   _____

Relationship to above person _____   _____

Postal Address in full _____   _____

Postcode: _____

Telephone No. _____   Date of Application: _____

Signature ....

Post to The Registrar,
Births, Deaths & Marriages,

DARWIN, N.T. 5794

or for Alice Springs District:
District Registrar,
P.O. Box 1394,
ALICE SPRINGS, N.T. 5750

Deliver to Births, Deaths & Marriages Office,
Ground Floor, North Wing,
Civic Centre,
Harry Chan Avenue,
DARWIN, N.T.

or: Law Courts Building,
Parsons Street,
ALICE SPRINGS, N.T.

1388.8410   G. L. DUFFIELD, Government Printer of the Northern Territory

NORTHERN TERRITORY OF AUSTRALIA

RG 2/5

OFFICE OF THE REGISTRAR BIRTHS, DEATHS AND MARRIAGES
APPLICATION FOR MARRIAGE CERTIFICATE

APPLICANT TO FURNISH PARTICULARS OF MARRIAGE		**FOR OFFICE USE ONLY**
(Please use Block letters)		Receipt No. ....
		Amount ....
Bridegroom's Given Names		Date ....
Surname		Reg. No. ....
		No. of Certified Copies ....
Bride's Given Names		No. of Extracts ....
		Total No. of Certificates..........
Surname before Marriage		No. to be posted ....
		No. to be collected ....
Date of Marriage		Date for Collection ....
		Certificate Nos......................
Place of Marriage	N.T.	Date Posted ....
		Date Collected.......................
		Received ....

Purpose for which certificate is required _____

Name of Applicant — Mr.
Mrs.
Miss
(Block Letters)

Postal Address in full — _____

Telephone No. — _____

Date of Application:

Signature ....

Post to — The Registrar,
Births, Deaths & Marriages,
G.P.O. Box 3094,
DARWIN, N.T. 5794

Deliver to — Births, Deaths & Marriages Office,
Ground Floor, North Wing,
Civic Centre,
Harry Chan Avenue,
DARWIN N.T. 5790

6-20   G. L. DUFFIELD, Government Printer of the Northern Territory

NORTHERN TERRITORY OF AUSTRALIA
OFFICE OF THE REGISTRAR BIRTHS, DEATHS AND MARRIAGES

RG 2/4

APPLICATION FOR DEATH CERTIFICATE

APPLICANT TO FURNISH PARTICULARS OF DECEASED (Please use BLOCK LETTERS)		FOR OFFICE USE ONLY
Given (Christian) Name		Receipt No. ....
		Amount ....
Surname		Date ....
Husband/Wife of		Reg. No. ....
		No. of Certified Copies ....
Date of Death		No. of Extracts ....
		Total No. of Certificates ....
Place of Death	N.T.	No. to be posted ....
		No. to be collected ....
Age last Birthday	YEARS	Date for Collection ....
		Certificate Nos. ....
Father's Full names		Date Posted ....
		Date Collected ....
Mother's full MAIDEN name		Received ....

Purpose for which certificate is required _____

Name of Applicant — Mr. Mrs. Miss (Block Letters) _____

_____

Postal Address in full — _____

Postcode: _____

Telephone No. — _____

Date of Application: _____

Signature ....

Post to — The Registrar,
Births, Deaths & Marriages,
P.O. Box 3094,
DARWIN N.T. 5794

Deliver to —

Births, Deaths & Marriages Office,
Ground Floor, North Wing
Civic Centre,
Harry Chan Avenue,
DARWIN N.T.

20705/80

AUSTRALIA—
Queensland

Send your requests to:

Office of the Registrar General
of Births, Deaths & Marriages
P.O. Box 188
Brisbane, North Quay
Queensland, Australia 4000

(011) (617) 224-6222

Cost for a certified Birth Certificate	Au $14.50
Cost for a certified short form Birth Certificate	Au $14.50
Cost for a certified Marriage Certificate	Au $14.50
Cost for a certified Death Certificate	Au $14.50

The Registrar has records from March 1, 1856.

The Family History Library of Salt Lake City, Utah has microfilmed many of the original and published vital records and church registers of Queensland's cities. They have microfiche copies of the indexes to births from 1850 to 1869, marriages from 1856 to 1899, and deaths from 1856 to 1894. For details on their holdings please consult your nearest Family History Center.

REGISTRAR-GENERAL'S OFFICE, BRISBANE

RECEIPT
(Not valid unless official cash register imprint appears hereon)
Payment by cheque or other negotiable instruments accepted subject to clearance.

BIRTH

Please Print
Name and Postal
Address of
Person to whom
Document is to
be Posted.

_____
_____
_____Postcode _____

Official receipts must be produced when taking delivery of documents.

REGISTRAR-GENERAL'S OFFICE, BRISBANE

OFFICE COPY ONLY

(Office Use Only)	
Entry No.:	
Certified Copy:	
Extract:	
Priority:	
Search:	
Change of Name:	
Alterations:	
Misc.:	
Suspense:	
Short:	
Cheque Refund:	
Amount Received:	
Assessor: _____	
Number of cheque/bank/money order and name of drawer of cheque if different from applicant.	
Copy No.(s):	
Date Copy Produced:	

BIRTH

Application for Search and/or Certified Copy or Extract

I hereby apply for a search for and/or
of the Registration of the undermentioned Birth.

☐ Certified Copy
☐ Short Extract

Name of Applicant: _____

Signature of Appplicant: _____

Address: _____

_____

Date of Application: _____ 19____

PARTICULARS OF BIRTH

1	Surname	
	First Names in Full	
2	Date and Year of Birth or Period of Years to be searched if Date of Birth is unknown	
3	Place of Birth	
4	Father's Name in Full	
5	Mother's First Names and Maiden Surname	
6	Applicant's Relationship to person described in Item 1	
7	Reason for which Certificate is Required	

Entry No.

Surname
& Initials

REGISTRAR-GENERAL'S OFFICE, BRISBANE
RECEIPT
(Not valid unless official cash register imprint appears hereon)
Payment by cheque or other negotiable instruments accepted subject to clearance.

MARRIAGE

Please Print
Name and Postal
Address of
Person to whom
Document is to
be Posted.

_____

_____

_____Postcode _____

Official receipts must be produced when taking delivery of documents.

REGISTRAR-GENERAL'S OFFICE, BRISBANE

OFFICE COPY ONLY

Entry No.:

Certified
Copy:

Extract:

Priority:

Search:

Change
of Name:

Alterations:

Misc.:

Suspense:

Short:

Cheque
Refund:

Amount
Received:

Assessor: _____

Number of cheque/bank/money order and name
of drawer of cheque if different from applicant.

Copy No.(s):

Date Copy Produced:

MARRIAGE

Application for Search and/or Certified Copy or Extract

I hereby apply for a search for and/or
of the Registration of the undermentioned Marriage.

☐ Certified Copy
☐ Short Extract

Name of Applicant: _____

Signature of Appplicant: _____

Address: _____

_____

Date of Application: _____19_____

PARTICULARS OF MARRIAGE

1	BRIDE GROOM	Surname	
		First Names in Full	
2	BRIDE	Surname before Marriage	
		First Names in Full	
3		Date and Year of Marriage or Period of Years to be searched if Date of Marriage is unknown.	
4		Place of Marriage	
5		Relationship to person described in Items 1 and 2	
6		Reason for which Certificate is Required	

Entry No.

Surname
& Initials

REGISTRAR-GENERAL'S OFFICE, BRISBANE

RECEIPT

(Not valid unless official cash register imprint appears hereon)

Payment by cheque or other negotiable instruments accepted subject to clearance.

DEATH

Please Print
Name and Postal
Address of
Person to whom
Document is to
be Posted.

_____

_____

_____Postcode_____

Official receipts must be produced when taking delivery of documents.

REGISTRAR-GENERAL'S OFFICE, BRISBANE

OFFICE COPY ONLY

(Office Use Only)

Entry No.

Certified
Copy

Extract

Priority

Search

Change
of Name

Alterations

Misc.

Suspense

Short

Cheque
Refund

Amount
Received

Assessor

Number of cheque/bank/money order and name
of drawer of cheque if different from applicant.

Copy No.(s)

Date Copy Produced

DEATH

Application for Search and/or Certified Copy or Extract

I hereby apply for a search for and/or
of the Registration of the undermentioned Death.

☐ Certified Copy
☐ Short Extract

Name of Applicant: _____

Signature of Applicant: _____

Address: _____

_____

Date of Application: _____ 19_____

PARTICULARS OF DEATH

1	Surname of Deceased	
	First Names in Full	
2	Date and Year of Death or Period of Years to be searched if Date of Death is unknown	
3	Place of Death	
4	Father's Name in Full	
5	Mother's First Names and Maiden Surname	
6	Applicant's Relationship to person described in Item 1	
7	Reason for which Certificate is Required	

AUSTRALIA—
South Australia

Send your requests to:

Principal Registrar
   of Births, Deaths & Marriages
Department of Public & Consumer Affairs
G.P.O. Box 1351
Adelaide, South Australia
Australia 5001

(011) (618) 226-1999

Cost for a certified Birth Certificate	Au $13.00
Cost for a certified Marriage Certificate	Au $13.00
Cost for a certified Death Certificate	Au $13.00

The Registrar has records from July 1, 1842. Enclose an additional Au $1.00 per certificate for air mail postage.

The Family History Library of Salt Lake City, Utah has microfilmed many of the original and published vital records and church registers of South Australia's cities. They have microfiche copies of the indexes to births and marriages from 1842 to 1906, and deaths from 1842 to 1905. For details on their holdings please consult your nearest Family History Center.

Births Deaths & Marriages Registration Division
59 King William Street
ADELAIDE 5000

BIRTH

G.P.O. Box 1351
ADELAIDE 5001
This Receipt MUST be produced when collecting documents

☐ **EXTRACT** (Tick appropriate boxes)

☐ **CERTIFICATE**

☐ **PRIORITY SERVICE**

COMPLETE IN **BLOCK** LETTERS

Reg. No.

Book .... Page...............................

Surname ....
(If Female; Insert Maiden Name)

Given Names ....

Date of Birth................................. Sex ....

Place of Birth...

Father's Name (in full).....................................

Mother's Maiden Name (in full) ....

You are advised that a certified copy includes **any former married name(s) of the mother.** A copy MAY be supplied omitting this information. Please indicate if you wish this information to be omitted.

☐ place tick in box

OFFICE USE ONLY

1. Name of Applicant ....
2. Relationship to above ....
3. Purpose for which document is required.............
   ....
4. Signature ....
   Address ....
   ....

NOTE:—If Birth occurred within 6 months of application, state at which hospital

....

PLEASE COMPLETE THIS SECTION IF DOCUMENT IS TO BE POSTED.

Name
Address and
Post Code

G7482

Births Deaths & Marriages Registration Division
59 King William Street
ADELAIDE 5000

MARRIAGE

G.P.O. Box 1351
ADELAIDE 5001
This Receipt MUST be produced when collecting documents

Received amount printed by
cash register

	(Tick appropriate boxes)	
Please supply	☐ Extract or	☐ Certificate
to be	☐ Posted ☐ Collected	☐ Priority Service

COMPLETE IN <u>BLOCK</u> LETTERS

Reg. No.

Book.........Page.........

Groom

Surname ....

Given Names ....

Bride

Maiden Surname ....

Given Names ....

Date of Marriage ....

Place of Marriage ....

Relationship of Applicant and

reason for application ....

NOTE:—If Marriage occurred within 6 months of
application, state name of celebrant

Signature ....

Address ....

....

....

TO BE COMPLETED IF DOCUMENT

TO BE POSTED

Name
Address and
Post Code

80230

Births Deaths & Marriages Registration Division
59 King William Street
ADELAIDE 5000

DEATH

G.P.O. Box 1351
ADELAIDE 5001
This Receipt MUST be produced when collecting documents

Received amount printed by
cash register

Reg. No.

Book   Page

```
┌─────────────────────────────────────────────┐
│                         (Tick appropriate boxes) │
│  Please supply    ☐  Extract or   ☐  Certificate │
│                                                  │
│  to be    ☐  Posted   ☐  Collected  ☐  Priority Service │
└─────────────────────────────────────────────┘
```

COMPLETE IN <u>BLOCK</u> LETTERS

Surname ....

Given Names ....

Date of Death— Day .... Month .... Year ..

Place of Death ....

Age of Death ....

Usual Residence ....

Relationship of Applicant and

reason for application ....

Signature ....

Address ....

....

NOTE:—If Death occurred within last 6 months,
state name of funeral director

....

**TO BE COMPLETED IF DOCUMENT
TO BE POSTED**

Name
Address and
Post Code

BD22D

AUSTRALIA—
Tasmania

Cost for a certified Birth Certificate	Au $12.00
Cost for a certified Marriage Certificate	Au $12.00
Cost for a certified Death Certificate	Au $12.00

The Registrar has records from December 1, 1838.

Application for Search

BIRTH – TASMANIA

To: Registrar-General,
Registrar.

I hereby apply for:— (Tick appropriate box)

EXTRACT search ☐   CERTIFICATE search ☐   EXTENDED search ☐

of birth on the following information:—

Christian names ....

Surname at birth (Maiden name) ....

Birthplace (City or Town) ....

Date of birth ..../ .... /............... (Age...............) OR if not known —

years to be searched .... to............................... inclusive.

Full names of natural/adoptive parents: (delete as necessary)

Father: ....

Mother: ....(Maiden name.......................................)

Purpose for which Extract or Certificate is required ....

Name of Applicant   Mr
                                    Mrs ....
(*Block Letters*)   Miss

Relationship to person registered ....

Address in full ....

.... Postcode........................

Telephone No. .... Date..................................

I enclose the amount of $ .... as payment for search.

PLEASE POST THE RESULT OF SEARCH TO ME.

(Tick One)

I WILL COLLECT THE RESULT OF SEARCH.

Signature..

Application for Search

MARRIAGE – TASMANIA

To: Registrar-General, G.P.O. Box 875 J, Hobart 7001

I hereby apply for:— (Tick appropriate box)

EXTRACT search ☐   CERTIFICATE search ☐   EXTENDED search ☐

of marriage on the following information:—

Full names of parties:—

    Bridegroom: ....

    Bride (prior to marriage): ....

    Date of Marriage................................ / .... / .... OR if not known

        years to be searched ....to............................ inclusive.

    Place of Marriage: .... in Tasmania.

    Purpose for which Extract or Certificate is required...

    ....

                  Mr
Name of Applicant Mrs...
  (Block Letters)   Miss

Relationship to person registered ....

    Address in full ....

    .... Postcode......................

    Telephone No. .... Date......................

I enclose the amount of $ .... as payment for search.

PLEASE POST THE RESULT OF SEARCH TO ME.

                (Tick One)

I WILL COLLECT THE RESULT OF SEARCH.

    Signature...

FOR OFFICE USE ONLY	{ Collected ....
	{ Posted ....

A. B. Caudell, Government Printer, Tasmania   DS.K 2172

Application for Search

DEATH — TASMANIA

To: Registrar-General,
    Registrar.

I hereby apply for:— (Tick appropriate box)

EXTRACT search ☐   CERTIFICATE search ☐   EXTENDED search ☐

of death on the following information:—

Full Names: ....

Place of Death: .... in Tasmania.

Date of Death ..../ ..../ .... OR if not known

    years to be searched .... to .... inclusive.

Purpose for which Extract or Certificate is required: ....

Name of Applicant   Mr
(Block Letters)   Mrs ....
                      Miss

Relationship to person registered ....

    Address in full ....

                    .... Postcode..............

    Telephone No. .... Date ....

I enclose the amount of $ .... as payment for search.

PLEASE POST THE RESULT OF SEARCH TO ME.
                                    (Tick One)
I WILL COLLECT THE RESULT OF SEARCH.

        Signature...

AUSTRALIA—
Victoria

Send your requests to:

The Government Statist
Registry of Births, Deaths & Marriages
295 Queen Street
P.O. Box 4332
Melbourne, Victoria, Australia 3001

(011) (613) 603-5800 *or* (011) (613) 609-9900

Cost for a certified Birth Certificate	Au $22.00
Cost for a certified Marriage Certificate	Au $22.00
Cost for a certified Death Certificate	Au $22.00

The Registrar has records from July 1, 1853.

The Family History Library of Salt Lake City, Utah has microfilmed many of the original and published vital records and church registers of Victoria's cities. They have microfiche copies of the indexes to vital records from 1 July 1853 to 1913. For details on their holdings please consult your nearest Family History Center.

PLEASE USE BLOCK LETTERS

APPLICATION FOR EXTRACT OR CERTIFICATE OF

BIRTHS IN VICTORIA

Registration of Births, Deaths & Marriages Regulations Form 4

THIS RECEIPT MUST BE PRODUCED WHEN COLLECTING DOCUMENTS

Applications to be made to:

Registry of Births, Deaths & Marriages
P.O. Box 4332
Melbourne 3001

or delivered to

295 Queen Street
Melbourne
Telephone: 603 5800

Insert family name and initials of the birth		Year of birth

Received amount printed by cash register

TICK APPROPRIATE BOXES

☐ **FULL CERTIFICATE**

☐ **EXTRACT**

☐ **PRIORITY SERVICE (Additional Fee)**

☐ **POST (Complete section below)**

☐ **COLLECT**

Enclosed is a cheque/money order/cash

for $...........................

DETAILS OF BIRTH REQUIRED

Official Entry No. If Known					Place of birth City/suburb/town Hospital	VICTORIA
Date of birth	Day	Month	Year	Or years to be searched 5 year period(s)	From.......................... to..........................	
		/	/			
Family name (at birth)				Christian or given names		
Fathers name	Family name				Christian or given names	
Mothers name	Family name (Maiden)				Christian or given names	

APPLICANTS DETAILS

Applicants name		Signature of applicant	
Applicants address			Tel:
Reason document is required		Relationship of applicant	

Office hours for making applications—8.30 a.m. to 4 p.m. Monday to Friday

IF THIS APPLICATION RELATES TO A LIVING PERSON OTHER THAN YOURSELF WRITTEN AUTHORITY MAY BE REQUIRED

PLEASE COMPLETE THIS SECTION IF DOCUMENT IS TO BE POSTED
PLEASE USE BLOCK LETTERS

Name	
Address and Postcode	

APPLICATION FOR EXTRACT OR CERTIFICATE OF

MARRIAGES IN VICTORIA

Registration of Births, Deaths & Marriages Regulations Form 9

THIS RECEIPT MUST BE PRODUCED WHEN COLLECTING DOCUMENTS

Applications to be made to:

Registry of Births, Deaths & Marriages
P.O. Box 4332
Melbourne 3001

or delivered to

295 Queen Street
Melbourne
Telephone: 609 9900

Insert family name of marriage party(ies)		Year of marriage

Received amount printed by cash register

TICK APPROPRIATE BOXES

☐ Full certificate

☐ Extract

☐ Priority Service **(Additional Fee)**

☐ Post (complete section below)   **FEES (Effective from 1.11.87 to 31.10.88)**

☐ Collect   **Reviewed Annually**

Enclosed is a cheque/money order/cash

for $....................................

DETAILS OF MARRIAGE REQUIRED

Registration Number (if known)			Place of marriage City/suburb/town		Victoria
Date of marriage	Day Month Year / /		Or years to be searched 5 year period(s)	From.......................... to..........................	
Bridegroom	Family name			Christian or given names	
Bride	Family name at time of marriage			Christian or given names	

APPLICANTS DETAILS

Applicants name		Signature of applicant	
Applicants address			Tel:
Reason document is required		Applicants relationship to parties	

Office hours for making applications—8.30 a.m. to 4 p.m. Monday to Friday

IF THIS APPLICATION RELATES TO LIVING PERSONS OTHER THAN YOURSELF **WRITTEN AUTHORITY** MAY BE REQUIRED

PLEASE COMPLETE THIS SECTION IF DOCUMENT IS TO BE POSTED

PLEASE USE BLOCK LETTERS

Name	
Address and Postcode	

Jean Gordon Government Printer Melbourne   4534(F4)

PLEASE USE BLOCK LETTERS

APPLICATION FOR EXTRACT OR CERTIFICATE OF

DEATHS IN VICTORIA

Registration of Births, Deaths & Marriages Regulations Form 8

THIS RECEIPT MUST BE PRODUCED WHEN COLLECTING DOCUMENTS

Applications to be made to:

Registry of Births, Deaths & Marriages
P.O. Box 4332
Melbourne 3001
or delivered to
295 Queen Street
Melbourne
Telephone: 603 5800

Insert family name of deceased and initials		Year of death

Received amount printed by cash register

TICK APPROPRIATE BOXES

☐ **FULL CERTIFICATE**

☐ **EXTRACT**

☐ **PRIORITY SERVICE (Additional Fee)**

☐ **POST (Complete section below)**

☐ **COLLECT**

Enclosed is a cheque/money order/cash

for $....................................

DETAILS OF DEATH REQUIRED

Registration Number (if known)		Place of death City/suburb/town	, Victoria
Date of death	Day Month Year / /	Search period **if** date unknown	From................................ to................................

Full name of deceased	.... (Surname) (Christian or given Names)	Age at death , years

Fathers full name		Mothers full name (maiden)	
Name of spouse (if applicable)		Other information e.g. birthplace, children, etc.	

APPLICANTS DETAILS

Applicants name		Signature of applicant	
Applicants address			Tel:
Reason document is required			

Office hours for making applications—8.30 a.m. to 4 p.m. Monday to Friday

PLEASE COMPLETE THIS SECTION IF DOCUMENT IS TO BE POSTED

PLEASE USE BLOCK LETTERS

Name	
Address and Postcode	

AUSTRALIA—
Western Australia

Send your requests to:

Registrar General
　of Births, Deaths & Marriages
Oakleigh Building
22 St. George's Terrace
Perth, Western Australia
Australia 6000

(011) (619) 425-7555

Cost for a certified Birth Certificate	Au $15.00
Cost for a certified Marriage Certificate	Au $15.00
Cost for a certified Death Certificate	Au $15.00

The Registrar has records from September 9, 1841.

The Family History Library of Salt Lake City, Utah has microfilmed many of the original and published vital records and church registers of Western Australia's cities. They have microfiche copies of the indexes to births from 1840 to 1895, marriages and deaths from 1841 to 1896. For details on their holdings please consult your nearest Family History Center.

APPLICATION FOR SEARCH—BIRTH

PLEASE FILL IN ALL DETAILS YOU KNOW

PERIOD to be searched: From .... to ....

PARTICULARS OF BIRTH

Surname ....

Other Names ....

Date of Birth ....

Place of Birth ....

Father's Name ....

Mother's Maiden Name in Full ....

....

Date of Parent's Marriage ....

Place of Parent's Marriage ....

Present Address of Parents ....

....

Names and Dates and Places of Birth of any Brothers and Sisters.

....

....

....

....

....

....

Has a Birth Certificate ever been issued   Yes/No

Was Birth Registered   Yes/No

Was this Birth Subject to an Order of Adoption.   Yes/No

Is Person Deceased.   Yes/No

Purpose for which Document is Required, e.g., Passport, Motor Driver's Licence,

Insurance, Probate, Employment, Social Security, etc.

....

Name of Applicant ....

Relationship If Not Person Concerned ....

Address of Applicant ....

....

Post Code ....

Telephone Number ....

Receipt No. ....

Date ....

APPLICATION FOR SEARCH—MARRIAGE

PLEASE FILL IN ALL DETAILS YOU KNOW

PERIOD to be searched: From .... to ....

PARTICULARS OF MARRIAGE

Surname of Bridegroom.. Age..................

First Names of Bridegroom...

Maiden Surname of Bride .... Age..................

First Names of Bride..

Date of Marriage...

Place of Marriage..

If Bride previously married, name of

former Husband ....

Children of Marriage (names, ages and places of birth)—

....

Reason for search ....

APPLICANT

Name ....

Address ....

Office Use Only

R.G. 445.

Receipt No..

Date ....

95300/6/80—60PDS—1854

REGISTRAR GENERAL'S OFFICE ● PERTH ● WESTERN AUSTRALIA

APPLICATION FOR SEARCH—DEATH

PLEASE FILL IN ALL DETAILS YOU KNOW

PERIOD to be searched: From .... to ....

PARTICULARS OF DECEASED PERSON

Surname.. Age...........................

First names...

Father's name...

Mother's name..

Supposed or approximate date of death ....

Place of death...

Place of birth..

If married, state to whom...

Date and place of marriage..

Reason for search...

APPLICANT

Name ....

Address ....

Office Use Only

Receipt No...

Date ....

R.G. 354.

95313/6/80—60PDS—2790

NEW ZEALAND

Send your requests to:

Registrar General's Office
Levin House
330 High Street
P.O. Box 3115
Lower Hutt, Wellington, New Zealand

(011) (64) 4-694-489

Cost for a certified Birth Certificate	NZ $14.00
Cost for a short form Birth Certificate	NZ $ 6.00
Cost for a certified Marriage Certificate	NZ $14.00
Cost for a certified Death Certificate	NZ $14.00

The fee plus postage costs may be paid in your local currency to the New Zealand Consulate, which will then forward your application to the Registrar General. Application forms sent directly to the Registrar General must be paid in New Zealand currency. The Registrar General has birth and death records from January 1, 1848 and marriage records from 1854.

The Family History Library of Salt Lake City, Utah has microfilmed many of the original and published vital records and church registers of New Zealand's cities. They have microfiche copies of the index to births and marriages from 1840 to 1920 and the index to deaths from 1848 to 1920. For details on their holdings please consult your nearest Family History Center.

DEPARTMENT OF JUSTICE
Application for Birth, Death or Marriage Certificate

Please supply a certificate for which particulars are given below. **ALL FEES MUST BE PREPAID.**

Enclosed is a postal note/cheque/cash for $ .... being the fees as set out below. (Stamps not acceptable tender).

Applicant: ....

(Please print or write clearly)

Address: ....

Date: ....

R.G.93

PLEASE READ CAREFULLY

NOTE 1: Applications for birth and death certificates can be made at the office where registration was made or at the Registrar-General's Office, Levin House, 330 High Street, Private Bag, Lower Hutt. Phone 694-489.

NOTE 2: Applications for marriage certificates can be made as follows:
  (i) Church marriages can only be obtained from the Registrar-General's Office, Lower Hutt.
  (ii) Registry-Office marriages can be obtained from the office where marriage performed or from Registrar General's Office.
  (iii) Other celebrant marriages can be obtained from the office which issued the licence or from Registrar-General's Office.

NOTE 3: Dates — Show the exact date if possible. If the entry is not found in the year stated an extended search can be made on request. If you require an extended search the years to be covered should be stated (e.g. 1926-1935) and search fees paid according to the scale set out below in addition to the certificate fee.

BIRTH (Note: Give Maiden name in case of married woman)	Surname or Family Name	First Names	Date & Year of Birth	Place of Birth	Father's Full Name	Mother's Name & Maiden Name
						(cont. over if required)

DEATH	Surname or Family Name	First Names	Date & Year Death	Place of Death	To Whom Married	Names of Parents
						(cont. over if required)

MARRIAGE	BRIDEGROOM		BRIDE		Date of Marriage	Place of Marriage
	Surname or Family Name	First Names	Surname or Family Name	First Names		
						(continue overleaf)

1500x50/8-95/240WP

	Surname or Family Name	First Names	Date & Year of Birth	Place of Birth	Father's Full Name	Mother's Name & Maiden Name
BIRTH (Note: Give Maiden name in case of married woman)						

	Surname or Family Name	First Names	Date & Year of Death	Place of Death	To Whom Married	Names of Parents
DEATH						

	BRIDEGROOM		BRIDE		Date of Marriage	Place of Marriage
	Surname or Family Name	First Names	Surname or Family Name	First Names		
MARRIAGE						

SOUTH AFRICA

Send your requests to:

Registration Office
Department of Home Affairs
Cape Town, Republic of South Africa

(011) (2721) 211-000

Cost for a certified Birth Certificate	No Charge
Cost for a certified Marriage Certificate	No Charge
Cost for a certified Death Certificate	No Charge

The Registration Office has records from 1924. The Director-General of Internal Affairs can at his discretion approve or refuse to issue a certificate.

The Family History Library of Salt Lake City, Utah has microfilmed many of the original and published vital records and church registers of South Africa's cities and counties. They have microfilm copies of South African church marriage records from 1696 to 1899 and death records from 1869 to 1939. For details on their holdings please consult your nearest Family History Center.

APPLICATION FOR BIRTH CERTIFICATE

(Complete in duplicate and write in block letters please)

Identity number: ☐☐☐☐☐☐ ☐☐☐☐ ☐☐ ☐

Surname ....

Maiden surname if a married woman ....

Full first names ....

Population group ....

Date of birth ....

District of birth ....

Full names and surname of father ....

....

Full names of mother ....

Maiden surname of mother ....

[*N.B.*—In terms of the regulations promulgated in terms of the Births, Marriages and Deaths Registration Act, 1963 (Act 81 of 1963), the Director-General: Internal Affairs may in his discretion approve or refuse the issue of a certificate.]

Make a cross (X) in the appropriate block:

☐ Abridged certificate is required.

☐ Full certificate is required.

(*N.B.*—An abridged certificate usually answers the purpose for which a birth certificate is required in South Africa).

Please state for what purpose the birth certificate is required...

....

....

Make a cross (X) in the appropriate block:

☐ Certificate to be collected.

☐ Certificate to be posted to applicant.

Name of applicant...

Address of applicant ....

....

.... Postal code ....

Date ....
                                                                                 Signature

(Vir Afrikaans—kyk keersy)

APPLICATION FOR MARRIAGE CERTIFICATE

(Complete in duplicate and write in block letters please)

Certificates not collected will be posted to the applicant.

Full names and surname of husband ....

....

Identity number of husband

Date of birth of husband ....

Full names and maiden surname of wife ....

....

Identity number of wife

Date of birth of wife ....

Date of marriage ....

Name of church or magistrate's office ....

Place where marriage took place ....

Name of marriage officer (if married in church) ....

Name of applicant..

Address of applicant ....

....

Make a cross (X) in the appropriate block—

☐ Abridged certificate is required.

☐ Full certificate is required.

If a full certificate is required, furnish the reasons briefly:

....

....

(*N.B.*—An abridged certificate usually answers the purpose for which a marriage certificate is required in South Africa.)

Make a cross (X) in the appropriate block—

☐ Certificate to be collected.

☐ Certificate to be posted to applicant.

Date of application...................... ....

Signature

APPLICATION FOR DEATH CERTIFICATE
PARTICULARS OF DECEASED

(Complete in duplicate and write in block letters please)

Certificates not collected will be posted to the applicant.

Identity number: ⬜⬜⬜⬜⬜⬜ ⬜⬜⬜⬜ ⬜⬜

Surname: ....

First names in full: ....

Date of birth: ....

Date of death: ....

District where death occurred: ....

If the death occurred after 1 February 1972, the name of the police station or regional office of the Department of Internal Affairs where the death was registered: ....

Name of applicant: ....

Address of applicant: ....

....

Make a cross (x) in the appropriate block —

⬜ Abridged certificate is required.

⬜ Full certificate is required.

If a full certificate is required, furnish the reasons briefly.

....

....

(N.B. An abridged certificate usually answers the purpose for which a death certificate is required in South Africa).

Make a cross (x) in the appropriate block —

⬜ Certificate to be collected.

⬜ Certificate to be posted to applicant.

DATE OF APPLICATION ....
                                                                        SIGNATURE

3. Europe

ALBANIA

Send your requests to:

Office of Civil Registration
(Town), Albania

Since Albania is a closed society it is difficult if not impossible to receive a reply from the government, and the current government has been in control since 1946. A civil registration and national identity card system are in place in Albania.

You might also consult the following libraries:

Biblioteka Kombëtare
(National Library)
Tirana, Albania

Biblioteka e Shtetit
(Durrës Public Library)
Durrës, Albania

Biblioteka e Shtetit
(Elbasan Public Library)
Elbasan, Albania

Biblioteka e Shtetit
(Gjirokastër Public Library)
Gjirokastër, Albania

Biblioteka e Shtetit
(Gramshi Public Library)
Gramshi, Albania

Biblioteka e Shtetit
(Korçë Public Library)
Korçë, Albania

Biblioteka e Shtetit
(Shkodër Public Library
Shkodër, Albania

ANDORA

Andora is a small principality with a population of just over 42,000 in seven towns. Catalan, the official language, is spoken by 30% of the people, while the majority speak Spanish. The government is jointly administered by France and the Bishop of Urgel.

AUSTRIA

Send your requests to:

Standesamt
(Town), Austria

There is no central office for vital records in Austria. To obtain copies of birth, marriage and death certificates write to the Civil Registration District Office in the town where the event occurred. Vital records are on file from 1784.

There are libraries and archives of value to researchers in every large city in Austria. It is impractical to list every one. The following, however, is a list of the key archives and libraries:

Österreichisches Staatsarchiv
(Austrian State Archives)
  Nottendorfergasse 2
  1030 Vienna, Austria

Österreichische Nationalbibliothek
(Austrian National Library)
  Josefsplatz 1
  1015 Vienna, Austria

Burgenlandisches Landesarchiv
Burgenlandische Landesbibliothek
  Landhaus
  Freiheitsplatz 1
  7001 Eisenstadt, Austria

Kartner Landesarchiv
  Landhaus
  A-9020 Klagenfurt, Austria

Bundesstaatliche Studien Bibliothek
  Kaufmanngasse 11
  9020 Klagenfurt, Austria

Archiv der Stadt Linz
  Postfach 1000
  4041 Linz, Austria

Niederösterreiches Landesarchiv
  Herrengasse 11-13
  1014 Vienna, Austria

Oberösterreichisches Landesarchiv
  Anzengruber Strasse 19
  4020 Linz, Austria

Bibliothek des Oberösterreichischen
  Landesmuseums
  Museum Strasse 14
  4020 Linz, Austria

Stadtarchiv und Stadtmuseum
  Prandtauer Strasse 2
  3100 St. Polten, Austria

Salzburg Landesarchiv
  Postfach 527
  5010 Salzburg, Austria

Steiermarkisches Landesarchiv
  Burgergasse 2A
  8010 Graz, Austria

Steiermarkisches Landesbibliothek
  Postfach 861
  8011 Graz, Austria

Stadtarchiv Innsbruck
  Badgasse 2
  6020 Innsbruck, Austria

Tiroler Landesarchiv
  Herrengasse 1
  6010 Innsbruck, Austria

Vienna Stadt und Landesarchiv
Vienna Stadt und Landesbibliothek
  Rathaus
  Felder Strasse 1
  A-1082 Vienna, Austria

Vorarlberg Landesarchiv
  Kirchstrasse 28
  6901 Bregenz, Austria

Voralberger Landesbibliothek
  Studienbibliothek
  Fluher Strasse 4
  6901 Bregenz, Austria

Archiv und Museum der Stadt Wels
  Bibliothek
  4600 Wels, Austria

BELGIUM

Send your requests to:

Registres de l'Etat Civil
(Town), Belgium

There is no central office for vital records in Belgium. To obtain copies of birth, marriage and death certificates write to the town where the event occurred. Vital records are on file from 1796.

There are libraries and archives of value to researchers in every large city in Belgium. It is impractical to list every one. The following, however, is a list of the key archives and libraries:

Bibliothèque Royale Albert 1er
(Royal Albert Library,
Belgian National Library)
  4 blvd de l'Empereur
  1000 Brussels, Belgium

Rijksarchief te Antwerpen
(Antwerp State Archives)
  Door Verstraetepl 5
  2018 Antwerp, Belgium

Stadsarchief
(Antwerp City Archives)
  Venusstraat 11
  2000 Antwerp, Belgium

Stadsbibliotheek
(Antwerp Public Library)
  Hendrik Conscienceplein 4
  2000 Antwerp, Belgium

Archives de l'Etat a Arlon
  Parc des Expositions
  6700 Arlon, Belgium

Rijksarchief te Brugge
  Academiestraat 14
  8000 Bruges, Belgium

Archives de la Ville de Bruxelles
  65 rue des Tanneurs
  1000 Brussels, Belgium

Archives Generales du Royaume
  2-4 rue de Ruysbroeck
  1000 Brussels, Belgium

Bibliotheek van de Rijksuniversiteit te Gent
  9 Rozier
  9000 Ghent, Belgium

Rijksarchief te Gent
  Geraard de Duivelsteen
  9000 Ghent, Belgium

Provinciaal Archief en Documentatiecentrum
  Begijnhof
  Zuivelmarkt 33
  3500 Hasselt, Belgium

Rijksarchief te Kortrijk
  Guido Gezelle Strasse
  8500 Kortrijk, Belgium

Archives de l'Etat a Liège
  79 rue du Chera
  4000 Liège, Belgium

Bibliothèque Publique de la Ville de Liège
  8 place des Carmes
  4000 Liège, Belgium

Archief en Stadsbibliotheek
  Steenweg 1
  2800 Mechelen, Belgium

Archives de l'Archeveche
  Archeveche de Malines
  Wollemarkt 15
  2800 Mechelen, Belgium

Archives de l'Etat
  23 place du Parc
  7000 Mons, Belgium

Archives de l'Etat a Namur
  45 rue d'Arquet
  5000 Namur, Belgium

Rijksarchief te Ronse
  2 Biezen Strasse
  9600 Ronse, Belgium

BULGARIA

Send your requests to:

Executive Committee
People's Council
(Town), Bulgaria

Civil registration began in 1881 in Bulgaria. Church registers are available before that time. It should be noted that Bulgaria is one of the most closed of the Eastern Bloc countries.

There are important libraries and archives in the major towns of Bulgaria. Each of the twenty-six District Centers has a District Archives. The key archives and libraries in Bulgaria are:

Cyril and Medodius National Library
  Boul. Tolbuhin 11
  1504 Sofia, Bulgaria

Central Archives Administration
  Alabin 58
  1000 Sofia, Bulgaria

Central Historical Archives
  A. Zdanov 5
  1000 Sofia, Bulgaria

Central Archives of Bulgaria
  Ul. Slavjanska 4
  1000 Sofia, Bulgaria

Ivan Vazov National Library
  N. Vapcarov 17
  4000 Plovdiv, Bulgaria

Military Historical Archives
  Veliko Tarnovo
  1000 Sofia, Bulgaria

Sofia City and District State Archives
  Ul. Vitosa 2
  1000 Sofia, Bulgaria

Sofia City Library
  Ul. Gurko 1
  1000 Sofia, Bulgaria

Zentralno Statisticesko Upravlenie
  Ul. Sesgi Septemvri 10
  1000 Sofia, Bulgaria

Send your requests to:

Registrar
District Office
(Town), Cyprus

Civil registration of births and deaths began in Cyprus in 1895, marriages in 1923. There are only a few libraries and archives in Cyprus. The key archives and libraries are:

Cyprus Historical Museum and Archives
  Pentelis 50
  Strovolos
  Nicosia, Cyprus

Cyprus Library
  Eleftheria Square Post Office
  Nicosia, Cyprus

Cyprus Research Center
  P.O. Box 1952
  Nicosia, Cyprus

CZECHOSLOVAKIA

Send your requests to:

Embassy of the Czechoslovak Socialist Republic
3900 Linnean Avenue, NW
Washington, DC 20008

(202) 363-6315

Cost for a certified Birth Certificate	$12.00
Cost for a certified Marriage Certificate	$12.00
Cost for a certified Death Certificate	$12.00

When applying for a certificate include a stamped self-addressed envelope for certified mail. The Embassy will translate the certificate for an additional fee of $18.00. Church records are available in Czechoslovakia from 1785, but modern civil registration did not begin until 1919.

DENMARK

There is no central office for vital records in Denmark. To obtain copies of birth, marriage and death certificates write to the town where the event occurred. Church registers are on file from the 1600s.

The Family History Library of Salt Lake City, Utah has microfilmed many of the original and published vital records and church registers of Denmark's cities and counties. For details on their holdings please consult your nearest Family History Center.

There are libraries and archives of value to researchers in every large city of Denmark. The following is a list of the key libraries and archives:

Danes Worldwide Archives
(Udvandrerarkivet)
 Ved Vor Frue Kirke
 P.O. Box 1731
 9100 Aalborg, Denmark

Rigsarkivets Bibliotek
(Danish National Archives)
 9 Rigsdagsgarden
 1218 Copenhagen K, Denmark

Det Kongelige Bibliotek
(Danish National Library)
 P.O. Box 2149
 1016 Copenhagen K, Denmark

Sønderjydske Landsbibliotek
 6200 Abenrå, Denmark

Landsarkivet for de sønderjyske Landsdele
 45 Haderslevvej
 DK 6200 Abenrå, Denmark

Nordjyske Landsbibliotek
 P.O. Box 839
 9100 Aalborg, Denmark

Københavns Stadsarkiv
(Copenhagen Archives)
 Radhuset
 DK-1599 Copenhagen V, Denmark

Københavns Kommunes Biblioteker
(Copenhagen Public Library)
 Kultorvet 2
 DK-1175 Copenhagen K, Denmark

Landsarkivet for Sjaelland m. m.
 10 Jagtvej
 DK 2200 Copenhagen, Denmark

Esbjerg Kommunes Hovedbibliotek
 P.O. Box 69
 6701 Esbjerg, Denmark

Frederiksberg Kommunes Biblioteker
  Solbjergvej 21-25
  2000 Frederiksberg, Denmark

Odense Centralbibliotek
  DK 5000 Odense C, Denmark

Landsarkivet for Fyn
  Jernbanegade 36
  DK 5000 Odense C, Denmark

Landsarkivet for Norrejylland
  5 Ll. Sct. Hansgade
  DK 8800 Viborg, Denmark

Send your requests to:

Pastor	or	Registrar
Lutheran Church		District Registrar
(Town), Finland		(Town), Finland

Records from the local parishes and the registrars are forwarded to:

Population Register Center
PL 7
SF-00521 Helsinki, Finland

(011) (358) (0) 189-3909

Over 90% of Finland's vital records are registered by the Lutheran Church. Non-Lutherans have been allowed to register with their respective churches or the government since 1917. These records are forwarded to the Population Register Center. A file is kept on every resident of Finland, immigrant or citizen, as well as those who have emigrated from Finland. Church registers date back to 1686.

The Family History Library of Salt Lake City, Utah has microfilmed many of the original and published vital records and church registers of Finland's cities. For details on their holdings please consult your nearest Family History Center.

There are libraries and archives of value to researchers in every large city of Finland. The following is a list of the key archives and libraries:

Valtionarkiston Kirjasto
(National Archives)
 P.O. Box 258
 00171 Helsinki, Finland

Helsingin Yliopisto
(National Library)
 Kirjasto
 Unioninkatu 36
 P.O. Box 36
 00171 Helsinki, Finland

Suomen Sukututkimusseuran Kirjasto
(Genealogical Society of Finland)
 Mariank 7C
 00170 Helsinki, Finland

Espoo Kaupunginkirjasto-maskuntakirjasto
(Espoo City/Provincial Library)
 Vanhamaantie 11
 02600 Espoo, Finland

Hämeenlinnan Maakuntaarkiston
Kasikirjasto (Hämeenlinna Provincial
Archives)
　Arvi Kariston Katu 2 A
　PL 73
　13101 Hämeenlinna, Finland

Helsingin Kaupunginarkiston
(Helsinki City Archives)
　Toinen Linja 4 F
　00530 Helsinki 53, Finland

Helsingin Kaupunginkirjasto
(Helsinki City Library)
　Rautatielaisenkatu 3
　00520 Helsinki, Finland

Joensuun Kaupunginkirjasto Pohjois
Karjalan Maakuntakirjasto (Central Library of
North Carelia; Joensuu City Library)
　P.O. Box 114
　80101 Joensuu, Finland

Jyväskylän Maakunta-Arkisto
(Provincial Archives of Jyväskylä)
　P.O. Box 25
　40101 Jyväskylä, Finland

Kuopion Kaupunginkirjasto Pohjois
Savon Maakuntakirjasto (Central Library
of North Savo; Kuopio City Library)
　P.O. Box 157
　70101 Kuopio, Finland

Mikkelin Maakunta-Arkisto
(Provincial Archives of Mikkeli)
　P.O. Box 2
　5101 Mikkeli, Finland

Oulun Maakunta-Arkisto
(Provincial Archives of Oulu)
　P.O. Box 31
　90101 Oulu, Finland

Pori Kaupunginkirjasto Satakunta
Maakuntakirjasto (Satakunta Library;
Pori City Library)
　P.O. Box 200
　28101 Pori, Finland

Tampereen Kaupunginkirjasto
Pirkanmaan Maakuntakirjasto (Pirkanmaa
Library; Tampere City Library)
　P.O. Box 152
　33101 Tampere, Finland

Turun Maakunta-Arkisto
(Provincial Archives of Turku)
　Aninkaistenkatu 11
　20110 Turku, Finland

Vassan Maakunta-Arkisto
(Provincial Archives of Vassa)
　Raastuvank 1 A
　PL 240
　65101 Vassa, Finland

FRANCE

Send your requests to:

> Le Mairie
> (Town), France

There is no central office for civil registration in France. To obtain copies of birth, marriage and death certificates write to the Mayor of the town where the event occurred. Vital records are on file from 1792. Records are also available in the local churches.

There are libraries and archives of value to researchers in almost every town and department in France. You might consult the following:

National Archives
Archives Nationales
    60 rue des Frances-Bourgeois
    75141 Paris, France

National Library
Bibliothèque Nationale
    58 rue Richelieu
    75084 Paris, France

The following agencies can provide you with the current addresses of the hundreds of libraries and archives in France:

French libraries are under the direction of:

> Direction des Bibliothèques
> 3-5 blvd Pasteur
> 75015 Paris, France

French archives are under the direction of:

> Direction des Archives de France
> 60 rue des Frances-Bourgeois
> 75141 Paris, France

GERMANY

Send your requests to:

Standesamt
(Town), Germany

There is no central office for vital records in either the German Democratic Republic or the Federal Republic of Germany. Civil registration locally began in 1876. Earlier records are available from the local church.

Both the German Democratic Republic and the Federal Republic of Germany maintain a system of personal photo identity cards (*personalausweis*) which every resident receives by the age of sixteen. These personal registration documents have been kept for most of this century.

There are libraries and archives of value to researchers in almost every town in the Federal Republic of Germany and the German Democratic Republic. The following is a list of the key libraries and archives:

Staatsbibliothek Preussischer Kulturbesitz
Postfach 1407
1000 Berlin 30, Federal Republic of Germany

Stadtarchiv und Wissenschaftliche Stadbibliothek
Stadtverwaltung
5300 Bonn, Federal Republic of Germany

Geh. Staatsarchiv Preussischer Kulturbesitz
Archivstr.
1000 Berlin 33, Federal Republic of Germany

Historic Emigration Office
Museum für Hamburgische Geschichte
Holstenwall 24
2000 Hamburg 36, Federal Republic of Germany

Deutsch Staatsbibliothek
Postfach 1312
1086 Berlin, German Democratic Republic

Deutsche Staatsbibliothek
(National Library)
Postfach 1312
1086 Berlin, German Democratic Republic

Deutsche Bucherei
Deutscher Pl
7010 Berlin, German Democratic Republic

Archenhold Sternwarte
Alt-Treptow 1
1193 Berlin, German Democratic Republic

Stadtarchiv Berlin
(Berlin Archives)
Postfach 660
Berlin, German Democratic Republic

Stadtarchiv Dresden
(Dresden Archives)
Archivstr. 14
Dresden, German Democratic Republic

GIBRALTAR

Send your requests to:

Registrar of Births, Marriages and Deaths
277 Main Street
Gibraltar

(011) (350) 72-289

Cost for a certified Birth Certificate	£ $6.50
Cost for a certified Marriage Certificate	£ $6.50
Cost for a certified Death Certificate	£ $6.50

While the Registrar has some birth and death records from 1848 and marriage records from 1862, the registration of deaths was not compulsory until 1869, births until 1887, and marriages until 1902.

Payment must be by certified check made out to the "Gibraltar Government Account." No personal checks are accepted. No application forms are provided by the Registrar.

Another useful source is the Gibraltar Garrison Library founded in 1793.

GREECE

Send your requests to:

Registrar
Civil Registry Office
(Town), Greece

Civil registration started in 1924. For prior records you should consult the local church. The National Library's address is: Odos El Venizelu 32, 106 79 Athens, Greece.

The Division on Citizenship of the Ministry of the Interior directs the work of the local Civil Registry Office.

HUNGARY

Send your requests to:

Civil Registration Office
(Town), Hungary

The government national identity card system is administered by:

National Office of Personal Registration
H-Budapest PF 81
1450 Hungary

There is no central office for vital records in Hungary. To obtain copies of birth, marriage and death certificates write to the Civil Registration District Office in the town where the event occurred. Vital records are on file from 1895. Early records are available from the local parish church. The National Office of Personal Registration also maintains files on residents of Hungary as part of the national identity card system.

There are libraries and archives of value to researchers in every large city in Hungary. It is impractical to list every one. The following, however, is a list of the key archives and libraries:

Országos Széchényi Könyvtár
(National Library)
  Budavári Palota F-épület
  1827 Budapest, Hungary

Muvelodesi Minisztérium Leveltari Osztaly
(National Board of Archives)
  Uri u. 54-56
  1014 Budapest, Hungary

Magyar Orszagos Leveltar
(Hungarian National Archives)
  Becsikapu-ter 4
  PF 8
  1250 Budapest, Hungary

Uj Magyar Kozponti Leveltar
(New Hungarian Central Archives)
  Hess Andras ter 4-5
  1014 Budapest, Hungary

Allami Gorkij Könyvtár
(Gorky State Library)
  Molnar u. 11
  1056 Budapest, Hungary

Budapest Fovaros Leveltar
(Budapest City Archives)
  Varoshaz u. 9/11
  1052 Budapest, Hungary

Fövárosi Szabó Ervin Könyvtár
(Budapest City Library)
  Szabó Ervin ter 1
  PF 487
  1371 Budapest, Hungary

Kozponti Statisztikai Hivatal
(Central Statistical Office)
  Kelenti Karoly u 5
  PF 10
  1525 Budapest, Hungary

Békés Megyei
(Békés County Library)
  Derkovits sor 1
  Bekescsaba, Hungary

Hajdu-Bihar Megyei Tanács VB Könyvtár
(Hajdu-Bihar County Library)
  PF 29
  4026 Debrecen, Hungary

Heves Megyei Könyvtár
(Heves County Library)
  PF 30
  3300 Eger, Hungary

Kisfaludy Karoly Könyvtár
(Gyor Sopron County Library)
  PF 9200
  120 Gyor, Hungary

Palmiro Togliatti Megyei Könyvtár
(Palmiro Togliatti County Library)
  PF 59
  7401 Kaposvár, Hungary

Katona Jozsef Megyei Könyvtár
(Bács-Kiskun County Library)
  Kossuth ter 1
  6000 Kecskemét, Hungary

Móricz Zsigmond Megyei és Varosi Könyvtár
(Móricz Zsigmond County Library)
  PF 23
  4400 Nyiregyháza, Hungary

Balassi Bálint Megyei Könyvtár
(Nograd County Library)
  PF 18
  3101 Salgótarján, Hungary

Somogyi Könyvtár
(Csongrad County Library)
  PF 441
  6701 Szeged, Hungary

Vörösmarty Mihály Megyei Könyvtár
(Fejér County Library)
  PF 65
  8001 Székesfehérvár, Hungary

Tolna Megyei Könyvtár
(Tolna County Library)
  PF 60
  7101 Szekszard, Hungary

Pest Megyei Müvelödési Központ
(Pest County Library)
  PF 67
  2001 Szentendre, Hungary

Verseghy Ferenc Megyei Könyvtár
(Szolnok County Library)
  PF 139
  5000 Szolnok, Hungary

Berzsenyi Daniel Megyei Könyvtár
(Vas County Library)
  PF 113
  9701 Szombathely, Hungary

József Attila Megyei Könyvtár
(Komárom County Library)
  PF 136
  2801 Tatabanya, Hungary

Eötvös Károly Megyei Könyvtár
(Veszprém County Library)
  PF 43
  8201 Veszprém, Hungary

Zala Megyei Könyvtár
(Zala County Library)
  PF 16
  8901 Zalaegerszeg, Hungary

ICELAND

Send your requests to:

The Statistical Bureau of Iceland
Althyduhusid
Hverfisgata 8-10
101 Reykjavík, Iceland

(011) (354) (1) 266-99

Cost for a certified Birth Certificate	No Charge
Cost for a certified Marriage Certificate	No Charge
Cost for a certified Death Certificate	No Charge

The Bureau has records on all residents of Iceland from 1953. They maintain these records as part of a national identity system. Prior to this time records were kept by the local, usually Lutheran, church. These church registers go back to 1785.

The following are the key archives and libraries in Iceland:

Thjodskjalasafu Islands
(National Archives of Iceland)
    P.O. Box 313
    121 Reykjavík, Iceland

Landsbókasafn Islands
(National Library of Iceland)
    Safnahusinu, Hverfisgotu
    P.O. Box 210
    121 Reykjavík, Iceland

Borgarbókasafn Reykjavikur
(Reykjavik City Library)
    Thingholtsstraeti 29-A
    101 Reykjavík, Iceland

Borgarskjalasafn Reykjavikur
(Reykjavik City Archives)
    Skulatuni 2
    105 Reykjavík, Iceland

ITALY

Send your requests to:

Ufficio di Stato Civile
(Town), Italy

There is no central office for vital records in Italy. To obtain copies of birth, marriage and death certificates write to the town where the event occurred. Vital records are on file from 1800, but more generally available from 1865 to the present.

There are libraries and archives of value to researchers in every state and large city in Italy. It is impractical to list every one. The following list is of the key archives and libraries.

Archivio Centrale dello Stato
(Italian Central Archives)
 Piazzale degli Archiv
 00144 Rome, Italy

Biblioteca Nazionale Centrale
 Vittorio Emanuele II
(Vittorio Emanuele II
 National Central Library)
 Viale Castro Pretorio 105
 00185 Rome, Italy

Archivio di Stato di Ancona
 Via Maggini 80/82
 60100 Ancona, Italy

Archivio Provinciale De Gemmis
 Piazza Corte del Catapano 5
 70122 Bari, Italy

Archivio di Stato di Bologna
 Piazza de Celestini 4
 40123 Bologna, Italy

Archivio di Stato di Cagliari
 Via Gallura 2
 09100 Cagliari, Italy

Archivio di Stato di Campobasso
 Via Orefici 43
 86100 Campobasso, Italy

Archivio di Stato di Catania
 Vittorio Emanuele 156
 95121 Catania, Italy

Archivio di Stato di Firenze
 Piazzale degli Uffizi
 50122 Florence, Italy

Archivio di Stato di Genova
 Via Tommaso Reggio 14
 16123 Genoa, Italy

Archivio di Stato di Lucca
 Piazza Guidiccioni 2
 55100 Lucca, Italy

Archivio di Stato di Macerata
 Corso Cairoli 175
 62100 Macerata, Italy

Archivio di Stato di Massa
 Via Giovanni Sforza 5
 54100 Massa, Italy

Archivio di Stato di Messina
Via XXIV Maggio 18
98100 Messina, Italy

Archivio di Stato di Modena
Corso Cavour 21
41100 Modena, Italy

Archivio di Stato di Napoli
Via Grande Archivio 5
80138 Naples, Italy

Archivio di Stato di Palermo
Corso Vittorio Emanuele 31
90133 Palermo, Italy

Archivio di Stato di Parma
Via Massimo d'Azeglio 43
43100 Parma, Italy

Archivio di Stato di Pisa
Palazzo Toscanelli
Lungarno Mediceo 17
56100 Pisa, Italy

Archivio di Stato di Potenza
Corso Garibaldi 4A
85100 Potenza, Italy

Archivio di Stato di Reggio Emilia
Corso Cairoli 6
42100 Reggio Emilia, Italy

Archivio di Stato di Roma
Corso del Rinascimento 40
00186 Rome, Italy

Archivio di Stato di Salerno
Piazza Abate Conforti 7
84100 Salerno, Italy

Archivio di Stato di Sassari
Via Angioy 1
07100 Sassari, Italy

Archivio di Stato di Siena
Via Banchi di Sotto 52
53100 Siena, Italy

Archivio di Stato di Teramo
Via Melchiorre Delfico 16
94100 Teramo, Italy

Archivio di Stato di Torino
Via Luzio 4
10123 Torin, Italy

Archivio di Stato di Trieste
Via La Marmora 17
34139 Trieste, Italy

Archivio di Stato di Venezia
Campo dei Frari 3002
30125 Venice, Italy

Archivio di Stato di Vercelli
Via A. Manzani 11
13100 Vercelli, Italy

Archivio di Stato di Verona
Via Franceschine 2
37100 Verona, Italy

LIECHTENSTEIN

Send your requests to:

Bureau of Civil Registration
9490 Vaduz, Liechtenstein

(011) (41) (75) 661-11

The Bureau of Civil Registration has records from 1878. For earlier records you should search the church parish registers.

You should also consult:

National Library of Liechtenstein
   Liechtensteinische Landesbibliothek
   PF 385
   9490 Vaduz, Liechtenstein

National Archives of Liechtenstein
   Liechtensteinische Landesarchiv
   9490 Vaduz, Liechtenstein

LUXEMBOURG

Send your requests to:

Registres de l'Etat Civil
(Town), Luxembourg

Copies of certificates before 1979 are also available from:

Archives de l'Etat
BP 6
2010 Luxembourg, Luxembourg

Cost for a certified Birth Certificate	No Charge
Cost for a certified Marriage Certificate	No Charge
Cost for a certified Death Certificate	No Charge

Vital records are on file at the local Civil Registration Office from 1795. Copies of records more than ten years old are also on file at the National Archives (Archives de l'Etat).

MALTA

Send your requests to:

Public Registry Department
Ministry of Justice
197 Merchants Street
Valletta, Malta

Vital records are on file at the Public Registry Department from 1863.
You might also consult:

The National Library of Malta
Old Treasury Street
Valletta, Malta

or

Principal Government Statistician
Central Office of Statistics
Auberge d'Italie
Merchants Street
Valletta, Malta

MONACO

Send your requests to:

> Mairie de Monaco
> Bureau de l'Etat Civil
> Monte Carlo, Monaco

Cost for a certified Birth Certificate	No Charge
Cost for a certified Marriage Certificate	No Charge
Cost for a certified Death Certificate	No Charge

Vital records are on file at the Bureau de l'Etat Civil from 1793.

You might also consult:

> The National Library of Monaco
> Bibliothèque Louis Notari
> 8 rue Louis Notari
> Monte Carlo, Monaco

THE NETHERLANDS

Send your requests to:

Civil Registration Office
(Town), The Netherlands

There is no central office for vital records in The Netherlands. To obtain copies of birth, marriage and death certificates write to the Civil Registration Office in the town where the event occurred. Vital records are on file from 1811.

There are libraries and archives of value to researchers in every large city in The Netherlands. The following list is of the key archives and libraries.

Algemeen Rijksarchief
(National Archives)
   Prins Willem Alexanderhof 20
   The Hague, The Netherlands

Koninklijke Bibliotheek
(National Library)
   Postbus 90407
   The Hague, The Netherlands

Provinciale Bibliotheek Centrale
Noord-Holland
   Hofplein 1
   1811 LE Alkmaar, The Netherlands

Gemeente Archief
   Oude Gracht 247
   1811 CG Alkmaar, The Netherlands

Gemeentelijke Archiefdienst
   Amsteldijk 67
   1074 HZ Amsterdam, The Netherlands

Stichting Provinciale Bibliotheek
Centrale Gelderland
   Zeelandsingel 40
   Postbus 9052
   6800 GR Assen, The Netherlands

Provinciale Bibliotheek Centrale Drenthe
   Postbus 78
   9400 AB Assen, The Netherlands

Provinciale Bibliotheek Centrale
Overijssel-Oost.
   Postbus 72
   7620 AB Borne, The Netherlands

Gemeentelijke Archiefdienst
   Stadserf 2
   4811 XS Breda, The Netherlands

Gemeentelijke Archiefdienst
   Groeneweg 32
   2801 ZD Gouda, The Netherlands

Provinciale Bibliotheek Centrale
Groningen
   Postbus 2503
   9704 CM Groningen, The Netherlands

Gemeentearchief
   Viaductstraat 3A
   9725 BG Groningen, The Netherlands

Gemeentearchief
   Jansstraat 40
   2011 RX Haarlem, The Netherlands

Rijksarchief in de Provincie
Noord-Brabant
  Zuid Willemsvaart 2
  5211 NW's-Hertogenbosch, The Netherlands

Stadsarchief
  Postbus 90158
  5200 MK's-Hertogenbosch, The Netherlands

Gemeentearchief
  Molenstraat 28
  8261 JW Kampen, The Netherlands

Provinciale Bibliotheek van Friesland
  Postbus 464
  8901 BG Leeuwarden, The Netherlands

Archief der Gemeente Leeuwarden en
Stedlijke Bibliotheek
(Leeuwarden City Archives and Library)
  Groote Kerkstraat 29
  8911 DZ Leeuwarden, The Netherlands

Gemeentearchief
  Boisotkade 2A
  2311 PZ Leiden, The Netherlands

Zeeuwse Bibliotheek
  Postbus 8004
  4330 EA Middleburg, The Netherlands

Gemeentearchief
  Marienburg 95
  6511 PS Nijmegen, The Netherlands

Provinciale Bibliotheek Centrale Limburg
  Godweerdersingel 34
  6041 CX Roermond, The Netherlands

Gemeentelijke Archiefdienst
  Swalmerstraat 12
  6041 CX Roermond, The Netherlands

Provinciale Bibliotheek Centrale Zuid-Holland
  Westfrankelandsedijk 1
  3115 HG Schiedam, The Netherlands

Provinciale Bibliotheek Centrale Noord-Brabant
  Postbus 90114
  5000 LA Tilburg, The Netherlands

Gemeentearchief
  Dokter Blumenkampstraat 1
  5914 PV Venlo, The Netherlands

Gemeentelijke Archiefdienst
  Plein Emaus 5
  3135 JN Vlaardingen, The Netherlands

Gemeentearchief
  Hogendijk 62-64
  1506 AJ Zaandam, The Netherlands

Genmeentearchief
  Spiegelstraat 15
  7201 KA Zutphen, The Netherlands

Centrale Bibliotheekdienst West-Overijssel
  Postbus 10068
  8000 GB Zwolle, The Netherlands

Gemeentelijke Archiefdienst
  Voorstraat 26
  8011 ML Zwolle, The Netherlands

Send your requests to:

> Pastor
> Lutheran Church
> (Town), Norway

or

> Local Office of the Population Register
> (Town), Norway

Information is also available from:

> The Central Office of the Population Register
>   P.O. Box 8131
>   0033 Oslo, Norway

Limited information is also kept on those who left Norway at:

> The Norwegian Emigration Center
>   Bergjelandsgt. 30
>   4012 Stavanger, Norway

Civil registration is carried out by the local churches or, for those not members of the state church, by the local Office of the Population Register. You will need to contact them for birth, marriage and death certificates. While church registers can go back to 1685, civil registration for birth and deaths is recorded only from 1915 and marriages from 1918.

The Central Office of the Population Register receives information from the Local Registrars and churches for statistical purposes.

You might also consult:

The National Archives:

> Riksarkivet
>   Folke Bernadottes vei 21
>   Postboks 10 Kringsja
>   N-0807 Oslo, 8 Norway

The National Library:

> Universitetsbiblioteket og Norges Nasjonalbiblioteket
>   Drammensvn 42
>   0255 Oslo, 2 Norway

The Regional Archives:

Statsarkivet i Oslo
    Folke Bernadottes vei 21
    Postboks 8 Kringsja,
    N-0807 Oslo 8, Norway

(For: Ostfold, Akershus, Oslo, Buskerud, Vestfold and Telemark fylker)

Statsarkivet i Hamar
    Strandgaten 71,
    N-2300 Hamar, Norway

(For: Hedmark and Oppland fylker)

Statsarkivet i Kristiansand
    Vesterveien 4
    4600 Kristiansand S, Norway

(For: Aust-Agder and Vest-Agder fylker)

Statsarkivet i Stavanger
    Domkirkeplassen 3
    4000 Stavanger, Norway

(For: Rogaland fylker)

Statsarkivet i Bergen
    Arstadveien 22
    N-5000 Bergen, Norway

(For: Hordaland and Sogn og Fjordane fylker)

Statsarkivet i Trondheim
    Hogskolevegen 12
    Postboks 2825 Elgesaeter
    N-7001 Trondheim, Norway

(For: More og Romsdal, Sor Trondelag, Nord-Trondelag, Tromsø and Finnmark fylker)

Statsarkivet i Tromsø
    Skippergaten 1 C
    9000 Tromsø, Norway

(For: Tromsø and Finnmark)

POLAND

Send your requests to:

Civil Registration District Office
(Town), Poland

There is no central office for vital records in Poland. To obtain copies of birth, marriage and death certificates write to the Civil Registration District Office in the town where the event occurred. Modern civil registration began in 1946 but records are available much earlier from the District Office and from the churches.

You might also consult:

Naczelna Dyrekcja Archiwow Panstowowych
(National Archives)
  Ul Dluga 6
  SKR Poczt 1005
  00-950 Warsaw, Poland

Biblioteka Narodowa
(National Library)
  Hankiewicza 1
  00-973 Warsaw, Poland

Biblioteka Slaska
(Silesian Library)
  U1 Francuska 12, 529
  40-956 Katowice, Poland

Central Statistical Office
  A1 Niepodleglosci 208
  00-925 Warsaw, Poland

PORTUGAL

Send your requests to:

Los Registros Civiles
(Town), Portugal

There is no central office for vital records in Portugal. To obtain copies of birth, marriage and death certificates write to the town where the event occurred. Vital records are on file from 1911. Some local registrars have records back to 1832. Estimates are that the current records are only 85% complete and that earlier records are even less so. Older records have been transferred to the District Archives.

You might also consult:

Biblioteca Nacional
(National Library)
   Ocidental do Campo Grande, 83
   1751 Lisbon, Portugal

Biblioteca Pública e Arquivo
de Angra do Heroismo
   Rua da Rosa, 49
   9700 Angra do Heroismo, Acores, Portugal

Arquivo Distrital de Aveiro
   Praca da Republica
   3800 Aveiro, Portugal

Biblioteca Pública e Arquivo Distrital
   Largo Conde de Vila Flor
   7000 Evora, Portugal

Arquivo Regional da Madeira
   Rua da Mouraria
   Palacio de Sao Pedro
   Funchal, Madeira, Portugal

Arquivo Distrital de Guarda
   Rua de Batalha Reis
   6300 Guarda, Portugal

Biblioteca Pública e Arquivo Distrital
   Largo da Republica
   2400 Leiria, Portugal

Biblioteca Pública e Arquivo Distrital
   Governo Regional dos Acores
   Rua Ernesto de Canto
   9500 Ponta Delgada, Acores, Portugal

Arquivo Distrital de Portalegre
   Rua do 15 de Maio
   Qu de San Francisco
   7300 Portalegre, Portugal

Arquivo Distrital de Porto
   Praca da Republica, 38
   4000 Porto, Portugal

Arquivo Distrital de Setubal
   Rua de Dama Braga, 15
   2900 Setubal, Portugal

Biblioteca Pública e Arquivo
Distrital de Vila Real
   Av de Carvalho Araujo, 7
   5000 Vila Real, Portugal

Arquivo Distrital de Viseu
   Largo de Santa Cristina
   3500 Viseu, Portugal

Send your requests to:

Civil Registration Office
(Town), Romania

There is no central office for civil registration in Romania. To obtain copies of birth, marriage and death certificates write to the Civil Registration District Office in the town where the event occurred. Vital records are on file from 1865; earlier records are in the churches. Older vital records have been transferred to the National Archives.

You might want to consult:

Arhivele Statululi
(National Archives)
 b-dul Gheorghe Gheorghiu-Dej 29
 Bucharest, Romania

Biblioteca Centrală de Stat
(National Library)
 Str Ion Ghica 4
 Bucharest, Romania

SAN MARINO

Send your requests to:

Parish Priest
Serravalle, Repubblica di San Marino

Send your requests for civil marriages from September 1, 1953 to:

Minister of Justice
Serravalle, Repubblica di San Marino

San Marino is a small republic with a population of just over 22,000, of whom more than half live in Italy or abroad. San Marino is a land-locked country surrounded by Italy.

Vital records are kept by the local parish church. Civil marriages have been allowed by the government since September 1953.

SPAIN

Send your requests to:

Registros Civiles
(Town), Spain

There is no central office for civil registration in Spain, though identity cards are issued to every resident at the age of fourteen. Copies of vital records are available from the Office of Civil Registration in the town where the event occurred. Civil registration began in 1870. Earlier records are available from the churches.

You might also consult:

Archivo Historico Nacional
(National Archives)
  Serrano, 115
  28006 Madrid, Spain

Biblioteca Nacional
(National Library)
  Paseo de Recoletos, 20
  28001 Madrid, Spain

Archivo General de la Diputacion
Provincial de Barcelona
(Barcelona Provincial Archives)
  Pza Sant Jaume
  08002 Barcelona, Spain

Archivo Historico Provincial
(Cordoba Provincial Archives)
  Pompeyos, 6
  14003 Cordoba, Spain

Archivo del Reino de Galicia
  Jardin San Carlos
  15001 La Coruna, Spain

Archivo Historico Municipal y Museo
de Historia de la Ciudad
(City Archives and Museum)
  Forca, 27
  17004 Gerona, Spain

Biblioteca, Archivo y Coleccion
Arqueologica Municipal
(City Library, Archives and
Archeological Collection)
  Pl. de la Asuncion, 1
  Jerez de la Frontera, Spain

Archivo Historico Municipal de Murcia
(City Archives)
  Palacio Almundi
  Plano de San Francisco
  30004 Murcia, Spain

Archivo del Reino de Mallorca
  C Ramon Llull, 3
  07001 Palma de Mallorca, Spain

Archivo Real y General de Navarra
  Avenida San Ignacio, 1
  31002 Pamplona, Spain

Archivo Historio Provincial de Salamanca
(Salamanca Provincial Archives)
  Patio Escuelas, 1
  37008 Salamanca, Spain

Archivo Municipal de Sevilla
(Seville City Archives)
  Pza Nueva, 1
  41001 Seville, Spain

Archivo Biblioteca Municipal de Vitoria
(Vitoria City Archives)
  Ayuntamiento de Vitoria
  General Alava, 26
  01005 Vitoria-Gasteiz Alava, Spain

SWEDEN

Send your requests to:

Pastor
Lutheran Church
(Town), Sweden

Your requests for records after 1947 can also be sent to:

County Registrar
County Administration
(County Seat, County), Sweden

Sweden is divided into twenty-four counties and 227 towns. To obtain copies of vital records in Sweden write to the Lutheran Church in the town where the event occurred; for records after 1947 you can write to the County Registrar where the event occurred. Church registers generally date from 1686.

Since 1960 Sweden has issued personal identity numbers to all persons living in the country. These numbers are based on the date of birth and are issued by the local registrars and administered by the Swedish National Tax Board.

The National Data Center for Administrative Data Processing maintains SPAR, or the Coordinated Register of Individuals and Addresses, which serves as a central population register. Information is only available from this agency by permission of the Data Inspection Board.

You might also consult:

Kungliga Biblioteket
(National Library)
Box 5039
102 41, Stockholm, Sweden

Stockholms Stadsbibliotek
(Stockholm Library)
Box 12199
102 55, Stockholm, Sweden

SWITZERLAND

Send your requests to:

Civil Registration Office
(Town), Switzerland

There is no central office for vital records in Switzerland. To obtain copies of birth, marriage or death certificates you need to write to the local town where the person was born. Civil registration began in 1876. Church registers began much earlier.

You might also consult:

Schweizerisches Bundesarchiv
(National Archives)
   Archivstr. 4
   3012 Bern, Switzerland

Schweizerische Landesbibliothek
(National Library)
   Hallwylstr. 15
   3003 Bern, Switzerland

Staatsarchiv des Kantons Aargau
(Aargau City Archives)
   Obere Vorstadt
   5001 Aargau, Switzerland

Staatsarchiv Basel-Stadt
(Basel Archives)
   Martinsgasse 2
   4001 Basel, Switzerland

Staatsarchiv des Kantons Bern
(Bern City Archives)
   Falkenplatz 4
   3012 Bern, Switzerland

Staatsarchiv des Kantons Graubunden
(Graubunden Archives)
   Reichsgasse
   Archivegebaude
   CH-7001 Chur, Switzerland

Archives de l'Etat
(Geneva Archives)
   1 rue de l'Hotel de Ville
   1211 Geneva 3, Switzerland

Staatsarchiv des Kantons Luzern
(Luzern Archives)
   Bahnhofstr. 18
   6003 Luzern, Switzerland

Archives de l'Etat
(Neuchatel Archives)
   Le Chateau
   CH-2001 Neuchatel, Switzerland

Staatsarchiv des Kantons Zurich
(Zurich Archives)
   Winterhurestr. 170
   8057 Zurich, Switzerland

Zentralbibliothek Zurich
(Zurich Central Library)
   Zahringerplatz 6
   8025 Zurich, Switzerland

UNION OF SOVIET SOCIALIST REPUBLICS

Send your requests to:

Central State Archives
Bolshaia Pirogovkaia ul. 17
119817 Moscow, USSR

Since the Soviet Union is still a closed society it is difficult if not impossible to receive a reply from the government, though a civil registration and national identity card system are in operation. It is a large country with fifteen distinct republics and well over 3,000 town, regional, and state archives.

Civil registration is carried out on the town or district level by registrars appointed by local Party officials. They prepare three copies of each record, keeping one and forwarding the second and third copies to the regional or Soviet Republic civil registration office and to the regional or Soviet Republic vital statistics office.

On 18 April 1989 the United States and the Soviet Union signed an agreement on joint archival projects which included a proposal for establishing a system for responding to genealogical inquiries. Contact Mr. Don W. Wilson, Archivist of the United States, National Archives and Records Administration, Washington, DC 20408 for the current status of this unfolding relationship.

YUGOSLAVIA

Send your requests to:

Local Registrar for Internal Affairs
(Town), Yugoslavia

There is no central office for civil registration in Yugoslavia, though identity cards are issued to each resident. Copies of vital records are available from the Local Registrar for Internal Affairs in the town where the event occurred. Civil registration began in 1946, but earlier records are available from the churches.

You might also consult:

Arhiv Jugoslavije
(National Archives)
 PF 65
 11000 Belgrade, Yugoslavia

Narodna Biblioteka SRS
(National Library)
 Ul Serkliceva 1
 Belgrade, Yugoslavia

Savenzi Zavod za Statistiku
(National Office of Statistics)
 PF 203
 11000 Belgrade, Yugoslavia

Arhiv Srjije
(Serbian Archives)
 Karnedzijeva 2
 11000 Belgrade, Yugoslavia

Arhiv Hrvatske
(Croatian Archives)
 Marulicev trg 21
 41000 Zagreb, Yugoslavia

Arhiv SR Slovenije
(Slovenia Archives)
 Zvezdarska 1
 61000 Ljubljana, Yugoslavia

Arhiv na Skopje
(Skopje Archives)
 Moskovska 1
 91000 Skopje, Yugoslavia

Centralna Narodna Biblioteka SR Crne Gore
(National Central Library of Montenegro)
 PF 57
 81250 Cetinje, Yugoslavia